Twin and Triplet Psychology

D1434559

Twin and Triplet Psychology provides professionals with clear, concise information on the special needs of multiples, from a range of professional settings.

The contributors examine the relationship between twins and triplets both before and after birth and as they mature. The education, language, growth and development of multiples are covered, along with issues surrounding adolescence, separation, special needs and the death of a twin. Implications for parents and the need for adequate counselling, information and support are also highlighted.

Twin and Triplet Psychology is essential reading for all professionals involved in the care of twins and triplets at every stage of their development.

Audrey C. Sandbank is a UKCP registered family psychotherapist in private practice. For the last ten years she has been Hon. Consultant Family Therapist to the Twins and Multiple Births Association (Tamba).

Twin and Triplet Psychology

A professional guide to working with multiples

Edited by Audrey C. Sandbank

London and New York

My affectionate thanks go to my husband Professor Charles Sandbank for his advice and support.

First published 1999
by Routledge
11 New Fetter Lane, London EC4P 4EE

Simultaneously published in the USA and Canada
by Routledge
29 West 35th Street, New York, NY 10001

Routledge is an imprint of the Taylor & Francis Group

© 1999 Selection and editorial matter, Audrey C. Sandbank;
individual chapters, the contributors

Typeset in Times by J&L Compositon Ltd, Filey, North Yorkshire
Printed and bound in Great Britain by
TJ International Ltd, Padstow, Cornwall

All rights reserved. No part of this book may be reprinted or
reproduced or utilised in any form or by any electronic, mechanical,
or other means, now known or hereafter invented, including
photocopying and recording, or in any information storage or
retrieval system, without permission in writing from the publishers.

British Library Cataloguing in Publication Data
A catalogue record for this book is available from the
British Library

Library of Congress Cataloguing in Publication Data
Twin and triplet psychology: a professional guide to working
    with multiples / edited by Audrey Sandbank.
        Includes bibliographical references and index.
        1. Twins – Psychology.   2. Triplets – Psychology.   I. Sandbank,
    Audrey.
        BF723.T9T85   1999
        155.44′4 – dc21   98–51543

ISBN 0–415–18397–9 (hbk)
ISBN 0–415–18398–7 (pbk)

Contents

Illustrations

Tables

Contributors

Britta Alin Åkerman is Associate Professor at Stockholm Institute of Education, Department of Special Education. She is an authorised psychologist and psychotherapist. She is the author of many books in Swedish, for example, *The First Seven Years – The Whole of Children's Development*, *My Child Would be Tested – What Does That Mean?*, *The Swedish Manual of the Griffith's Mental Development Scales*, and *They are Two – Twins and Triplets from Fetus to Teenager*. She also works with the education departments in Sweden, Estonia, Russia and Japan.

Elizabeth M. Bryan is honorary Consultant Paediatrician at Queen Charlotte's and Chelsea Hospital, London, Reader in Paediatrics at Imperial College Medical School and Founder and Medical Consultant to the Multiple Births Foundation. She is President for of the International Society for Twin Studies. She established her first clinic specifically for twins in 1987 in London and has now started clinics in Birmingham and York. She has written four books on twins including *Twins, Triplets and More* (Penguin 1992); *Twins and Higher Multiple Births: A Guide to their Nature and Nurture* (Edward Arnold 1992); and one with her husband, *Infertility. New Choices, New Dilemmas* (Penguin 1995).

John M.H. Buckler was educated at King Edwards School, Birmingham and trained in medicine at Brasenose College, Oxford and St Bartholomew's Hospital, London, qualifying BM, B.Ch. (Oxford) in 1959. Early medical and surgical appointments were mainly in and around London, but paediatric experience included three years at The Hospital for Sick Children, Great Ormond Street, London, and one year at the Children's Hospital of Philadelphia, USA between 1965 and 1970. He was appointed Senior Lecturer in paediatrics (combined for the first five years with chemical pathology) in the University of Leeds with an honorary NHS paediatric post at consultant grade from 1972. Further qualifications included MRCP (London 1965), FRCP (London 1977), DM (Oxford 1970) and D.Sc. (Oxford 1992). In the paediatric appointments in Leeds he specialised in growth and endocrinology and has written four books on these subjects involving considerable research into growth, notably at adolescence. He retired from clinical paediatrics in 1995 but retains an honorary appointment in the Leeds University Department and continues his research and publications.

David A. Hay was born in Aberdeen and trained there and in Birmingham before moving to Australia in 1972. In 1977 in Melbourne he began the LaTrobe Twin Study of Behavioural and Biological Development which followed some 600 multiple birth families through childhood and adolescence. With his move to Western Australia in 1996, he was one of the founders of the population-based WATCH (WA Twin Child Health) Study. In 1991, he and colleagues began the Australian Twin ADHD project which is an ongoing longitudinal study of Attention Deficit Hyperactivity Disorder in some 2,000 twin pairs and their families. He is the National Patron of the Australian Multiple Birth Association (Inc).

Kay Mogford-Bevan is currently Senior Lecturer in the Department of Speech, Newcastle University. She first trained and practised as a speech and language therapist, then moved on to study psychology and child development at Bristol and Nottingham Universities. Her research interests are in the field of child communication disorders. Her interest in twins stems from both family and clinical experience.

Alessandra Piontelli trained in medicine and neuropsychiatry in Italy. She also trained at the Tavistock Clinic in London where she became part of the teaching staff. She is now visiting professor at the Department of Child Psychiatry and a researcher at the Department of Maternal–Fetal Medicine, University of Milano.

Pat Preedy is Head Teacher of Knowle Church of England Primary School, Solihull, West Midlands. She became interested in twins and higher multiples in 1992 when nine sets of twins were registered to start school. This event prompted her to embark upon a major piece of research focusing upon the education of twins and higher multiples. As an Education Research Consultant for the

Twins and Multiple Births Association (Tamba) she is very involved in training professionals and supporting families.

Audrey C. Sandbank is married with a son, twin daughters and six grandchildren. She is a UKCP registered family psychotherapist and was a member of the working party concerned with developing standards of practice for psychotherapists. She has practised family therapy for twenty years in health service clinics for children and families as part of a multidisciplinary team. She is now in private practice. For the last ten years she has been Hon. Consultant Family Therapist to the Twins and Multiple Births Association which prompted her to write *Twins and the Family*, a parenting manual, also translated into Italian, based on her own research and clinical practice. She was on the Young Minds working party which set up the UK Information Service Helpline for parents and professionals and is currently a professional adviser working as part of a team providing a professional telephone advice service. Young Minds is a UK organisation promoting child mental health. She is a regular writer and broadcaster on 'multiple' issues.

Jane A. Spillman was in charge of a neonatal unit for many years. She developed a keen interest in families who had a multiple birth. Years of research into the emotional and physical effects of such experiences followed. The results of her studies have been widely reported. She was for fifteen years the Hon. Medical Research Consultant for the Twins and Multiple Births Association and remains a member of their Advisory Board.

Foreword

I was delighted to be asked to write the foreword to this book. As a founder member of the Twins and Multiple Births Association (Tamba) in 1978, I am aware that much has changed about our perceptions of twins and higher multiples. Not only has public interest in multiple births increased but there has been interest from professional, voluntary and commercial organisations as well.

When Tamba was set up, we hoped to increase awareness of the needs of families who were expecting or had multiples – this included the risks of multiple pregnancy. I am pleased that the general awareness has increased but there is still a gap in the knowledge and skills among professionals, carers and families. Audrey Sandbank's book will help fill this gap. It will give professionals and parents of multiples the information, advice and support they need to care for multiples.

The book highlights the practical and emotional needs of multiple birth families and the growth and development of twins, triplets and more. Medical and technological improvements have ensured that the survival rate for babies has improved.

Audrey has edited a book where distinguished authors have highlighted current and specific areas of need. The book can also be used as a reference at various stages of the children's development. It offers the professional practical advice on the development of twins and higher multiples from conception to adulthood. The early chapters are devoted to pregnancy and birth, and later chapters include growth, education issues, development and relationships.

This book offers an insight into how it feels to be a twin and emphasises the importance of allowing individuality and independence to develop from birth onwards. Several authors are, or have been, Tamba members and are therefore also aware of the fact that having a multiple birth is a unique experience which, with the right information and advice, can be enjoyable and fulfilling.

Judi Linney
Head of Health Promotion – West Surrey Health Authority
President of Tamba

1 Introduction

The importance of understanding the psychology of twin and triplet relationships

Audrey C. Sandbank

Social change

There has been a steady increase in the number of live multiple births in the developed nations over the last few years due to healthier populations, medical advances and fertility treatment, and social changes which have led many women to delay starting their families or continuing to bear children at a later age – there has been found to be a direct correlation between the age of the mother and the chance that she will conceive dizygotic (DZ), non-identical, twins (Lazar *et al.* 1981). Correspondingly, there has been a growing public interest in multiples and an awareness by professionals that they need to be better equipped to offer help and advice to parents and twins alike. This book collects the accumulated knowledge of leading professionals on the subject of multiples and how they may differ in their needs from singletons in the current social environment.

Many of the aspects concerning twins which are treated in detail throughout the book are reflected by Associate Professor Dr Britta Alin Åkerman in Chapter 7, dealing with triplets. Unfortunately we have not been able to cover quads or quins but the reader should be able to extrapolate from the information presented here. In Chapter 9 Dr John Buckler also covers the subject of triplets in his specialised treatment of growth and development and in Chapter 5 Dr Elizabeth Bryan includes triplets in her statistics on the risk of cerebral palsy. She also points out that monozygotic (MZ) pairs are more at risk than DZ and this includes identical members of higher multiple groups. As the numbers increase, so also do the risks.

Separate and shared environments

Comprehensive studies of MZ twins who have been reared both apart and together (Bouchard *et al.* 1990) have demonstrated that our genes account for appoximately half of the development of most psychological traits with non-shared environment contributing to the rest, i.e. prenatal and perinatal differences, birthweight and birthorder, individual friends and school experiences. IQ has been shown to be much more gene dependent and recent Swedish studies have shown that this increases with age and that 80-year-olds are more alike in this respect than the younger age groups (McClearn *et al.* 1997). Why then, it may be asked, at least in the case of MZ twins, do we need a book on twin and triplet psychology?

Professor David Hay convincingly points out (Chapter 8) that even in the case of MZ twins, we need to be aware of the importance of the non-shared and shared environment as twins (or triplets) go through life, the former creating differences between MZ twins, the latter sometimes making DZ twins more alike, sometimes less alike. This is even more noticeable if they are identical di-chorionic twins (MZDC) as discussed by Dr Alessandra Piontelli in Chapter 2. First, as Piontelli has shown with the use of ultrasound, there are physical differences in utero that may favour one or other of the twin pair and the intra-uterine environment itself is modified by the behaviour of the fetus. There are also differences in activity patterns which are predictors of postnatal differences. Jane Spillman (Chapter 3), as well as Piontelli (Chapter 2), Åkerman (Chapter 7) and Buckler (Chapter 9), have demonstrated that inequality in the intra-uterine environment has an effect on each twin or triplet, leading to differences between the two. Prenatal and perinatal factors which may sometimes lead to one twin or triplet having special needs are discussed by Elizabeth Bryan in Chapter 5. Bryan reminds us with sensitivity that their are implications for every member of the family, particularly the co-twin, and gives some thoughtful advice on management based on her experience of those attending her twins clinics which have been a lifeline for many parents. Buckler (Chapter 9) demonstrates that growth is strongly genetically controlled with 'a significant role for environmental factors' and that any disadvantages that twins may have *per se* as regards growth are usually ironed out by the time they reach adulthood.

The unshared environmental component results in subtle differences which may be exaggerated or depressed depending on the twins themselves and those around them. Spillman (Chapter 3) shows how birthweight differences may lead to unequal bonding and a preference for the heavier baby, resulting in behavioural and even IQ differences. Research reported by Hay in Chapter 9 shows that some differences perceived by parents may have little foundation in fact and owe more to labelling, birthweight, or more importantly, which twin came home from hospital first, and these perceived differences tend to persist.

Family relationships

In Chapter 10 the Editor, Audrey Sandbank, points out that those closest to MZ twins find it easiest to detect small differences which may influence outside relationships and eventually partners. Sandbank also looks at the separation issue from a psychodynamic point of view and at the possible pitfalls in adolescence. Hay looks at adolescence rather more pragmatically from the educational perspective in Chapter 8.

Contrary to the popular view, twins do not simply consist of the MZ population. DZ twins, with all their normal sibling differences, most notably in the case of DZos (opposite sex) twins, need to have their twinness taken into account. MZ twins also need to have their individuality and separate identity acknowledged. When both twins have most of their traits in common, and even when they are no more alike than any two brothers or sisters, the psychology of the couple requires to be taken into consideration, as Sandbank (Chapter 10) and Hay (Chapter 8) point out, not least when separation looms or even death occurs. Bryan (Chapter 11) tells us how the death of a twin at any age is a trauma which those of us who are singletons may never fully understand, which is why, she says, it is so important for twins to help twins. It was for this reason that Bryan set up the Lone Twin Network for twins who have lost a co-twin. They are able to share their feelings with others and discover that they are not unique, and find help and support. Bryan also emphasises the importance of the sympathetic treatment and counselling of mothers who have lost a twin prenatally or perinatally, particularly if they have had to make the choice of selectively reducing the number of fetuses.

In Chapter 3, Spillman, a midwife and veteran researcher into the effect on the family not only of the arrival but also the news of the arrival of twins or more, gives us an insight into the emotional impact on parents and its subsequent effect on parent–twin relationships. This, as we can see from Chapters 8 and 10, may have long-term effects. She suggests that adequate counselling for those undergoing infertility treatment and for all those expecting multiples, an awareness of their needs through pregnancy, birth and afterwards, can greatly improve the well-being of the families. She emphasises the important role of self-help organisations and those supporting professionals in disseminating information. Åkerman also gives us a thoughtful overview of this area, but more from the psychodynamic point of view, and includes many firsthand accounts. She does give us background medical information, for, as she points out, having triplets is a very different experience from having a singleton, or even twins. (It is not within the brief of this book to cover fully the biological or obstetric aspects of twinning which are more than adequately covered in other works.)

Åkerman, Hay and Sandbank all mention the problems for mothers (and fathers) who lose their special role when their multiples grow up and Bryan (Chapters 11 and 5) makes the same point more poignantly if one or more babies die, or the 'perfect' pair is lost through disability. The mother may try to maintain the fiction of 'normal' twinship inappropriately to the detriment of both members of the pair. In the UK, Tamba offers various support groups including 'special needs' and 'bereavement'. Sharing experiences with others is seen as the most valuable help that can be offered, as well as acknowledging that those who have lost a twin still have the right to be under the 'multiple' umbrella.

Education

All twins and those involved in their care require us, the professionals, to be aware of what will make their path through life a little easier. All the contributors to this book have demonstrated their dedication to this cause, none more so than Pat Preedy who, in Chapter 6, draws attention to the benefits which would be derived from an education policy on twins and also that twins themselves should have a voice. As a head teacher she is well aware of the importance of the right educational environment in getting the best out of the young children in her care, and the results of her pupils testify to her methods. Faced with a large influx of twins she at once set herself to discover what their particular needs might be, recognising that these might be different from those of singletons. Following in the path which Hay in Australia has trod for the past twenty years she was able to replicate some of his pioneering research. Hay himself (Chapter 8) has given us an impressive overview of his work, and of the subject, and is now breaking new ground in examining the problems of ADHD in twins and singletons.

Åkerman (Chapter 7) has given education policy in Sweden a high priority for triplets – there are so many more choices to be made! Bryan also reminds us (Chapter 5) that physical disability is not necessarily linked to mental disability and, importantly, that any perceived differences may be due to timing of milestones or diversity of gifts, particularly in the case of DZ pairs where the children will differ in the same way as any two siblings in a family.

The nature/nurture question is one that Dr Kay Mogford-Bevan rigorously explores in Chapter 4 on language and encourages us not to overlook the possibility of a shared language disorder when looking at language delay in twins, or possibly a disorder in only one if one twin appears to be dominant in the use of language. At the same time, she looks at the twin situation and how we can best encourage the development of language, an area which Preedy highlights from the point of view of education in Chapter 6 and Hay in Chapter 8, where he also looks at the ADHD connection. Mogford-Bevan points out that being a twin may not lead to language delay at all, but may even give some twins an advantage. Åkerman also looks at language delay in triplets in Chapter 7.

Telepathy

Some readers may be disappointed that we have not covered the vexed question of telepathy, but, so far as the editor is aware, there is no evidence, on the standard method of testing, that twins are any more telepathic than the rest of the population. The fact that so many report amazing coincidences and synchronicity of events, whether together or apart (Sommer *et al.* 1961) may, as the Minnesota study seems to show (Bouchard *et al.* 1990), owe more to their genes than it does to telepathy. However, there is plenty of anecdotal evidence of telepathic experiences, particularly if one twin is in pain or danger. To dismiss these as of no importance is to deny the very real experiences that many twins have had and which are by no means confined to MZ twins but have also been reported by DZss and DZos twins.

Playfair (1999) suggests that researchers have been doing the wrong kind of experiments and that they should be designed to fit the type of experiences that twins themselves report where the sender appears to do more than transmit an image, but actually influences the physiology of the receiver. This effect is rarely reported by other than close relations, and one will view results of further research with interest.

References

Bouchard, T.J., Lykken, D.T., McGue, M., Segal, N.L. and Tellegen, A. (1990) 'Sources of human psychological differences: the Minnesota study of twins reared apart', *Science* 250, 223–228.

Lazar, P., Berger, C. and Hemon, D. (1981) 'Preconceptual prediction of twin pregnancies' in Twin Research 3, *Twin Biology and Multiple Pregnancy*, ed. W. Nance, pp. 175–181. New York, Alan R. Liss.

McClearn, G.E., Johansson, B., Berg, S., Pedersen, N.L., Ahern, F., Petrill, S.A. and Plomin, R. (1997) 'Substantial genetic influence on cognitive abilities in twins 80 or more years old', *Science* 276, 1560–1562.

Playfair, G. (1999) 'Telepathy and identical twins', *Journal of the Society for Psychical Research* 63(854), 86–89.

Sommer, R., Osmond, H. and Pancyr, L. (1961) 'Selection of twins for ESP experimentation', *International Journal of Parapsychology* 3, 55–73.

2   Twins in utero

Temperament development and intertwin behaviour before and after birth

Alessandra Piontelli

Myths and facts

Many myths, legends and popular beliefs have always grown around the intra-uterine life of twins. In the public imagination their shared life during pregnancy has frequently been fantasised as being a specially animated and already social affair.

Fights abound from Esau and Jacob struggling for their birthright, to Rebecca, Isaac's wife, sensing her children battling in utero 'and the children struggled together within her' (Genesis 25). But we also hear about twins entertaining each other in all sorts of ways and being generally involved in adult and complex social interchanges which clearly only belong to life after birth. Such legends die hard. Even recently, intentional fights and kisses in utero have been 'scientifically' described.

Until fairly recently the study of human behaviour was necessarily limited to postnatal life, and the dramatic event of birth marked the limit beyond which it was impossible to observe the infant. The advent of ultrasound towards the middle of the 1970s, has opened a window into prenatal life. Ultrasounds are primarily of clinical importance and it was mainly their use in clinical practice which permitted fetal medicine to develop into a well-established, autonomous field. In all respects the fetus has now become a patient in its own right.

Ultrasounds are of special clinical relevance in twin pregnancies. Such pregnancies, being generally considered at risk, often need frequent monitoring and are usually subject to repeated ultrasonographic examinations.

However, ultrasounds are not only of purely clinical importance. Albeit with various limitations, they have made it feasible to observe and investigate the spontaneous behaviour of the undisturbed fetus within its natural environment. The studies by Prechtl (1984), De Vries *et al.* (1982, 1985, 1988), Manning *et al.* (1979) and several others have all given us fundamental knowledge of behavioural 'developmental milestones' (Birnholz *et al.* 1978) in utero. A wealth of data about fetal competencies is now available and rapidly accumulating. Nevertheless, prenatal life is either still ignored by most researchers in various branches of psychology or, at the opposite extreme, findings in this field, most frequently made available by purely medical sources, are often subject to unrestrained and far-fetched interpretations.

Possibly due to difficulties in enrolling sufficiently large samples, twin fetuses have also been largely ignored by prenatal behavioural studies. Apart from a few notable examples (Melnick *et al.* 1978, Ramos-Arroyo *et al.* 1988, Piontelli 1989, 1992, Riese 1990, Sokol *et al.* 1995), twin research is no exception to this general neglect. In addition, most twin researchers, probably for purposes of analysis, generally assume that monozygotic (MZ) twins share a common intra-uterine environment, even when they recognise that this assumption is probably false (see, for example, Bouchard and Propping (1993) for a collection of recent studies).

Intra-uterine effects are however far from being negligible in all pregnancies and are possibly doubly so in the case of twins. Far from being static, the intra-uterine environment undergoes constant dynamic and developmental changes (Alberts and Cramer 1988, Smotherman and Robinson 1988). These changes in turn further modify fetal behavioural development and may, at the same time, be modified by behavioural differences in the fetus. Intra-uterine effects become all the more important in twin pregnancies, as twins usually do not share even such macroscopic components as a single placenta, umbilical cords or amniotic sacs. However, even when they do, their common placenta is never equally shared, their amniotic fluid (except in very rare cases of mono-amniotic pregnancies) is never equally distributed, and umbilical cords never carry identical blood supplies even in the exceptional occurrence of a joint insertion. Weight discrepancies amongst dizygotic (DZ) twins can be explained by their different genetic make-up which renders them no less different from ordinary siblings. However, almost universally, weight discrepancies amongst MZ twins at birth are probably the most macroscopic end-result of the unequal partaking of the intra-uterine environment. Many other consequences, sometimes of even catastrophic proportions, are derived from this non-symmetric sharing.

Until fairly recently, zygosity determination in utero was only possible in the presence of opposite-sex twins. Since prenatal studies are extremely time-consuming and labour-intensive, this limitation has presumably had a restraining influence on extending twin research to intra-uterine life. However, recent diagnostic advances allow us to assess with reasonable accuracy (Barss *et al.* 1985) zygosity already in utero even in the case of mono-chorionic (MC) twin pregnancies. MZ twins can have different types of placentation according to the timing when the splitting originating the twinning phenomenon took place (Baldwin 1994). Seventy per cent of them share the same placenta and inhabit two different amniotic sacs and are hence called mono-chorionic (MC)-di-amniotic (DA). The remaining 30 per cent have two separate placentas and are therefore named di-chorionic (DC) (Bryan 1992). Determination of type of placentation is again primarily of clinical importance. MC pregnancies, being subject to greater risks, have to be monitored particularly carefully. In fact early assessment of placentation is now increasingly becoming routine practice in most civilised countries. MC pregnancies are then usually referred to centres of advanced care.

Though zygosity always has to be reassessed at birth, this distinction has also opened up the possibility of applying twin research to prenatal behaviour. Only same-sex DC twins are excluded from this possibility, as it is impossible to appraise in utero if they are MZ or not. In this case we have to wait and carry out cord blood sampling at birth or serological analyses at later stages in postnatal life.

Applying twin research in utero does not mean having the possibility of employing the same sophisticated methods normally used after birth. Prenatal investigations, besides being extremely labour- and time-consuming, are also plagued by the difficulty of collecting sufficiently large samples of comparable gestational ages even remotely equivalent to the magnitude of those usually put together after birth. Furthermore, while twin research often centres around psychological features in twins, when discussing the twin fetus we must be very careful how we assess each particular age and stage.

Ultrasounds provide a fairly reliable picture of the entire behaviour of the fetus only up to about 20 to 22 weeks' gestation. After this, current limitations in our equipment only allow accurate visualisation of progressively smaller body segments. While in the singleton fetus the use of two or more probes has been described (de Vries *et al.* 1982), this proved to be impossible in the case of twins. Given the complex and intricate spatial distribution of both fetal bodies, the probes were seen to interfere with each other (Piontelli *et al.* 1997). A first/early-second trimester fetus is clearly developmentally very different from its third trimester counterpart. While a fetus approaching birth can be reasonably thought to be already equipped with functions which will allow it to live in a relational/social world, the same may not apply to a premature fetus whose survival is closely linked to purely physical factors. However, it is frequently the case that no distinction of gestational age is made within the turbulent and rapidly evolving fetal stage.

In addition to this, another important confusion often arises. All fetuses, but particularly early ones, move around a lot. Only too frequently fetal activity is equated with wakefulness and therefore possibly with intentionality and consciousness. In reality a behaviourally active fetus is not awake at all, but presumably just in a different phase of 'sleep' or some such similar prior condition arising during early development. Brief episodes of wakefulness have only been described close to term (Nijhuis *et al.* 1982).

Intra-uterine behaviour

What can the study of the intra-uterine behaviour of the twin fetus reasonably tell us?

First of all, it teaches us that MZ twins are never behaviourally identical. From the time they first start moving around they already show important differences in their levels of activity. Such discrepancies increase rapidly and progressively. Though initially MZ twins show greater behavioural similarities than do DZ twins, nevertheless by 20 to 22 weeks' gestation they have already reached the same level of dissimilarity as DZ twins in the amount of time they spend in motion within a given period of observation. Only approximate estimations are possible thereafter, but these seem to indicate that such behavioural differences persist throughout pregnancy. Postnatal observations show that these tendencies extend well beyond birth, the more active twin remaining so. The same applies to reactivity levels, though, as I will explain below, twins do not react to each other from the start.

If one decides to analyse their motion in detail, MZ and DZ twins all merge together. Some move their arms more, some their legs, still others their heads, etc. Examined in more detail, the greater original macroscopic similarities shown by MZ twins are found to be lacking. In addition, each twin when measured against its co-twin generally shows a certain consistency over time in its greater or lesser degree of activity. However, it is easy to imagine how various factors and complications could intervene to alter this trend. For instance, a previously more active twin could become constrained in its motion if oligo-hydramnios (reduced amount of amniotic fluid) intervened. On the contrary, the lack of motion of a relatively inactive twin could become enhanced by a greater amount of amniotic fluid. Nevertheless, even when initial trends are altered and twins modify their behavioural characteristics during their uneven and often rough journey through prenatal life, behavioural differences between them are the rule. Such diversity is all the more striking and enhanced during prenatal life, as ultrasounds remove the often confounding factor of similarities in physical appearance among MZ twins.

If only in a purely behavioural sense, the intra-uterine environment leaves its mark. During prenatal life the basis for future development is paved and prenatal life clearly renders MZ twins behaviourally different. Their shared intra-uterine sojourn contributes towards making them distinct individuals. Non-shared intra-uterine environmental factors certainly play a large part in creating these differences and as such can no longer be ignored. Only too often, all that is prenatal is still regarded as 'constitutional' and confused with genetic inheritance.

A glimpse of the future

In addition to the beginnings of behavioural diversity, ultrasounds allow us to catch a glimpse of the primordia of future temperamental traits. The dawning of individual dispositions can be caught in the diversity of fetal movement patterns, of preferential positions and of favoured activities. However, this too should be treated with caution. What we can realistically observe is individuality and the first signs of temperament in an embryonic form. Within broader similarities, each fetus moves differently and has dissimilar rhythms, adjustments and clock times. Some cycle more regularly, others alternate fairly irregularly between rest and activity cycles. Some move more, some move less, some seem to need more prompting to show signs of activity, some appear more jerky in their movements, some react more strongly to intra-pair stimulation, etc. These traits show the same behavioural continuity after birth. Furthermore, these differences are all the more evident in the case of twins as, in their case, there is the unique opportunity of using each co-twin as a control.

In addition, ultrasounds allow us to detect some sign of their future intra-pair relationship. Some twins seem to be contact-seeking, showing an inclination towards touch or proximity of some kind.

Others appear to be avoidant, possibly already showing fastidious-ness or irritation towards contact. These traits seem to continue after birth. This however does not mean that twins entertain complex and already properly social relationships in utero. They may feel and sense the stimulation originating from the other twin, but sensing and perceiving, a more complex operation involving the interpreta-tion of sensations and instilling them with meaning, may not coincide in the fetus (Hepper 1992) and, if they do, it is possibly so only in the more mature one. Neither may complicated feelings of love, jealousy or longing be postulated as being exchanged between them at any stage.

Even twins born at term and in favourable circumstances do not show any sign of 'social' recognition towards their co-twin. Being placed together and next to each other seems to have little or no significance at this point. Often parents are actually surprised and disappointed by the scarcity or even absence of interactions between their newborn twins. Many, in order to try to re-create their union within the womb and to offer them some form of comfort, put them in the same cot, only to find that they cry over the apparent lack of space. Most twins when reunited lie in distant corners of their cradle and show fastidiousness to any stimulation originating from the other twin. Only a few seek physical proximity with their co-twin. However, initially, even these few seem to derive a purely physical warmth from this closeness, similar to the comfort which could be procured by the proximity of a cuddly and lively puppy. The same probably applies to prenatal life or at least to the later stages of it. Again one should make a distinction between early and mature fetuses.

Longing and loss

This brings us to the question of when and how a twin fetus could 'long for' the presence of the other in case of a shockingly untimely prenatal death. So far we have only anecdotal evidence of this, mainly from children or adults reporting a sense of loss which they can only explain in terms of the yearning for a reunion with their dead co-twin. However, in such cases it is impossible to tease out how much this sense of loss derives from real recollections of the living sensa-tions felt in utero or from later constructions belonging to postnatal life alone.

The longing for a double, an ideal companion who understands us even without words, is fairly universal among adults and children alike. The abundance of 'doubles' in the mythology and literature down through the ages testifies to this universal yearning. In addition, it is not difficult to imagine how the terrible shock suffered by the parents due to the loss of a twin in utero could reverberate in only too many ways on the surviving twin. Here again we ought to make a distinction about the time and the circumstances when such a loss occurred. Much has been made about the so-called 'vanishing twin' phenomenon (Landy *et al.* 1982), the occasional discovery of another gestational sac (empty or not) during an early first trimester ultra-sonographic examination. It is difficult to imagine that such a discovery could be perceived as a devastating blow by the parents. Furthermore, it is also hard to imagine that an early fetus could 'miss' something that it has never felt. Intra-pair stimulation usually starts when the 'vanishing twin' would have already ceased to exist. Quite different for a mother is a later fetal loss, whether spontaneous or through excruciating choice. By 'choice' is meant selective feticide and fetal reduction, i.e. procedures by which a malformed or genetically compromised twin fetus is selectively terminated (selective feticide) or a higher multiple gestation is reduced to twins (fetal reduction) in order to give the remaining fetuses a better chance of survival. Fetal reduction in particular is most frequently perceived by parents (and by those performing it) as a kind of cruel 'Russian roulette'. No matter how rationally this painful decision is made, a sense of agonising guilt remains. Furthermore, this procedure evokes in all those involved a giddy sense of precariousness, making us feel that we are all near-misses, the products of pure chance. Had our parents made love on a different day or during a different month we would not have existed at all.

Once the mother has got used to the idea of having twins, any fetal loss is always a deep wound. When this occurs near term it is often a devastating blow. Nevertheless, only once intra-pair stimulation has become a consistent feature of the intra-uterine life of twins could one postulate that some kind of sense of 'loss' might be felt by the surviving twin. This would obviously increase with advancing gestational age when fetal crowding renders regular contact inevitable. In any case, we should not forget that the overwhelming majority of twins are separated by a dividing membrane; therefore what a twin fetus might 'miss' is clearly not a whole, distinct person, but just the more or less strong stimulation arising from the other twin and some rather 'animal' sense of comfort similar to that due to the presence of a live litter mate. Though intra-pair stimulation is certainly an important factor in the intra-uterine life of twins, we have so far only scanty and unconvincing evidence to judge whether all this will remain forever embedded in the subconscious of a surviving twin. Prospective not retrospective studies are greatly needed in this delicate area. It is only by studying individuals in this way that we will be able to get the answers that we seek. Again some basic questions will only be solved by looking deeply, rigorously and directly into the intrauterine past.

Experiments in nature

Besides showing us how their individuality and some temperamental traits and features in their reactions to the other are all implanted during prenatal life, twin fetuses can also tell us other facts which make it worthwhile to study their behaviour in utero.

Intra-pair stimulation beautifully demonstrates that tactile and proprioceptive sensibility are already present and functioning in utero. The simple fact that the twin fetus does respond to the light strokes (touch) or deep pressure (proprioception) originating from the other twin allows us to confirm this. These sensory capabilities had so far only been investigated by Hooker (1952) and Humphrey (1964) in pre-agonic fetuses extracted from the womb and stimulated in the few minutes preceding their death. Not until we (Piontelli *et al.* 1997) used the twin fetus as a model to show the functioning of such sensory capabilities was it thought possible to ascertain this in the unimpaired fetus within its natural environment.

Intra-pair stimulation, however, does not coincide with the onset of movement at 7 to 7.5 weeks' gestational age (Piontelli *et al.* 1997), but is usually delayed by a few weeks. It is not possible to tell whether this may be due to a discrepancy in the onset of motor and this specific type of sensory functioning or to the weakness of the initial motions of the fetus. Only if one had the chance to observe a very rare monoamniotic twin pregnancy at such an early age and, moreover, one in which the insertion of the cords would be close enough to allow sufficient physical proximity for stimulation to take place, could this question be answered. Until about 10 weeks' gestational age twin fetuses do not usually stimulate each other. Between 10 and 12 weeks' gestational age intra-pair stimulation is a feature possibly pertaining to MC twin pregnancies alone. Sharing the same placenta and being divided by a thin membrane favours earlier contact in most MZ twins. From 13 weeks DC twins usually join in as well. By 15 weeks' gestational age intra-pair stimulation is a constant feature of all twin pregnancies.

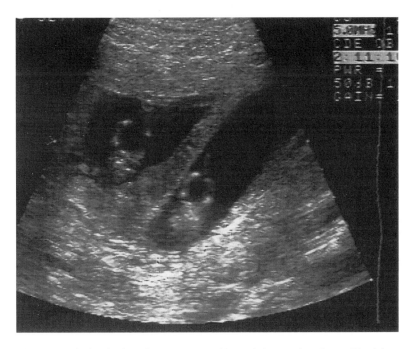

Plate 2.1 Di-chorionic twin pregnancy, 10 weeks' gestational age. Fetal legs are visible. A thick septum divides two amniotic sacs. Inter-twin stimulation is not possible at this early stage.

Intra-pair stimulation indicates that the intra-uterine life of twins, if only in this respect, is fundamentally different from that of a singleton fetus. This means that twins ought to be studied as a particular group in their own right.

In addition, intra-pair stimulation shows another interesting finding (Piontelli *et al.* 1997). Twin fetuses are not always responsive to stimulation, but show periods of sensory-motor inhibition. Though their body is passively displaced within the amniotic fluid by a blow from their co-twin, during such periods of sensory-motor unresponsiveness they show no apparent reaction to this. Intra-pair stimulation being a random event, the duration of such periods cannot be measured. However, the frequency with which the stimuli of a twin in an active state reach the body of the other twin assures that this is not an accidental occurrence. This finding is significant as it allows us to link the still unclarified function of rest–activity cycles in the fetus to later stages of well-organised sleep.

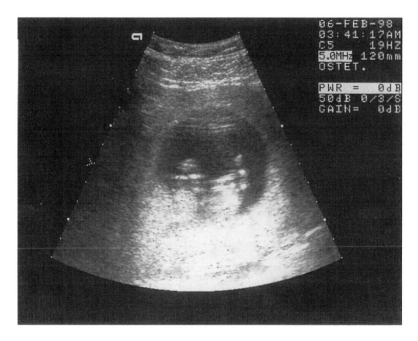

Plate 2.2 Mono-chorionic, mono-amniotic twin pregnancy, 10 weeks' gestational age. Fetal legs are visible. Twin fetuses are contained within the same amniotic sac. Early contact is inevitable.

In other respects, too, the intra-uterine behaviour of twins could prove to be a simple yet important 'experiment in nature', enabling us to understand some basic elements of fetal physiology. However, this may not be relevant in a chapter of a book on the psychology of twins.

Nevertheless, what most clearly emerges from studying the behaviour of twins from its first manifestations is how individual differences which will reverberate into postnatal life are created in utero. Though I am talking about behaviour alone, scholars from other fields are also showing how the twinning phenomenon in itself is not as simple and clear-cut as was previously imagined. Furthermore, local events during prenatal life ensure increasing variance. No individual emerges from this period as an identical copy of someone else. Studying twins from their first manifestations in intra-uterine life will certainly prove to be of great value in understanding why we are all quite different and unique human beings.

References

Alberts, J.R. and Cramer, C.P. (1988) 'Ecology and experience. Sources of means and meaning of developmental change', in E.M. Blass (ed.) *Handbook of Behavioural Neurobiology, Vol. 9. Developmental Psychobiology and Behavioural Ecology*, New York: Plenum Press.

Baldwin, V.J. (1994) *Pathology of Multiple Pregnancy*, New York: Springer Verlag.

Barss, V., Benacerraf, B.R. and Frigoletto, F.D. (1985) 'Ultrasonic determination of chorion type in twin gestation', *Obstetrics and Gynecology*, vol. 66, 779–783.

Birnholz, J.C., Stephens, J.D. and Faria, M. (1978) 'Fetal movement patterns: a possible means of defining neurologic developmental milestones in utero', *American Journal of Roentgenology*, vol. 130, 537–540.

Bouchard, T.J. and Propping, P. (eds) (1993) *Twins as a Tool of Behavioural Genetics*, Chichester: Wiley.

Bryan, E.M. (1992) *Twins and Higher Multiple Births: A Guide to their Nature and Nurture*, London: Arnold.

de Vries, J.I.P., Visser, G.H.A. and Prechtl, H.F.R. (1982) 'The emergence of fetal behaviour. I. Qualitative aspects', *Early Human Development*, vol. 7, 301–322.

de Vries, J.I.P., Visser, G.H.A. and Prechtl, H.F.R. (1985) 'The emergence of fetal behaviour. II. Quantitative aspects', *Early Human Development*, vol. 12, 99–120.

de Vries, J.I.P., Visser, G.H.A. and Prechtl, H.F.R. (1988) 'The emergence of fetal behaviour. III. Individual differences and consistencies', *Early Human Development*, vol. 16, 85–103.

Hepper, P.G. (1992) 'Fetal psychology: an embryonic science', in J.G. Nijhuis (ed.) *Fetal Behaviour: Developmental and Perinatal Aspects*, Oxford: Oxford University Press.

Hooker, D. (1952) *The Prenatal Origin of Behaviour*, Lawrence: University of Kansas Press.

Humphrey, T. (1964) 'Some correlations between the appearance of human fetal reflexes and the development of the nervous system', *Brain Research*, vol. 4, 93–135.

Humphrey, T. (1978) 'Function of the nervous system during prenatal life', in U. Stave (ed.) *Perinatal Physiology*, New York: Plenum.

Landy, H.G., Keith, L. and Keith, D. (1982) 'The vanishing twin', *Acta Geneticae Medicae et Gemellologiae*, vol. 31, 179–184.

Manning, F.A., Platt, L.D. and Sipos, L. (1979) 'Fetal movements in human pregnancies in the third trimester', *Obstetrics and Gynaecology*, vol. 54, 699–702.

Melnick, M., Myrianthopoulos, N.C. and Christain, J.C. (1978) 'The effects of chorion type on variation in IQ in the NCPP Twin Population', *American Journal of Human Genetics*, vol. 36, 425–433.

Nijhuis, J.G., Prechtl, H.F.R., Martin, C. and Bots, R.S.G.M. (1982) 'Are there behavioural states in the human fetus?', *Early Human Development*, vol. 6, 177–195.

Piontelli, A. (1989) 'A study of twins before and after birth', *International Review of Psycho-Analysis*, vol. 16, 413–426.

Piontelli, A. (1992) *From Fetus to Child*, London: Routledge.

Piontelli, A., Bocconi, L., Kustermann, A., Tassis, B., Zoppini, C. and Nicolini, U. (1997) 'Patterns of evoked behaviour in twin pregnancies during the first 22 weeks of gestation', *Early Human Development*, vol. 50, 39–45.

Prechtl, H.F.R. (1984) 'Continuity and change in early neural development', in H.F.R. Prechtl (ed.) *Continuity of Neural Functions from Prenatal to Postnatal Life*, London: Spastics International Medical Publications.

Ramos-Arroyo, M.A., Ulbright, T.M., Yu, P.L. and Christian, J.C. (1988) 'Twin study: relationship between birthweight, zygosity, placentation and pathologic placental changes', *Acta Geneticae Medicae et Gemellologiae*, vol. 37, 229–238.

Riese, M.L. (1990) 'Neonatal temperament in monozygotic and dizygotic twin pairs', *Child Development*, vol. 61, 1230–1237.

Smotherman, P.W. and Robinson, R.R. (1988) 'The uterus as environment: the ecology of fetal behaviour', in E.M. Blass (ed.) *Handbook of Behavioural Neurobiology, Vol. 9. Developmental Psychobiology and Behavioural Ecology*, New York: Plenum Press.

Sokol, D.K., Moore, C.A., Rose, R.J., Williams, C.J., Reed, T. and Christian, J.C. (1995) 'Intrapair differences in personality and cognitive ability among young monozygotic twins distinguished by chorion type', *Behavioural Genetics*, vol. 25, 457–465.

3 Antenatal and postnatal influences on family relationships

Jane A. Spillman

Introduction

Research has shown that unresolved anxieties can affect relationships between parents of twins and higher multiples both postnatally and in the longer term (Spillman 1984). It is therefore desirable that all professionals caring for such families are aware of the problems they experience and how these undesirable effects might be avoided or minimised.

It is not within the brief of this chapter to discuss the biology or medical aspects of a multiple pregnancy but rather to explore the psychological implications and how those who care for such families can best support them. (Various books are available which address the medical and biological aspects of Twinning. See, for example, MacGillivray *et al.* 1988, Bryan 1992, Spillman 1997.)

Until recently, it was possible to say that twins, triplets and more were never planned. However, as treatment for infertile couples has become almost commonplace, many of such parents are warned that a multiple birth may result. Some parents may even be disappointed if the outcome is only a singleton pregnancy. Surprisingly, the author found in her own research (Spillman 1984) and more recently in that of Linney (1995) that not all parents who presented themselves for infertility treatment actually expected to become pregnant, let alone have multiples and were quite upset when the treatment was successful. Because their families and obstetricians were delighted at a pregnancy being achieved, they were unable to voice their true feelings and sometimes became quite depressed.

When procedures such as ovulation induction, in-vitro fertilisation and GIFT (gamete intrafallopian transfer) were first introduced, the numbers of multiples that were being born increased dramatically. It was realised that in the latter two methods the more embryos or gametes that were implanted, the greater the chance of a successful pregnancy. Such multiple implantation contributed to the upsurge in the incidence of twins and particularly of triplets and higher order births. To control this explosion of higher multiples, the Human Fertilisation and Embryology Authority was set up to regulate the procedures. Their guidelines, issued in 1991, recommend that a maximum of three embryos are implanted. However, more twins, triplets and quadruplets are the result of ovulation induction than are due to IVF and GIFT and in the past few years the twinning and triplet rates have continued to rise, although less swiftly (Cooper 1997) (see Figure 3.1 and Table 3.1). It can be an even greater shock for parents who have not planned pregnancy at all when a multiple pregnancy results. Sometimes mothers have been refused a termination of their unplanned pregnancy because they appeared to be at a later gestational stage than their last monthly period suggested. It then transpired that their increased size was due to a multiple pregnancy. Needless to say, such babies might be less than welcome. Nowadays, with the introduction of reliable early ultrasound scanning techniques, this scenario is less likely.

Professional responsibility

With the escalation in the incidence of multiple births it becomes increasingly important for all professionals involved in the care of

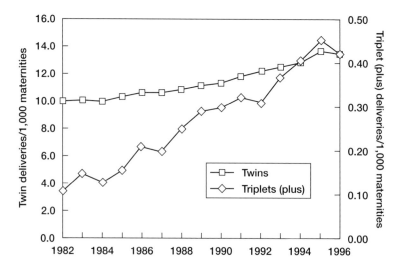

Figure 3.1 Multiple births in England and Wales, 1982–1996.
Source: OPCS (stillbirths included). Crown Copyright.

Table 3.1 Incidence of multiple births in the UK, 1996

	Number of maternities England and Wales	Scotland	N. Ireland
All maternities	643,862	58,831	24,398
Twins	8,615	800	311
Triplets	259	29	11
Quads+	9	0	2
Quins+	n/a	0	0
All multiples	8,883	829	324
Multiple birth rate per 1,000 maternities	13.8	14.1	13.3

Source: ONS London; GRO Scotland; GRO Northern Ireland.

Note: Figures include live and still births.

such families to be aware of their needs through pregnancy, birth and afterwards. There should be close communication between obstetricians, general practitioners, paediatricians, anaesthetists, midwives, health visitors, sonographers, dieticians, physiotherapists, social workers, and later, schoolteachers, speech therapists, educational psychologists and many others. Optimum care from all of these professionals can greatly improve the well-being of the families (Linney 1995).

Contrary to what many doctors, midwives, family and friends believe, for most parents the news that the longed-for baby they are expecting is bringing along one or two playmates comes as a shock. Research has shown that most parents experience very negative feelings at first (Figure 3.2). If their anxieties remain unresolved there can be lasting problems in some cases affecting relationships through to adulthood (Spillman 1984).

Anxieties of parents expecting a multiple birth

What then are the unanswered questions and anxieties which are identified by parents, particularly mothers? In two separate research projects the author identified the same persisting problems (Spillman 1984, 1992). The younger mothers in these studies were particularly concerned about the financial and practical implications of having twins or more, whereas the older mothers worried more about the health and welfare of the forthcoming infants and their own health. They were particularly concerned about the risk of pre-term delivery and whether the babies would be small (see also Linney 1995). In the

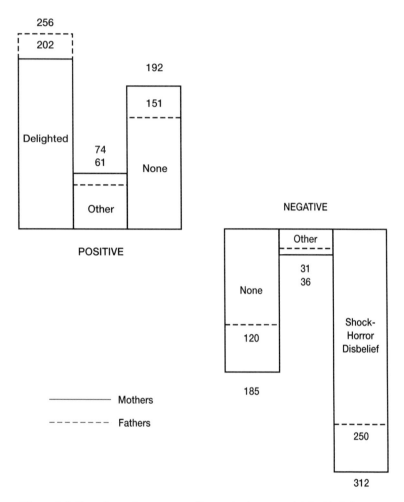

Figure 3.2 Reaction of parents to diagnosis that a multiple birth is expected.
Source: © J.R. Spillman.

event it was generally the babies of the younger mothers who arrived early and gave cause for anxiety in the first days of life. In the second study, midwives were also asked what they felt would worry the mothers when they were told about the great expectations. Few of them identified the same factors as those mentioned by the mothers. They thought the mothers would be most concerned about their own health, the delivery and how to feed two or more babies. The worry about the size of twins is one about which reassurance is particularly important. Parents should be told that twin babies do tend to be born smaller and earlier than their singleton counterparts but this does not mean they are not healthy.

Effects of the diagnosis

The first period of anxiety for mothers, and sometimes fathers, often started when the diagnosis was made in the scan room by the sonographer (Spillman 1985, Linney 1995). Most mothers stated that they were made aware by the reactions of the scan operator that something was amiss or not quite as expected. In some hospitals the sonographer was not allowed to break the news to the mother, who was told to return in a day or two to see the consultant. This led to great anxiety in the interim period. Mothers stated that they thought the baby was abnormal or even dead. When the scan operator was permitted to give the news, it was often shared less than diplomatically. For example, mothers were asked if they wanted the 'bad' news. One mother was told she had one-and-a-half babies in there! One can imagine what she visualised. Several mothers reported screaming, feeling faint or sick and crying uncontrollably. Ideally, when the diagnosis is made, the scan operator should present it as good news and an experienced midwife or doctor should be available to answer immediate questions. It is also very helpful if the mother is given the contact telephone number of the local twins club or another mother of twins who, having been through the experience can offer support, reassurance and encouragement. Many mothers report a feeling of total isolation. Most say that the best person to help other than their partner is another mother of twins. Although midwives were considered to be sympathetic, general practitioners were on the whole not thought to be understanding and obstetricians even less so. For example, one mother, Mrs S.K., describes her first visit to see the consultant at her local hospital:

> At our *first* meeting with my consultant, his first words were 'I need triplets like I need a hole in the head!' It was at this point that my husband and I decided to ask our GP if I could be referred to another hospital and consultant. . . . Given that we were already under considerable stress, how much nicer it would have been if we hadn't had to endure this totally negative and uncaring approach. Empathy, negotiation and discussion were sadly lacking.

Antenatal care and advice

Unfortunately, specific advice relating to the effects of a multiple birth on a family has been rarely available. Although those parents undergoing treatment for infertility do appear to be given counselling and warned of the risk of a multiple pregnancy, often no information is given of the implications of having and rearing an 'instant family' (Linney 1995). Mothers whose multiples are naturally conceived seem unlikely to receive any counselling whatsoever (Figure 3.3).

In one or two hospitals where there are obstetricians or midwives with a specific interest in multiple births, sound advice is available and gradually, over recent years, hospitals are beginning to set up specific clinics for mothers who are expecting two or more babies. Where this has happened it has been much appreciated. Parents receive specific advice on diet and rest, are given invitations to relaxation classes earlier than those with a singleton pregnancy, visit the neonatal unit and delivery suite sooner than those having one baby and are encouraged to finish work at an earlier stage.

These measures can result in healthier more confident mothers when the delivery date approaches. Because of the special input antenatally it is often possible for shared care with the general practitioner and practice midwife, resulting in a reduction in hospital visits for the parents.

In 1984 Dr Barbara Broadbent studied two groups of mothers in

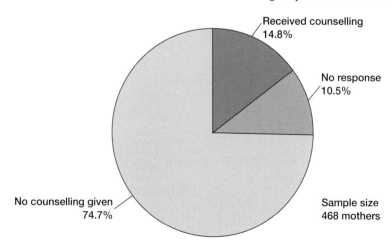

Figure 3.3 Antenatal counselling of mothers expecting a multiple birth.
Source: © J.R. Spillman.

Greater Manchester who were expecting multiple and singleton births respectively. Mothers expecting a multiple birth were required to travel more frequently to the hospital clinic for their antenatal care than were the singleton mothers. This involved them in greater expense, longer time commitments, difficulties in arranging child care and extreme tiredness, particularly in the last months of their pregnancy (Broadbent 1984). In the author's more recent research (Spillman 1992), many of the mothers received shared care which lessened the difficulties described by Broadbent, but the remainder found their frequent visits to distant consultant units tiring and inconvenient. They complained particularly about the lack of parking facilities, long waiting times, and seeing different members of staff at each visit, thus having to tell their histories repeatedly. They found all these difficulties stressful. It would seem that with good liaison between hospitals and GPs and practice midwives, most of the mothers could receive the bulk of their care at their own health centres.

Provision of literature and counselling

Many of the anxieties already mentioned might be relieved if adequate information and literature was made available to families. In my own research (Spillman 1992), very few parents received any (Figure 3.4). Much of what they learned was gleaned from women's and parents' magazines and from neighbours and family members.

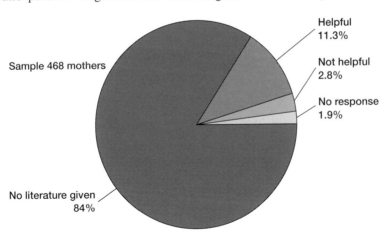

Figure 3.4 Literature given to mothers expecting multiples.
Source: © J.R. Spillman.

Unfortunately there was a dearth of such information from the professionals who cared for the families. Those interviewed thought that adequate advice and counselling was forthcoming if the 'parents asked for it'. When I asked them about their awareness of appropriate literature only 5 per cent could quote any suitable publication. The same was true when I enquired about their knowledge of local twins clubs and what service they offered. It would much enhance the practice of these professionals if they could point the parents in the right direction where excellent literature and appropriate advice is available and where baby equipment and clothing can be purchased at very low cost.

When midwives and nurses were aware of local clubs, they often thought that parents should wait until after the arrival of their multiples before they made contact. The usual reason they gave for this was that both or not all of the babies might survive. They were unaware that bereavement and special needs groups existed within Tamba to give appropriate support in those very situations. Mothers of twins still remain mothers of twins, even when one baby is lost. It is their special status and the pride in it that helps them to cope. Chapter 11 goes into such experiences in depth. When twins clubs have good liaison with their local hospital, the families' well-being and confidence is enhanced (Spillman 1992).

Antenatal hospitalisation

Another concern that parents have is the possibility of hospitalisation in the antenatal period. This used to be commonplace when twins were expected, but although it does still happen in a few centres the practice has largely fallen into disrepute as studies have found it to be unhelpful in the prevention of pre-term delivery, even in high risk cases (MacGillivray 1986, Crowther et al. 1989, Bryan 1996).

There are many advantages to keeping the mother at home as long as is practicable. First-time parents have often never been apart before and can become very depressed. Where there are other children, in particular toddlers, mothers become very anxious about periods of separation. Such little ones will have to make a great adjustment when two or more competitors arrive on the scene. Another advantage is that mothers often sleep more soundly in their own beds and prefer home cooking to hospital fare (Tresmontant and Papiernik 1983, Hay et al. 1990). Although, for those expecting twins admission for bed-rest has almost disappeared unless there are complications, for mothers having triplets or more it continues to be used in many cases. The author found that of twenty-eight mothers of triplets in her study, all but two experienced at least one term in hospital antenatally. The admissions were for periods extending from a few days to over three months.

The 'birth plan'

Another dilemma facing mothers having twins and more is the birth plan. These days this is a popular method of including the parents in how and where babies will be born. Although in my research I found that two mothers had delivered at home by prearrangement and another did not make it to the hospital, all the rest had a hospital confinement.

Although it is not in the brief of this chapter to comment on the medical aspects of multiple pregnancy, it is relevant to mention epidural anaesthesia and Caesarean section because the postnatal repercussions of these procedures affect the well-being of the family.

Epidural anaesthesia and Caesarean section

Even though many mothers wished to have a 'natural' birth it was commonplace for pressure to be put on them to undergo epidural anaesthesia, and in my research I found that many were given no choice (Spillman 1992). When the procedure was carried out by inexperienced professionals the mothers often found it was ineffective or had unpleasant side effects (Figure 3.5). Dr Elizabeth Bryan, a

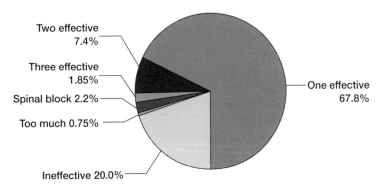

Figure 3.5 Effectiveness of epidurals in deliveries of multiples.
Source: © J.R. Spillman.

paediatrician internationally acknowledged as an expert in the management of the delivery of multiples, states:

> No medical team prepared for the delivery of twins can be complete without an experienced anaesthetist. General and epidural anaesthesia are frequently required, sometimes in the case of the second twin, at short notice.
>
> (Bryan 1992)

Mothers who were asked antenatally how they felt about having an 'epidural', having had the reasons and benefits explained to them, often accepted readily, although when the time for delivery came, many did not actually receive the anaesthesia because no anaesthetist was available to administer it.

I found in my research that the Caesarean section rate varied dramatically in different parts of the country. It was particularly high in the London area. Patients who underwent this operation tended to find their postnatal period much more difficult than the mothers who had normal deliveries. For example, they were less likely to succeed in their desire to breastfeed their infants and they were significantly more likely to suffer from postnatal depression. Many described their health postnatally as unwell or very unwell (Spillman 1993) (and see Figure 3.6).

Whether the babies are born naturally or by Caesarean operation, the delivery is likely to be more physically and emotionally stressful

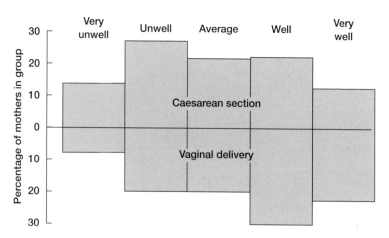

Figure 3.6 Mothers' assessments of their own health after delivery.
Source: © J.R. Spillman.

than for those who have a single baby. Apart from the risk of premature delivery with all its inherent anxieties, the presence of many attendants and on-lookers and the use of a multiplicity of monitoring and other equipment can prove unnerving for the parents. It has been shown that the presence of a partner or close family member or friend can do much to alleviate this anxiety (Spillman 1987a). Professionals who are aware of these difficulties can be sensitive to them and ensure that the parents are happy with the arrangements, particularly the presence of observers. My research showed that when the father is not present, mothers may not remember the birth of the second twin because of anxiety about the welfare of the firstborn infant. These mothers sometimes found difficulty in accepting and bonding with the second twin.

Twin babies frequently need to spend varying lengths of time in the neonatal unit after birth. This can be very worrying for their parents. It should be the aim of all staff caring for the mother and babies to help them cope with the separation involved. There are many strategies which can help make parents feel welcome and which are essential to the well-being of their babies. For example, here are some comments from mothers:

> 'I was encouraged to visit the babies at all times day or night or even to ring in the middle of the night if I wanted reassurance that the babies were OK.'

> 'The unit was beautifully decorated – lots of happy pictures and success stories.'

> 'The babies were dressed in pretty, well-cared-for clothes and had handmade cot covers.'

> 'Staff were in the main caring, supportive and encouraging, although with the shift system continuity was difficult. There were differences in approach which was confusing.'

In general, most mothers felt that the staff were supportive and caring although sometimes too busy to realise there were problems for families, especially if one baby was being nursed in the postnatal or transitional care ward with the mother and the other/others in the neonatal unit. This particularly affected feed times for the babies, which could clash with both sets of staff expecting the mother's presence simultaneously!

Interestingly, I found in my research that mothers whose infants were in the neonatal unit were more likely to successfully breastfeed their infants than those on the postnatal ward, where several mothers who had intended to breastfeed their babies gave up during the first few days, probably reflecting the amount of professional support they received (Spillman 1987a). Broadbent reported the same in her study (Broadbent 1984).

Discharge home of multiples

It should be realised that parents often feel secure in the hospital environment and may wish to postpone the return home because of the responsibility they will then have to undertake. It is important that the time of discharge is discussed with parents and agreement reached. The health visitor should meet the parents and assure them of her interest and support as soon as the babies go home. Some parents may wish to take one baby home before the other so as to be 'broken in gently'. Others may wish a well baby to be kept in the hospital until his or her brother or sister is ready for discharge. Where possible, a sympathetic ear and consideration should be given to such requests, though Hay (Chapter 8) does not recommend that one baby should come home before the other.

It is vital that adequate help is arranged for the family when the babies do come home. This is particularly so when there are toddlers to be considered. Mothers are usually exhausted following a multiple pregnancy and delivery. They may well have had a sleep deficit stretching over much of the final trimester of pregnancy. The stresses of coping without help can exacerbate the situation and lead to postnatal illness and/or depression.

Twin mothers face a dilemma. They want to care for their babies and to be seen to cope, but do not have the physical strength to do so. Toddlers who have been model children during the pregnancy can often become raging 'monsters' when two competitors for mum's attention arrive on the scene. If adequate help is provided, the whole situation will be less fraught and relationships can develop. Nursery nurse training colleges are often pleased to release their students to spend their practical experience time with a family with twins and this can be rewarding for both the student and the family.

The parents' anxieties about the birthweights of their expected twins or triplets have already been mentioned. When I asked mothers what weight they would define as satisfactory, those expecting twins, almost without exception, said that 5.5 lb (2.5 kg) would be acceptable and mothers of forthcoming triplets said they would be happy if their babies weighed in at 4.5 lb (2.04 kg) or more (Spillman 1984). In the event, in many cases, when the babies arrived, the mothers found that they developed an early preference for the infant who was heavier or, in the case of triplets, heaviest, even if the smaller babies weighed well above the desirable weight. The greater the weight difference, the more likely the preference. It seems that these smaller babies could become the epitome of the parents' antenatal anxieties. This even happened when the smaller baby was healthier and more active than the larger.

The professionals caring for the families were often unaware of the mother's ambivalent feelings, as most women tried to cover these up, fearing they would be labelled 'unsatisfactory mothers'. If doctors, nurses and other practitioners appreciate the possibility of a strong preference for the larger baby developing, by reassuring the mother that this is a normal feeling which will soon pass, the guilt can be relieved and support given to have time with each baby so as to allow relationships to develop. If this reassurance and support are not forthcoming, the preference can continue even into adulthood. There are warning signs that can alert carers to a bonding difficulty. For example, preferred twins are likely to be easier to feed, to vocalise earlier, are less likely to have temper tantrums and to be generally more sociable than those to whom the mother has difficulty in relating. The less favoured baby, on the other hand, may be more destructive and less sociable and be described as a 'loner' (Spillman 1987b). In a longitudinal study undertaken in Louisville, USA, it was reported that the smaller twins had more problems with sleeping, feeding and toilet training (Matheny and Brown 1971). These same researchers elicited that the smaller twins, more commonly, exhibited a larger number of temper tantrums, had attention deficits and were likely to suffer more accidental injuries when young (Matheny *et al.* 1971).

Another American study showed birthweight to be a factor in how mothers perceived their twin babies and suggested that the way they cared for their infants was affected by this (Allen *et al.* 1976).

Earlier research had shown that when IQ scores of twins were studied there was a correlation between the intra-pair weight difference and the intelligence quotients in favour of the larger baby. This held good for full-term and pre-term infants alike. The conclusion was that 'bigger is better' (Scarr 1969). Hay (Chapter 8), however, reports that apart from birthweight, 'the one variable that really mattered was which twin left hospital first'. There is a need to look at the overall picture.

The father

If mothers experience problems in building relationships with two babies, siblings and fathers may also find difficulties. In Chapter 10 the sibling experience is defined. However, it is important to look in more detail at the role of fathers. In my studies (Spillman 1984, 1992) I found a high incidence of marital breakdown, not only following the birth of multiples but in several instances at the time of diagnosis and before the birth. It seems that some fathers can be overwhelmed by the responsibilities imposed on them by the arrival of two or more babies simultaneously. This effect was exacerbated when the pregnancy had been unplanned or when triplets or higher multiples were involved (Price 1991).

Fathers have a vital role to play throughout twin pregnancy, birth and afterwards (Salvesen 1991). They should be involved right from the beginning. When this happens, most fathers come to enjoy their greater participation in the day-to-day care of the children, their partners cope better, siblings are less likely to feel left out and the family functions well. Fathers who do not share feel left out and seek satisfaction elsewhere, either at work or in relationships outside the home. It is desirable that the parents try to share time together on a regular basis, although this is often difficult to arrange. Mrs M.R. explains how she felt in the early days:

> 'Physically I was very tired and suffered from bouts of depression – emotionally I felt very vulnerable, stressed and isolated. I am concerned that this has had an adverse effect on my relationship with my husband. Because we are so tired and have no time to communicate, our relationship is suffering – we do try to mitigate this by trying to find time together alone. It's difficult to find someone to look after four children for any length of time.'

She then goes on to express her anxieties about how her husband is coping with the situation:

> 'He has had to give up any leisure/sporting activities as he recognises the need to relieve me if there is any spare time. As a result I am worried about his physical state of health – i.e. a classic case for heart problems, stressful job, stressful home life – no time for exercise or relaxation.'

She continues:

'The toll on our relationship is considerable. We hope we will get through it with support from our family and friends.'

Mrs M.R. portrays very graphically the stresses that can result from a multiple birth. It is likely that, as she was able to voice her concerns so articulately, she and her husband would be able to work through those early difficult days. For those parents who are unable to confide or discuss their anxieties, breakdowns in health and relationships may well occur. Professionals should be aware of the strains experienced by the families and offer support and counselling to help them adjust to their new situation. Health visitors have a vital role to play as carers with access to the home.

Parent support groups

The value of membership of a twins club for parents cannot be overstated. These clubs exist in most countries and throughout the United Kingdom. Ideally, parents should join in the antenatal period in order to get to know other parents who have survived the experience. There will usually be a good range of appropriate literature available on all aspects of rearing twins, triplets and more. For example, in the UK the Twins and Multiple Births Association (Tamba) offers advice on feeding the babies, mobility with multiples, potty training and many other subjects. Most UK clubs are affiliated to Tamba which publishes the various booklets. An excellent magazine, *Twins, Triplets and More*, is published three times annually and is full of interesting articles about raising multiples.

There are special groups within Tamba to support triplets and higher multiples, twins with special needs, lone parents of twins, families who have suffered bereavement, and adoptive parents of multiples. There is also a comprehensive group of professional consultants on hand to offer advice to members on most subjects. Access to these experts is directly through Tamba.

Professionals should be aware of the facilities offered by organisations such as Tamba as well as the professional support available from the Multiple Births Foundation (see Chapter 11) to enable them to offer quality care to these special families.

Tamba telephone helpline

Within the last few years Tamba has set up a listening service in the UK called Twinline, which has proved particularly supportive of parents concerned about their expectation of multiples, as well as the ongoing problems of caring for multiples, or of being a multiple. The Twinline listening service operates in the evenings and at weekends when statutory services are not always easily accessible. The most frequent calls concern maternal health and antenatal issues which include questions about zygosity, amniocentesis, breastfeeding and infertility.

However, once parents learn to cope with their special situation, there are many rewards and great joy to be had in having twins, triplets and more within the family. It is the duty of the professionals to do all in their power to help make this possible.

References

Allen, M.G., Greenspan, S.I., Pollin, W. (1976) 'The effect of parental perceptions on early development of twins', *Psychiatry*, 39 (February), 65–71.

Broadbent, B.A. (1984) 'A study of the effect on the family of a multiple birth', unpublished Ph.D. thesis, University of Manchester.

Bryan, E. (1992) *Twins and Higher Multiple Births – A Guide to their Nature and Nurture*, London, Edward Arnold.

Bryan, E. (1995) *Twins, Triplets and More – Their Nature, Development and Care*, London, MBF.

Cooper, C. (1997) *Twins & Multiple Births – The Essential Parenting Guide from Pregnancy to Adulthood*, London, Vermilion.

Crowther, C.A., Neilson, J.P., Verkuyl, D.A.A., Bannerman, C. and Ashurst, H.M. (1989) 'Preterm labour in twin pregnancies, can it be prevented by hospital admission?', *British Journal of Obstetrics and Gynaecology*, 96, 850–853.

Hay, D.A., Gleeson, C., Davies, C., Lorden, B., Mitchell, D. and Paton, L. (1990) 'What information should the multiple birth family receive before, during and after the birth?', *Acta Geneticae Medicae et Gemellologiae*, 39, 259–269.

Linney, J. (1995) 'Multiple births: assessing the mental health needs of mothers', M.Sc. dissertation.

MacGillivray, I. (1986) 'Epidemiology of twin pregnancy', *Semin Perinatology*, 10, 4–8.

MacGillivray, I., Samphier, M., Little, J. (1988) 'Factors affecting twinning', in I. MacGillivray, D.M. Campbell and B. Thompson (eds) *Twinning and Twins*, Chichester, John Wiley & Sons, pp. 67–98.

Matheny, A.P., Brown, A.M. (1971) 'The behaviour of twins: effects of birthweight and birth sequence', *Journal of Child Development*, 42, 251–257.

Matheny, A.P., Brown, A.M., Wilson, R.S. (1971) ' Behavioural antecedents of accidental injuries in early childhood: a study of twins', *Journal of Paediatrics*, 79, 122–124.

Price, F. (1991) 'Extraordinary circumstances: coping with triplets, quads and more', in D. Harvey and E. Bryan (eds) *The Stress of Multiple Births*, London, The Multiple Births Foundation, pp. 119–126.

Salvesen, S. (1991) 'A parent's view of early childhood', in *The Stress of Multiple Births*, London, The Multiple Births Foundation, pp. 68–73.

Scarr, S. (1969) 'Effects of birthweight on later intelligence', *Social Biology*, 16, 249–256.

Spillman, J.R. (1984) 'The role of birthweight in mother–twin relationships', unpublished M.Sc. thesis, University of Cranfield.

Spillman, J.R. (1985) 'You have a little bonus, my dear', *British Medical Ultrasound Bulletin*, 39, 6–9.

Spillman, J.R. (1987a) 'Emotional aspects of experiencing a multiple birth', *Midwife, Health Visitor and Community Nurse*, 23, 54–58.

Spillman, J.R. (1987b) 'Double exposure – coping with newborn twins at home', *Midwife, Health Visitor and Community Nurse*, 23(3), 92–94.

Spillman, J.R. (1992) 'A study of maternity provision and multiple births in the UK', *Acta Geneticae Medicae et Gemellologiae*, 41(4), 353–364.

Spillman, J.R. (1993) Multiple pregnancy – effects of caesarean section and epidural anaesthesia on postnatal health. *Proceedings: 23rd International Congress of Midwives*, Vancouver, Canada, 1V, 1766–1776.

Spillman, J.R. (1997) 'Multiple pregnancy', in B.R. Sweet and D. Tiran (eds) *Mayes Midwifery*, London, Balliere Tindall Ltd.

Tresmontant, R. and Papiernik, E. (1983) 'Economic analysis of the prevention of preterm births in twin pregnancy', *European Journal of Obstetrics and Gyncological Reproduction Biology*, 15, 277–279.

Tamba leaflets (regularly updated)

Twins, Triplets and Higher Order Pregnancies (a pamphlet for midwives).
Twins, Triplets and More (a pamphlet for health visitors).
Bottle Feeding Twins.
Healthy Eating for a Multiple Pregnancy.
Multiple Births Fact Sheet.
Postnatal Depression in Mothers of Multiples.
So You Are Expecting Twins.
The Arrival of Twins.
Twins, Triplets and Higher Multiples in Special Care Baby Unit.

Tamba booklets

Breastfeeding Twins, Triplets or More (ISBN 0–9518705–1–3).
Guide for Parents with Twins (ISBN 0–9518705–2–1).

4 Twins and their language development

Kay Mogford-Bevan

Introduction

In the twentieth century, the language of twins has been of special interest to psychologists. As the century progressed, linguists and speech and language pathologists also came to study the special characteristics of language development in twins and to help unravel the many interacting factors that shape its development.

The study of language development requires more than plotting the emergence of such milestones as the age of a child's first spoken words or sentences. Language has a complex structure, involving different levels of organisation. In child language the levels which have been studied are phonology, syntax (grammar) and semantics. In simple terms, phonology is the level at which speech sounds are used contrastively to differentiate word forms; grammar is the system of rules that governs the way that different meaningful units are combined to convey more complex meaning; semantics is concerned with the relationship between linguistic units and their meaning; and the way that language is used to fulfil the intentions of speakers is referred to as pragmatics. Although these levels interact, each has typically been analysed separately by linguists to show its structure. The study of child language has used similar linguistic techniques to describe and analyse the development of these systems and the same methods have been used to describe and understand the developing language of twins. However, despite popular interest in the topic, much remains to be investigated.

Language development in twins has attracted interest for a variety of reasons, some not directly related to twinship itself. For example, some studies have attempted to estimate how much variation in language ability between individuals can be attributed to genetic rather than environmental factors by using the variation in genetic make-up of monozygotic and dizygotic twins as a natural experiment (e.g. Munsinger and Douglass II 1976). Twins also provide a natural experiment in the social environment because twin siblings share from birth the environment and developmental resources usually available to a single child. The effect of sharing these resources can contribute to the understanding of critical features of the language learning environment (Mogford 1993).

This chapter, however, reviews research that aims to describe and understand the process of language development in twins for its own sake, as a special case of socialisation, where two siblings with the same developmental needs share the resources that are typically dedicated to rearing a single child. For twin children this also creates a unique personal psychological circumstance of sharing experiences with another individual throughout their development. (See Rutter and Redshaw (1991) for a review of psychological factors involved in 'growing up as a twin'.)

There have been two main approaches to the study of language development in twins: detailed individual case studies and group studies, where twins are compared on a variety of language measures with singletons. Both approaches have produced valuable insights, though disappointingly, the descriptions of the language of twins, even in case studies, have often been limited. Case studies are especially useful in highlighting the complexity of factors which bear on language development in individual pairs of twins and in providing the opportunity to record, often longitudinally, and to analyse aspects of language development in depth. Group studies, on the other hand, reveal trends and tendencies but generally use more restricted measures of language.

Group studies that compared singletons and twins with singleton norms have established that language development in twins is especially vulnerable to delay (Day 1932, Davis 1937, Mittler 1971). However, it seems that this vulnerability is marked in the early stages of development but diminishes as twins mature. Thus the onset of speech is frequently reported as later than in singletons (Zazzo 1960, Lenneberg 1967) which causes concern to parents and professionals alike. In middle childhood these differences persist but diminish (Zazzo 1960, Wilson 1977, Watts and Lytton 1981). By the time children reach the later stages of schooling, differences are still measurable and systematic but the degree of difference is so small as to be of little practical significance (Fischbein 1978). Psychologists have also established that language is not the only aspect of development that seems to be delayed in twins in infancy. Early investigations questioned whether the delay in language was explained as part of a delay in intellectual development, reflecting the demands made by twins on the environmental resources that promote development. Similar theories have been advanced to explain delays found in the younger children of large families, especially where births are closely spaced (e.g. Breland 1974).

It was shown that when children born as twins were reared as singletons, the delay in intellectual performance was smaller (Record *et al.* 1970). It gradually became clear, however, that although measures of intellectual performance might show a systematic if small deficit for twins this was almost entirely explained by the difference between verbal and performance elements in tests which measured intelligence (Koch 1966, Zazzo 1978). It was concluded that what needed explanation was language delay rather than slow intellectual development.

Studies also suggested that not only was language delayed, but it might also have distinctive characteristics reflecting the special social relationship between twin siblings. One version of this argument is that the especially close relationship between twin siblings and degree of shared experience compromises the development of individual identity and reduces the need for explicit interpersonal communication. This view is eloquently expressed by John Barth, a writer and a twin.

> But twins of any sort (i.e. monozygotic, dizygotic same or opposite genders) share the curious experiences of accommodating to a peer companion even from the beginning; even in the womb; of entering the world with an established side-kick, rather than alone, of acquiring speech and other skills a deux, while in the meanwhile sharing a language beyond speech and before speech. Speech, baby twins may feel is for Others. As native speakers of a dialect regard the official language, we may regard language itself: it is for dealing with outsiders; between ourselves we have little need of it.
>
> (Barth, quoted in Farmer 1996, p. 468)

It was from this perspective that the French psychologist Zazzo suggested that language delay resulted when twins developed their own jargon form of communication before they acquired the language of 'others'. Zazzo termed this *cryptophasia*: literally, a secret language. Zazzo thought that this early secret language was later replaced by the language of others but that language development was delayed as a result. Although other terms such as *idioglossia, twin talk* and *twin language* have been employed, *secret language* has become the most widely used. Bakker (1987a) rejects all these terms. He points out that these language forms are not restricted only to twins and multiple birth sets, and that the term *secret language* is misleading. The phenomenon is very different from true secret languages, where the intention of the inventors is to obscure meaning from others. These are usually created by peers and are rule-governed transformations of standard language forms. These secret languages are used in limited situations and exist alongside competence in the language of the community to which the children belong. Bakker rightly points out that the intention to obscure meaning cannot be attributed to twins who use their only form of language with all others and may show frustration when not understood. In addition, there is no evidence that the language is invented. Bakker favours another term, *autonomous language.* This term is associated with the Russian psychologist Luria, who used it to describe the language he studied in a single pair of twins with language delay (Luria and Yudovitch 1959). It appears that Luria and Yudovitch (1959) and Zazzo (1960) were actually referring to different phenomena. Although Luria's description is the more extensive, the description and analysis of the linguistic forms are relatively limited. None the less, it is apparent that he is describing an early form of speech rather than jargon, which shares characteristics with the earliest stages of language development in singletons. As cases of twins were identified who shared a speech system that was unintelligible to others, the belief that many twins develop a secret or autonomous language grew, although the nature of this language was rarely made explicit. Studies often report the incidence of secret language but offer no definition of what is meant by this (Mittler 1971). Despite the popular belief in the secret language of twins, the language has rarely been described in detail or analysed satisfactorily by linguists. Bakker (1987a) suggests that this is because linguists abandon detailed analysis as soon as they discover that these languages are primarily distorted versions of the child's mother tongue rather than entirely new creations. Another explanation is the practical difficulty involved. The degree of unintelligibility is often so extreme in twins that linguists find it difficult to determine what words were intended and are unable to use young children as reliable informants about what meaning they were trying to convey with their speech (see case illustration 4, p. 56).

The possibility that the unintelligible speech of twins might be the result of a shared speech disorder has been frequently debated. However, it is argued that the phenomenon of autonomous language only develops in instances where the models available to twins from adults are extremely restricted (Bakker 1987b). The relative unintelligibility of the speech of twins in comparison to singletons is often explained by suggesting that each twin uses the other as a model, thus reinforcing and stabilising their earliest forms of speech. This then contributes to the delay evident in the forms of language used and understood by twins. Bakker suggests that the lack of intelligibility further reinforces the parents' exclusion and reduces language input.

How inevitable is language delay in twins?

Risk factors and normally developing children

The emphasis given to language delay in twins should not lead to the conclusion that twins will inevitably show delayed language development. Even where a statistically significant difference is found between a singleton sample and a sample of twins, there will often be some twins whose language development is superior to some in the singleton group. This was clearly shown by Wilson (1977), who compared the verbal and performance scale scores of twins on the WISC with siblings from the same families at 7 and 8 years of age. Although there was a significant but small difference in favour of siblings on the verbal scale, 44.5 per cent of the twins scored as well or better than siblings. Wilson concluded that twins 'are not routinely handicapped in the development of their verbal abilities' and there is 'no across the board pervasive effect that suppresses the verbal development of all twins' (p. 215).

According to Pinker (1984), language acquisition is 'a stubbornly robust process' and the developmental outcome of a complex interaction of factors. In addition, development is characterised by plasticity (Siple 1985), which means that there exists the capacity to adapt to a range of varying circumstances and disadvantages in language learning. The circumstance of twinship alone is unlikely to have inevitable negative consequences for language development although the increased incidence of speech and language problems found in twins (Watts and Lytton 1981, McEvoy and Dodd 1992) testifies to the increased risk.

There have been no studies that have set out to look at factors which reduce or increase the risk of language delay, although some clues have emerged incidentally. It is clear from some of the most well-known case studies that rearing twins puts such a strain on some parents that the overall quality of parenting may suffer, especially for parents in disadvantaged circumstances (Luria and Yudovitch 1959, Douglas and Sutton 1978). This is supported by Robarge *et al.* (1982). Twins may also affect family dynamics with implications for language development (Sandbank and Brown 1990).

Some of the variables associated with language development in twins have been explored but with contradictory results: these include gender and social class (Davis 1937, Koch 1966, Lenneberg 1967, Mittler 1970, Conway *et al.* 1980, Hay *et al.* 1987).

There are a few case studies of twins whose language is developing normally. The identical twin girls studied by Malmstrom and Silva (1986) are reported to have developed conventional syntax and vocabulary. Waterman and Shatz's (1982) study of twin boys aged 2:1–3:7 provides longitudinal data indicating no overall delay in language development. The twin boys Toby and David (Keenan 1974, Keenan and Klein 1975) aged 2:9 appear also to be developing close to the norms though data are limited. All three pairs were from middle-class families with parents who had high levels of education. The three pairs of twins learning Serbo-Croat studied by Savic (1980) also showed no delay. These twins were deliberately chosen from advantaged backgrounds so that only the effects of twinship would be studied. In particular, in all three families, both parents had higher education and childcare was shared by at least three adults. Stafford (1987) also studied children from advantaged backgrounds and although she found that twins were relatively delayed on a standard language measure, all twins performed within the norms for their age. It appears that the effects of advantage and disadvantage may be magnified in language development in twins.

Comparing twins with singletons – difference or delay?

The work of Savic (1980) raised a question that had not previously been considered: whether language development in twins is different in quality from that of singletons. When twin language is studied longitudinally, as a developing system in its own right, what may look like a delay when cross-sectional comparisons between singletons and twins are made may be seen as a difference in the sequence of development. A similar point was made by Waterman and Shatz (1982) in relation to the development of names and personal pronouns in their twins. Savic argued that utterances are found to be shorter in twins. This is not because they are delayed in grammatical development but is a consequence of the conversational conditions in which they typically communicate. Conversations between caregivers and twins typically involve at least three participants and so conversational turns need to be brief. Savic suggested that twinship might confer some advantages on twins in some aspects of language development, particularly in the acquisition of personal pronouns and using social speech. She presented some evidence from her twin study to support both of these suggestions. Apart from Savic, relatively few investigations have been made of the ability of twins to handle triadic interaction and conversation. Studies tend to concentrate on assessing the quantity and quality of adult speech directed to twins in the triad or to study the intra-twin dialogues of twins when no adult is present. In one of these studies (Keenan 1974, Keenan and Klein 1975) twins as young as 2:9 years were found to demonstrate conversational turn-taking. Savic reports conversational co-ordination between twins prior to their second birthday. She suggests that twins have greater opportunities to practise dialogue skills which appear to emerge later in singletons (Garvey 1984).

Some key concepts in language acquisition and language disorder

The complexity of language acquisition

Language development is a complex and multidimensional aspect of development. Normally there will be chronological and functional relationships between the different systems of language during development, although it has also been shown in exceptional circumstances that some systems are impaired or delayed while others develop as expected. For example, typically, understanding and use of language develop in a related and predictable way. With a small number of children, however, while language understanding approaches normality, expressive speech is markedly delayed. Other children may show an isolated difficulty in producing the speech sound (phonological) patterns of a language. There may be difficulties with forming correctly mature grammatical forms, acquiring appropriate expressive vocabulary or recalling appropriate words when needed. Further, competent communication demands not only the ability to produce acceptable and intelligible forms but also the ability to vary forms in different contexts in order to convey the intention of the speaker in appropriate ways. Some children lack this ability despite competence in other systems.

When studying the language of any child, it is not enough to describe the child's errors by comparing the child's language with that of an adult. The study of language development has shown that each child gradually creates their own rules, based on the system that they experience in communication, which they use to produce and understand language. As a result, the child may use language forms that they are unlikely to have heard spoken by adults. However, over time the rules are refined and reformulated until the language used and the interpretation of other speakers matches that of the adult community. Over the last thirty years typical developmental sequences and rates of development have been described for singleton children in phonology (speech sounds), syntax (grammar), semantics (meaning) and pragmatics (language use and function) for many languages. Since each child needs to acquire rather than be taught these rules, there may be individual variation in the process and different routes to mature language forms. The same systems of analysis that have been applied to the study of the language of normal children have also been applied to children with difficulties in developing speech and language.

Language delay and language disorder

A conceptual distinction has been made between language that is delayed and language that is disordered. Although the distinction is controversial it is useful in the context of twin language development. Until now only two possibilities have been considered: first, that language development in some twins can be delayed or second, develops normally. In this section the distinction between language delay and language disorder is outlined and a third possibility examined: that language development in some twins may be disordered.

Although there is some variation in the way these two terms are used, in this chapter *language delay* is used to refer to language development that seems to be following the typical pattern of singleton children but at a slower rate. The term is used also to suggest that language delay arises as a consequence of inadequacies in the language learning environment. In this sense of *language delay*, improvements in language learning opportunities should lead to a rapid restoration of the normal rate of development. The implication is that all the components of the child's psycholinguistic system which processes and facilitates the acquisition of language function effectively.

With a *language disorder*, different levels of language development may proceed at different rates so that some will be delayed relative to others. In addition, when the rules that underlie the child's language are analysed, these may differ from those that are typical. Furthermore, the normal rate of development and the typical pattern cannot be restored simply by increasing language input. The effects of a *language disorder* are typically persistent and require more specifically targeted teaching over a period of time than is the case with language delay. Even though spoken language disorders may be resolved, there may be difficulties with reading and writing. The implication is that the child has difficulty in acquiring language which is due to a weakness in one or more psychological processes that make language acquisition possible. This is not pure supposition: these weaker elements can be identified if they are systematically assessed, using appropriate assessments and models of language processing.

Factors causing language disorder in singletons

Language disorder was first described in singleton children midway through the nineteenth century. It was recognised that, in acquiring language, some children experienced difficulty that could not be attributed to any of the primary causes of language difficulties such as hearing or intellectual impairment, neglect and deprivation, or psychiatric disorder. Indeed, what seemed to be outstanding in these children was the degree to which their competence and intellectual capacities were preserved in the face of significant difficulties in acquiring speech and language. From the 1970s onwards psychologists, linguists and speech and language pathologists have exhaustively studied the linguistic and behavioural characteristics of these children and have developed methods to assess and describe the patterns of language development which characterise what has come to be known as *specific language impairment* (SLI). A wide range of possible causes for SLI have been investigated (Bishop 1987). While the evidence for some causes has proved inconclusive or negative, genetic explanations have looked promising. The study of language development in twins, using the twin method, has played a major part in this investigation.

Factors causing difficulties in acquiring language in twins

For many years language disorder was not considered as an explanation for language difficulties in some twins. When twins were compared with singletons, twins with speech and language difficulties due to hearing impairments, motor impairments affecting speech, autism or intellectual impairment were excluded. However, the possibility that some twins might have a primary language disorder was not explicitly considered in many studies and it is not clear if some of the verbal deficit found for twins could be due to the inadvertent inclusion of twins with specific language disorders.

One common presentation of SLI is failure to develop intelligible speech because of delayed or disordered phonology (speech sounds) (Ingram 1976, Grunwell 1981). The child typically uses a smaller number of different speech sounds than are used in the adult language. The structure of words may be simplified and there are systematic substitutions of one sound for another. In a volunteer sample of nineteen multiple birth sets at 3 years of age, McEvoy and Dodd (1992) found that only 10 per cent showed normal development in the language profile used to assess development. All the remaining sets showed an uneven profile of development and three-quarters evidenced delayed and atypical phonological (speech sound) development characteristic of such a disorder in singleton children. In the sets where one child showed a phonological delay or disorder, this was shared by the other sibling, to some degree, in all but two cases.

Further support for the finding that twins sometimes share a language disorder is demonstrated by research that finds higher levels of such patterns in monozygotic than in dyzygotic pairs (Lewis and Thompson 1992, Bishop *et al.* 1995). Indeed, the recognition that twins could have a specific language impairment (Levi and Bernabei 1976) rather than, or as well as, a delay in language provided evidence for the genetic basis of specific language impairments. The 'twin method' is an experimental design which compares the co-occurrence of a disorder in both members of monozygotic and dizygotic twins. A higher co-occurrence of a condition in monozygotic than dyzygotic twins suggests that there is a significant genetic component involved in the aetiology, since it is assumed that the environment is common to both members of each pair. Although previously a familial tendency to SLI had been recognised (Tomblin 1989, Lewis and Thompson 1992) an investigation using the twin method had not previously been undertaken. Two studies (Lewis and Thompson 1992, Bishop *et al.* 1995) have now used this method and findings indicate a significant genetic factor in the causation of SLI and that this factor is higher in male twins than female twins.

These studies are not unproblematic because there is also a high level of language delay in twins which could be misdiagnosed as SLI. Lewis and Thompson overcame this difficulty by studying children only at an age when language delay should have resolved in twins. Bishop *et al.* (1995) used very stringent diagnostic criteria. Both studies found a significantly higher concordance for language disorder in monozygotic twins than for dizygotic pairs.

Explanations for language delay in twins

Birth hazard

As discussed in the previous section, twin language development may not only show the special characteristics of 'the twin situation' but may also be influenced by the same factors that produce speech and language difficulties in singletons, like specific language disorder. In addition, there is an increased risk of some disabilities, particularly those that result from birth injury. This is because twins are at greater risk from the hazards of birth than singletons (MacGillivray *et al.* 1988). Although children with birth injury are typically eliminated from studies which show language delay in twins, there is still the possibility that twin language development is put at risk through the greater incidence found in twins of prematurity and low birthweight even where hard neurological signs are absent (Rutter and Redshaw 1991). This is one explanation for language delay in twins that has been investigated systematically. However, there is little evidence to suggest that language delay in twins can be attributed to prenatal and perinatal factors. Indeed, Lytton *et al.* (1977) claimed that the majority of difference in twin language development from which children with frank impairment had been excluded could be attributed to the postnatal environment.

The twin situation

Since the increased birth hazards of twinship cannot explain language delay in twins, the cause may lie with the special social and psychological situation into which twins are born. In this section different interpretations of this view will be examined.

Identity and motivation

The first of these explanations is based on the difficulty which twins experience in establishing separate identities and the reduced motivation they supposedly show to communicate with others. There are suggestions in the literature that twins suspend communication in the presence of 'outsiders'. The evidence for this claim is not well established although it clearly does happen in some cases, notably when twins show elective mutism. However, the number of recorded instances of this condition in twins is limited (Mora *et al.* 1962, Tachibana *et al.* 1982, Wallace 1996). Elective mutism is a rare and persistent condition in which a child who has the ability to talk chooses to talk only in familiar settings while not talking to unfamiliar people, typically in school. Although relationships within the family may explain many cases, elective mutism is associated with speech and language disorders in one-third of cases (Steinhausen and Juzi 1996). It may be that the diagnosis is often not made in the case of twins because the situation is usually thought to be explained by twinship. For example, in the case of S. and D., identical male twins of 4:5 years studied by myself, the twins were judged by their nursery school to have failed to develop speech and language because they had not been heard to talk in the classroom over an eighteen-month period. The twins' parents reported that they spoke at home, although their speech was very difficult to understand. When the twins' communication was recorded in both settings it was found that they would talk at home and with other adults in private but not to adults or children in the classroom. Their speech was severely unintelligible and their language delayed. They relied heavily on context and gesture to make themselves understood. Although they behaved as electively mute in the classroom, they communicated energetically with others elsewhere. Investigation of their family circumstances suggested that their speech and language disorder was the cause of their reluctance to speak at school and not the 'symbiotic' relationship associated with other cases of elective mutism.

Evidence to support the view that twins routinely have difficulty with establishing separate identities is sometimes advanced from studies of the way that twins refer to themselves. However, the detailed studies that have been carried out on this phenomenon (Malmstrom and Silva 1986, Waterman and Shatz 1982) have clearly demonstrated that the use of a single name for the twin pair, for example, *Krista–Kelda* (Malmstrom and Silva 1986) was neither the consequence of language delay nor a failure to differentiate their names. Rather it was a way of marking their twin status. In both cases the phenomenon was of relatively short duration and had disappeared by age 3–3:5.

When twins are recorded in the presence of adults, it is not uncommon for the majority of the interaction to involve the adult. Malmstrom and Silva (1986) cited this as a reason for recording crib-dialogues as a way of collecting data on co-twin interaction. Savic (1980) found that the three normally developing twin pairs whom she studied most frequently addressed or sustained dialogue with adults. In two pairs of identical male twins (4:1 and 4:5 years respectively) referred for speech and language therapy, video-recordings were made by the author of each pair interacting with an adult. Of the utterances used by pair one, K. and J., when interacting in a free-play setting with their mother, twice as many turns in dyadic interaction were addressed to the adult by each twin as were addressed to their co-twin. Interaction between the adult and a single child accounted for 74 per cent of the interaction. In the second pair, S. and D., the adult who was present in the playroom filmed them as they played together. Here 47 per cent of turns were addressed by one of the twins to the adult present and only 5 per cent to their co-twin. Adult–child dyadic interaction accounted for 85 per cent of the verbal turns exchanged. In neither case was there any evidence of lack of motivation to communicate with the adult.

Another explanation for language delay, especially when it is apparent in only one of the siblings, is that of dominance. It has been recorded (Savic 1980) that twins develop distinct roles within their relationship in which each specialises in a specific set of skills. One of these is speaking. This has been thought to cause delay in the language of the non-dominant twin. However, it could equally be that the dominance of one twin in verbal exchanges is caused by a speech or language delay or disorder in the other twin. Although specialisation in verbal skills is often reported by parents, it is not always a stable feature of the relationship over time.

Autonomous language

The second explanation is that twin language development is delayed because they develop an autonomous language. As was indicated in the introduction, ideas about the nature of this language have differed. There have been few substantive accounts of this language. Bakker (1987a) reviewed thirteen published studies, not all in multiple birth situations. He claims that autonomous languages are acquired as the children's only form of language and are phonologically reduced forms of the language models of their parents which is why they are unintelligible. He estimates that about 90 per cent of words are derived in this way and a further 10 per cent are idiosyncratic onomatopoeic words. The words tend not to be inflected and many grammatical components are deleted. The remaining elements tend to be combined in a free order so that the syntax is considered deviant. However, as the autonomous language is continuously changing in the direction of the community language model, it eventually disappears. Bakker also considers that autonomous languages only arise in twins who live in relative isolation from peers and adults but not when language models are virtually absent as when children suffer extreme forms of deprivation (Kulochova 1972, 1976).

Another element in the autonomous language theory of language delay is that each pair develops its own form of language because they use each other as a model. If this were the case it would be expected that the forms used by each twin would be very close. Indeed, evidence from twins with unintelligible speech suggests that systems may be similar but rarely identical. In the study by Dodd and McEvoy (1992), three aspects of the spoken forms of twins' language were examined to distinguish between autonomous language and disordered phonology. In addition to the similarity of phonological (speech sound) systems used by seventeen sets of twins and two of triplets, the difference between systems in use in adult–child discourse and intra-twin discourse was analysed. The ability of co-twins to understand the non-standard spoken forms of their siblings' speech was also assessed relative to matched peers. All three measures favoured the explanation of language disorder rather than autonomous language. Although twins understood their siblings' words better than matched peers, their understanding was better the closer the forms sounded to the adult version. However, in the two case studies of twins with very unintelligible speech, K. and J. (4:1) and S. and D. (4:5), the patterns of speech identified were those of very early speech development, and though very similar were not identical. Both pairs showed some patterns of speech sound substitution that were shared but they also used some patterns not used by their co-twin. Little spontaneous change in these patterns was reported, which tends to support the view that the patterns were reinforced by the presence of the co-twin.

Triadic interaction and child-directed speech

The third explanation for language delay in twins is based on the reduction in the quantity of language used with each twin by the adult caregiver. Initially, studies quantified the amount of language directed to twins by parents. Lytton's (1980) study found that parents of twin boys (2 to 3 years) spoke less and responded less to their children than parents of singletons of the same age. It has already been established that the interactive style commonly associated with advanced language development in singletons in the early years is typically high levels of shared visual attention and relevant responses by the caregiver to the child's communication and interests. Bornstein and Ruddy (1984) found that although there were no developmental differences between a sample of twins and singletons at age 4 months, there were differences in the way that mothers spoke to their infants and directed their attention. By age 12 months significant differences had developed between these twins and singletons, particularly in early language. Tomasello *et al.* (1986) also showed that the language input of mothers to twins and singletons differed but that this was not explained by the children's language delay. Differences in mothers' speech remained even when singletons and twins were matched for language level.

Reduced language input is now understood to be a consequence of the predominance of triadic interaction in childrearing of twins as opposed to the dyadic interaction which tends to occur more frequently in the language learning experience of singletons. Stafford (1987), however, found that differences between mothers of twins and singletons were present when both were studied in a triadic situation. Savic argued that in dyadic interaction between a mother and a single child, there is an obligation to respond in turn to the communicative partner, whereas with two potential respondents, an utterance addressed to a pair carries the option rather than the obligation of a response. She concludes, 'twins are as interested in adults as singletons, because they too need to interact verbally with adults, but in the twin situation, adults react differently because they have to interact with two children'. Adults have a largely directive role and often do not respond to speech of twins that is not clearly directed to them. She attributes parents' briefer utterances to the speed and efficiency needed to exploit pauses in order to gain conversational turns in triadic conversations. A test of this explanation was a study of parents of seven pairs of twins (1:11 to 3:9 years) looking at picture- and story-books with their children (Jones 1998). Conversations between one (twin) child and the mother were compared with conversations between both children and the mother. It was found that mothers initiated the same amount of conversations in both situations. The children however responded more to these initiations in dyadic situations (73 per cent) than in the triadic situation (47 per cent). The difference was greater when the child's initiations were considered. In the dyadic situation mothers responded to 100 per cent of their child's initiations but in the triadic situation this dropped to 53 per cent.

This and the study by Tomasello *et al.* (1986) demonstrate that it is the triadic situation rather than the language level of the twins that determines the reduced amount of caregivers' speech to twins. Although a causal link between reduced input and delayed language has yet to be established, this seems the most plausible explanation of those who suggest that it is 'the twin situation' which produces a language delay.

Conclusions

Complexity of factors influencing language development in twins

Although language difficulties in twins are not inevitable, there is a greater risk in twins than singletons that language development may at some stage deviate from the norms expected in singletons. Sometimes the difference may be a direct result of twinship but indicate neither a delay nor a disorder. At other times the difference follows a pattern of delay or a disorder but the two can also overlap (see case illustration 2, p. 54). This gives those with a clinical responsibility a complex diagnostic problem in trying to determine which factors in any particular case are responsible for the language difficulties of twins.

Clinicians will need to assess the contribution of these factors carefully, through talking to parents and observing the twins in different communicative situations. They should try to discover ways in which parents have attempted to develop the personal identity of the twin siblings. Robin *et al.* (1994) found that French parents differed in the way they interpreted advice on developing individual identity in twins. Another factor to explore is the amount of available dyadic adult–child interaction. This will depend on the childcare support which main caregivers receive from their partners and the involvement of the extended family. The resources available for the care of twins, the time available and the motivation to carry out language activities can be affected by a range of factors including the health of the mother and the twins, the family composition and parents' employment, education and material circumstances. Where possible, observation of interaction in the home may help to assess the degree to which the children are motivated to communicate with adults. If the twins attend a nursery group, systematic observation can establish how much twins communicate with one another, and with peers and teachers. These investigations have two purposes: first, to assess ways to enhance the language learning situation; second, to assess the extent to which the language difficulties of the twins under investigation can be attributed to delay rather than to language disorder since this distinction carries implications for intervention.

In the case of a language delay, optimising the language learning environment may be sufficient to accelerate language development, especially if investigations have identified factors that may have reduced the effectiveness of the language learning environment (see case illustration 3, p. 55). If these factors are negligible, then a language disorder may be suspected, especially where there is a positive family history of language impairment. In this case, more specific language teaching and therapy is indicated (Lewis and Thompson 1992).

Although birth hazard is not thought to explain language delay in twins, there will be a number of twins who do suffer speech and language difficulties as a result of perinatal injury (see case illustration 1, p. 53). Where this is the case, the medical history should support this diagnosis. In these circumstances, the child may suffer from cerebral palsy, which may affect speech co-ordination. If this is associated with an intellectual impairment, language will also be delayed. In some cases, in the absence of motor disorders, the difficulties may be those associated with extreme prematurity.

Epilogue: four main patterns of presentation

To aid the clinician, four typical patterns of presentation are described and illustrated with brief case reports. There is also a brief discussion of management.

The first pattern is when one member of the pair, though sometimes both twins, suffers the consequences of a birth injury that leads to an impairment of speech. Where one child only is affected and the impairment is mild, there may be problems associated with the expectations of each member of the twin pair. Parents may need help in adjusting to the different communication abilities of each twin. Parents may also report that the more able, verbal twin seems to dominate interaction and anticipate the needs of the other child. This imbalance needs to be managed to give the less intelligible twin greater opportunities for verbal expression (see case illustration 1).

The second pattern is when one member of the twin pair presents with a primary language delay or disorder. This may be more common in dizygotic twins, especially when the pair are of different genders (Haden and Penn 1985, Clements and Fee 1994). Here again, the difficulty may be maintained by the dominance of the more advanced verbal member of the pair. A case study by Haden and

Case illustration 1

Michael was an identical twin who suffered a birth injury which left him with a unilateral facial weakness, poor concentration and mild learning difficulties, while his brother Raymond was unaffected. Although Raymond and Michael attended the same school, they were in different classes and had different friends. Raymond rarely played with his brother. Michael was referred to speech therapy at 6:5 years because his speech was not very intelligible. As well as delayed speech sound development he was also found to have difficulty articulating speech sounds requiring lip movements. His lack of confidence reduced his willingness to communicate, especially at home where he had to compete with his brother Raymond, whose speech and language were normal. Although he had a speech difficulty, Michael's language development was within normal limits for his age and ability. Michael's family found it difficult to accept the difference between the boys in ability and behaviour. Michael responded successfully to speech therapy. He benefited from the individual attention and his confidence increased. His family began to understand the reasons for his problems and his parents tried to ensure that he was given more opportunities to speak and that his contributions were respected and encouraged. This meant that he made greater efforts to communicate at home. However, he continued to show learning difficulties and behaviour problems at school.

Penn (1985) addressed this problem. They studied a pair of opposite sex fraternal twins from age 3:7–5:2 and found that the speech of both twins was affected by the presence of the co-twin when language samples were elicited. The twin with normal language development tended to dominate the interaction, competing for attention, breaking turn-taking rules, correcting and completing her sibling's speech. The effect was lessened after the twin with delayed language development was given individual speech and language therapy (see case illustration 2, p. 54).

The third and most common pattern is when both members of the pair present with a pattern of delay though there may be a difference in the degree of delay. Parents may think that the less advanced child is using the more advanced twin as a model because similar delayed forms are used by both twins, but one after the other. Intervention may succeed in enhancing the language learning environment of each twin by increasing the amount of adult–child dyadic interaction. Extra resources may not always be available within the family and

Case illustration 2

Fraternal twins, Kieran and Stacey, were born into a family with two older sisters, one of whom was attending a special language unit as a result of her specific language impairment. The twins were referred to speech and language therapy at age 2:6 by their health visitor, who felt they were showing a significant language delay. Unusually, Kieran, the boy, was found to be more advanced than his sister. He spoke in single words and had just begun to make some two-word combinations to accompany his age-appropriate play. Stacey, however, was withdrawn, spoke very little and showed delayed play development. Her mother indicated that with four children and a disabled husband she had little time to spend with the twins. Further investigation revealed that Kieran, the much desired and only son, was favoured by his father, who gave him a great deal of his time and attention. Stacey received little attention from either mother or father. A relative, who befriended the children's mother, expressed concern that Stacey was neglected and undertook to give her daily one-to-one attention and language stimulation. The twins were also admitted early to the local nursery school which ran a continuing language programme for children with speech and language delay. Kieran made steady progress and his language and speech were soon within the range of children attending the local nursery, indicating that he probably showed a language delay. Although Stacey made an initial spurt in development following the intervention of her aunt, she later made limited progress and at age 4:0 showed a severe delay in expressive speech and language, although her language understanding had shown much improvement. In this respect, her difficulties seemed to be following a path similar to her older sister who attended a language unit, and so she began to receive individual speech and language therapy and to be considered for a place in a language unit. It was felt that Stacey's difficulties resulted from the combination of a reduction in language input and from a familial tendency to language disorder.

supplying them may require liaison with extended family, nursery school or voluntary agencies which can provide practical support for parents in the home. Intervention programmes aimed at optimising parent–child interaction are also of value here; for example, the Hanen Early Language Parent Program (Girolametto *et al.* 1986) (see case illustration 3).

The fourth pattern is when both children present with a language disorder. In such cases, factors suggesting language delay are negligible and the pattern of language development on assessment shows

Case illustration 3

Julia and Marie were identical twin girls who had one older brother. There was no history of speech and language difficulties in the family. Although the girls' mother took pleasure in dressing them alike she tried to emphasise their individual identities in other ways. She reported that her husband had a demanding job and was unable to share much in the care of the twins and she had little time to give them individually, although she did play with them together at home. Their older brother had his own interests and friends and spent little time with the girls. At 4 years of age both girls showed a delay in all aspects of speech and language, which included the speech sound system (phonology), the understanding and use of grammatical sentences and vocabulary. Both children showed a typical pattern of development but Julia was more advanced than Marie, although the difference between them was not great. Julia was more outgoing and Marie tended to rely on her sister in interaction with strangers and the girls were very reluctant to be separated in the speech clinic. Their mother believed that Marie copied the patterns used by Julia. However, since both children were following the same typical pattern of development it was more likely that this impression resulted from one child being more advanced than the other. Three strategies were adopted to encourage further language development. First, the children's father agreed to share a story reading programme so that each child had some daily one-to-one time with a parent. The children both attended a block of language therapy sessions in a group with other children which aimed to improve listening and language comprehension. At the nursery class, attached to their local primary school, the girls were placed in different family groups managed by different members of staff although they were still in the same class. At age 5, both girls' speech and language had developed considerably and could be considered to be within the low normal range.

an uneven profile. This pattern is more common in monozygotic twins, particularly males. It is also most likely that the problem will be a phonological (speech sound system) disorder where development is atypical. Difficulties are likely to be persistent and to require speech and language therapy. Later there may be associated difficulties with reading (Dodd and Envoy 1992, Johnston *et al.* 1984). Although the form of intervention provided will depend on locally available resources and services, some children may be treated while attending mainstream schools while others may need the intensive provision of a language unit (see case illustration 4, p. 56).

Case illustration 4

When John and Derek were aged 3:11 they attended the local speech and language therapy clinic for assessment. Although they were outgoing and very talkative the speech and language therapist found them severely unintelligible. When she analysed their speech patterns used in single words, produced when naming pictures, she found that their speech sound system was severely delayed but also atypical and disordered. Although some of these atypical patterns were shared, each boy had some patterns not used by his brother. The pattern of language development was also uneven. For example, their understanding of grammatical structures and vocabulary was appropriate for their age, as was their play. It was difficult to tell if their conversational utterances were grammatically well-formed because it was often difficult to decide if grammatical words and affixes were being used. The children's mother and older sister were able to understand them, although their 'translation' was based on recognising key words and using the context and their own knowledge of grammar to suggest utterances that they thought the boys intended. Both boys communicated willingly and energetically with adults. Their older sister had no language problems and was considered to be very advanced in language by her school. The boys' mother felt that the twins' language development had been impaired as a result of her own ill-health. During the first few years of their life she had suffered a chronic illness that left her very tired and unable to give them much attention. She had been grateful that they played well together and felt that they had received far less attention than their sister. However, the boys showed a good knowledge of the world and were well used to co-operating in activities with adults which, taken together with their level of language understanding, indicated that their difficulties could not be entirely explained by a deprivation of language input. Although identical and often dressed alike, they were treated as individuals with different personalities, likes and interests. Neither was regarded as consistently dominant in speaking. The boys received speech and language therapy from age 4 to age 7:6. As their difficulties with the speech sound system were resolved it became clear that they also omitted grammatical elements from sentences. This difficulty was successfully remedied through therapy. They remained within their local mainstream school where they received sympathetic handling. This helped them to develop relationships with local children and at age 7:6, when discharged from speech and language therapy, the school felt that both boys were well integrated within their peer group.

References

Bakker, P. (1987a) 'Autonomous languages', *Publikaties Van Het Institute Voor Algamene Taalwetenschap* 53, University of Amsterdam.

Bakker, P. (1987b) 'Autonomous language in twins', *Acta Geneticae Medicae et Gemellologiae: Twin Research* 36, 233–238.

Barth, J. (1982) 'The making of a writer', *New York Times*, in P. Farmer, *Two or The Book of Twins and Doubles*, London: Virago Press.

Bishop, D. (1987) 'The causes of specific developmental language disorder ("developmental dysphasia")', *Journal of Child Psychology and Psychiatry* 28, 1–8.

Bishop, D.V.M., North, T. and Donlan, C. (1995) 'Genetic basis of specific language impairment: evidence from a twin study', *Developmental Medicine and Child Neurology* 37, 56–71.

Bornstein, M.H. and Ruddy, M.G. (1984) 'Infant attention and maternal stimulation: prediction of cognitive and linguistic development in singletons and twins', in H. Bouma and D.G. Bouwhuis (eds) *Attention and Performance X: Control of Language Processes*, London: Lawrence Erlbaum.

Breland, H. (1974) 'Birth order, family configuration and verbal achievement', *Child Development* 45, 1011–1019.

Clements, A. and Fee, E.J. (1994) 'An intra-twin phonological study: the phonologies of an SLI twin and her normally developing brother', *First Language* 14, 213–231.

Conway, H.C., Lytton, H. and Pysh, F. (1980) 'Twin–singleton language differences', *Canadian Journal of Behavioural Sciences* 12, 264–271.

Davis, E.A. (1937) 'The development of linguistic skill in twins, singletons with siblings, and only children from five to ten years', Monograph 14, Minneapolis: Institute of Child Welfare, University of Minnesota.

Day, E.J. (1932) 'The development of language in twins: 1. A comparison of twins and single children', *Child Development* 3, 179–199.

Dodd, B. and McEnvoy, S. (1994) 'Twin language or phonological disorder?', *Journal of Child Language* 21, 273–290.

Douglas, J.E. and Sutton, A. (1978) 'The development of speech and mental processes in a pair of twins: a case study', *Journal of Child Psychology and Psychiatry* 19, 49–56.

Fischbein, S. (1978) 'School achievement and test results for twins and singletons in relation to social background', in W.E. Nance, G. Allen and P. Parisi (eds) *Twin Research: Progress in Clinical and Biological Research: Psychology and Methodology*, New York: Liss.

Garvey, C. (1984) *Children's Talk*, London: Fontana.

Girolametto, L., Greenberg, J. and Manolson, A. (1986) 'Developing dialogue skills: the Hanen Early Language Parent Program', *Seminars in Speech and Language* 7, 367–382.

Grunwell, P. (1981) *The Nature of Phonological Disability in Children*, London: Academic Press.

Haden, R. and Penn, C. (1985) 'The twin situation and its effect on syntax and interactional language over time', *British Journal of Communication Disorders* 20, 19–30.

Hay, D.A., Prior, M., Collett, S. and Williams, M. (1987) 'Speech and language development in preschool twins', *Acta Geneticae Medicae et Gemellologiae: Twin Research* 36, 213–223.

Ingram, D. (1976) *Phonological Disability in Children*, London: Edward Arnold.

Johnston, C., Prior, M. and Hay, D. (1984) 'Prediction of reading disability in twin boys', *Developmental Medicine and Child Neurology* 26, 588–595.

Jones, R. (1998) 'Picture book reading in twins in dyadic and triadic situations', unpublished B.Sc. dissertation, Department of Speech, University of Newcastle upon Tyne.

Keenan, E.O. (1974) 'Conversational competence in children', *Journal of Child Language* 1, 163–183.

Keenan, E.O. and Klein, E. (1975) 'Coherency in children's discourse,' *Journal of Psycholinguistic Research* 4, 365–380.

Koch, H.L. (1966) *Twins and Twin Relations,* Chicago, IL: Chicago University Press.

Koluchova, J. (1972) 'Severe deprivation in twins: a case study', *Journal of Child Psychology and Psychiatry* 13, 107–114.

Koluchova, J. (1976) 'The further development of twins after severe and prolonged deprivation', *Journal of Child Psychology and Psychiatry* 17, 181–188.

Lenneberg, E.H. (1967) *The Biological Foundations of Language*, New York: Wiley.

Levi, G. and Bernabei, P. (1976) 'Specific language disorders in twins during childhood', *Acta Geneticae Medicae et Gemellologiae: Twin Research* 25, 366–368.

Lewis, B.A. and Thompson, L.A. (1992) 'A study of developmental speech and language disorders in twins', *Journal of Speech and Hearing Research* 35, 1086–1094.

Luria, A.R. and Yudovitch, F.I. (1959) *Speech and the Development of Mental Processes in the Child*, London: Staples Press.

Lytton, H. (1980) *Parent–Child Interaction: The Socialisation Process Observed in Twins and Singleton Families*, Calgary, Canada: Plenum Press.

Lytton, H., Conway, D. and Sauve, R. (1977) 'The impact of twinship on parent–child interaction', *Journal of Personality and Social Psychology* 35, 97–107.

McEvoy, S. and Dodd, B. (1992) 'The communication abilities of 2- to 4-year-old twins', *European Journal of Disorders of Communication* 27, 72–88.

MacGillivray, I., Campbell, D.M. and Thompson, B. (eds) (1988) *Twinning and Twins*, Chichester: Wiley.

Malmstrom, P.M. and Silva, M.N. (1986) 'Twin talk: manifestations of twin status in the speech of toddlers', *Journal of Child Language* 13, 293–304.

Mittler, P. (1970) 'Biological and social aspects of language development in twins', *Developmental Medicine and Child Neurology* 12, 741–757.

Mittler, P. (1971) *The Study of Twins*, Harmondsworth, Middlesex: Penguin.

Mogford, K. (1993) 'Language development in twins', in D. Bishop and K. Mogford (eds) *Language Development in Exceptional Circumstances*, Hove, Sussex: Lawrence Erlbaum.

Mora, G., Devault, S. and Schopler, E. (1962) 'Dynamics and psychotherapy of identical twins with elective mutism', *Journal of Child Psychology and Psychiatry* 3, 41–52.

Munsinger, H. and Douglas, A. II (1976) 'The syntactic abilities of identical twins, fraternal twins and their siblings', *Child Development* 47, 40–50.

Pinker, S. (1984) *Language Learnability and Language Development*, Cambridge, MA: Harvard University Press.

Record, R.G., McKeown, T. and Edwards J.H. (1970) 'An investigation of the difference in measured intelligence between twins and single births', *Annals of Human Genetics* 34, 11–20.

Robarge, J.P., Reynolds, Z.B. and Groothuis, J.R. (1982) 'Increase in child abuse in families with twins', *Research in Nursing and Health* 5, 199–203.

Robin, M., Josse, D., Casati, I., Kheroua, H. and Tourrette, C. (1994) 'Dress and physical environment of twins at 1 year: French mothers' attitudes and practices', *Journal of Reproductive and Infant Psychology* 12, 241–248.

Rutter, M. and Redshaw, J. (1991) 'Annotation: growing up as a twin: twin–singleton differences in psychological development', *Journal of Child Psychology and Psychiatry* 32, 885–895.

Sandbank, A.C. and Brown, G.A. (1990) 'An examination of the psychological and behavioural factors in the development of language retardation in twins', *Acta Geneticae Medicae et Gemellologiae: Twin Research* 39, 497–500.

Savic, S. (1980) *How Twins Learn to Talk. A Study of the Speech Development of Twins 1–3*, London: Academic Press.

Siple, P. (1985) 'Plasticity, robustness and language development: an introduction to research issues relating to sign language and spoken language', *Merrill-Palmer Quarterly* 31, 117–126.

Stafford, L. (1987) 'Maternal input to twin and singleton children: implications for language acquisition', *Human Communication Research* 13, 429–462.

Steinhausen, H. and Juzi, C. (1996) 'Elective mutism: an analysis of 100 cases', *Journal of American Academy of Child and Adolescent Psychiatry* 35, 606–613.

Tachibana, R., Nakamura, K., Schichiri, K. and Usada, S. (1982) 'Elective mutism in identical twins', *Japanese Journal of Child and Adolescent Psychiatry* 23, 277–286.

Tomasello, M., Mannle, S. and Kruger, A.C. (1986) 'Linguistic environment of 1–2–year-old twins', *Developmental Psychology* 22, 169–176.

Tomblin, J.B. (1989) 'Familial concentration of developmental language impairment', *Journal of Speech and Hearing Disorders* 54, 587–595.

Wallace, M. (1996) *The Silent Twins*, London: Random House.

Waterman, P. and Shatz, M. (1982) 'The acquisition of personal pronouns and proper names by an identical twin pair', *Journal of Speech and Hearing Research* 25, 149–154.

Watts, D. and Lytton, H. (1981) 'Twinship as handicap: fact or fiction?', in L. Gedda, P. Parisi and W.E. Nance (eds) *Twin Research: Progress in Clinical and Biological Research: Intelligence, Personality and Development*, New York: Liss.

Wilson, R.S. (1977) 'Twins and siblings: concordance for school-age mental development', *Child Development* 48, 211–216.

Zazzo, R. (1960) *Les jumeaux: le couple et la personne*, Paris: Presses Universitaires de France.

Zazzo, R. (1978) 'Genesis and peculiarities of the personalities of twins', in W.E. Nance, G. Allen and P. Parisi (eds) *Twin Research: Progress in Clinical and Biological Research: Psychology and Methodology*, New York: Liss.

5   Twins with special needs

Elizabeth M. Bryan

Introduction

If disability is difficult for a family with a single child, having a twin with a disability can be nearly overwhelming. All members of the family may, of course, suffer, but the very special needs of the healthy twin are often inadequately recognised. Parents who have two (or three) children plainly have two (or three) times the chance of having a child with special needs. The risk of disability is even higher with twins (or more) as many forms of disability, including congenital malformations, cerebral palsy and learning difficulties, are significantly more common among twins. Inevitably therefore, some parents find that both twins have special needs – a particularly heavy burden.

A child with special needs is defined here as one who, due to a physical or psychosocial impairment, requires help in addition to that needed by most children, whether singletons or multiples, of the same age. The problems that arise when there is a conspicuous difference in some aspect of physical or mental development between twin siblings will also be discussed. These problems may occur even where the development of each twin is well within the range expected for a child of the same age.

Throughout this chapter the terms the 'disabled' twin and the 'healthy' twin are used. However, it is fully recognised that the healthy child, like all of us, will have some disabilities and that the disabled child can otherwise be perfectly healthy and possessed of many skills. The term 'disability' is not used in the conventional way but only for the sake of brevity and only with these important qualifications.

The special considerations that apply to the care of all multiple birth children will not be included. These are covered elsewhere in this book.

Causes of disability

Congenital anomalies

Abnormalities in fetal development are more common in twins than in singletons, but the higher incidence is probably limited to monozygotic (MZ) twins (Little and Bryan 1988). Many of the severe malformations, such as those of conjoined (Siamese) twins and some forms of congenital heart disease, are unique to monozygotic twins. Others are caused by an inequality in the shared blood circulation between some MZ twins (particularly – but not only – if one baby dies in utero). Two-thirds of MZ twins share the same chorionic sac and therefore share a blood circulation. If one of mono-chorionic twins dies in utero, the sudden change in the blood flow between the two fetuses can result in a catastrophic fall in blood pressure in the survivor, causing permanent damage to many of her or his organs, including the brain.

Learning difficulties

It is generally agreed that learning difficulties occur more commonly in twins than in singletons. This is so whether or not both children survive. Of the various forms of learning difficulties the only one that appears to be less common in twins is that associated with Down's syndrome (trisomy 21).

Cerebral palsy

Cerebral palsy can be defined as a non-progressive disorder of posture and movement arising from damage to the developing brain.

All previous studies had suggested a much higher incidence of cerebral palsy among multiple birth children and this has now been confirmed in the few population-based studies that have been reported (Petterson *et al.* 1990, Grether 1993). The chances of having a single child with cerebral palsy are about 0.2 per cent whereas for twins the risk is about six times as great and for triplets over thirty times. But the chances of a family having at least one child with cerebral palsy is higher still – eightfold for twins and over fifty for triplets.

There is a variety of reasons for this much higher incidence of cerebral palsy, including the circulatory imbalance in some MZ pregnancies (even when both babies survive) and the complications of prematurity – with the high risk this carries of brain haemorrhage and consequent neurological impairment.

Although improvements in obstetric and neonatal care over the past thirty years have greatly reduced the risk of death in the new-born period there has been little change in the prevalence of cerebral palsy. This may be due to the still increasing number of very small survivors – who are clearly at greater risk. The causes of many types of mental retardation are often the same as those causing cerebral palsy.

The intellectual abilities of children with cerebral palsy vary from superior to severe impairment. The intellectual potential of a child with cerebral palsy is too often under-estimated and it is vital that any assessments are only undertaken by a psychologist with the necessary special experience.

The diagnosis

The diagnosis of a potential long-term disability may be made early in pregnancy, as with a neural tube defect or Down's syndrome. It may also be discovered at birth in a child with a clear physical abnormality. With a neurological impairment, such as cerebral palsy, the problem may not be recognised for many months, or in the case of intellectual or communication disorders, for several years.

However, abnormalities in development will often be detected in twins earlier than in single children. This may be due to the extra clinical attention they attract whether as twins or as being, for example, babies of relatively low birthweight. The mother may also become more aware of the defects of one twin (especially in MZ twins) as she watches the progress of the other.

Conversely, many parents worry unnecessarily when, for instance, one child has not taken its first steps although the other has been walking confidently for several months. This is not unexpected in DZ twins and in any case parents often forget the breadth of the normal range and therefore how children will have different weaknesses and strengths.

The parents

A parent's response to having a disabled child may be similar to that of bereavement, especially if the discovery comes as a shock because the parents have had no grounds for anxiety until the news is broken by the clinician. Denial, anger, guilt and grief are all common. The parents often mourn the healthy child that 'might have been' and parents of MZ twins have no difficulty in imagining this because the image of the healthy child is constantly present in the unimpaired one. Rather than remaining grateful for the normality of the one twin the parents may unconsciously blame her or him for the disability of the other.

All parents of a disabled child have to come to terms with a mixture of often powerful emotions, not least that of a special kind of loss: that of a perfect child. Parents who have twins can have an added and more subtle bereavement, the loss of the twinship as such. Because most parents are proud of having twins they may find it hard to stop treating their children the same, for example, in dress, even if they share neither the same mental nor physical appearance. This artificial imposition of twinship can clearly become an added burden for either or both children.

Responding appropriately to each child may become an objective problem particularly in the pre-school period, when the healthy child may still not understand the implications of his twin's disability. Encouraging and praising the two children appropriately can be difficult. A healthy 3-year-old may well find it hard to understand that his brother with cerebral palsy deserves praise for taking his first steps when his own physical achievements appear to pass unnoticed. Indeed the comfort offered to a disabled brother following his frequent falls may encourage his twin to contrive his own accidents.

As they grow beyond babyhood, the intellectual and physical needs of the two children will of course increasingly diverge. Balancing the needs of the disabled child with those of his siblings always causes problems. In the case of twins there is some danger that, by emphasising the twinship, the development of the more advanced child may be held back. The healthy twin's needs, and particularly her or his feelings – often including a kind of guilt – may be just as complex, and a family may need skilled counselling in coping with them (Bernabei 1976).

Needless to say, all parents with a disabled child deserve ready access to whatever help or advice they need. With twins, practical help can be a key factor. The care of a healthy pair of twins already presents practical, emotional and financial difficulties. Only with extra help can a mother of twins give the disabled twin the necessary attention and treatment and still have adequate time alone with and for her healthy children.

Reactions of the healthy twin

A child will often be aware, even at an early age, that his twin is being treated differently. It is therefore important that, within the level of his understanding, he should understand why this is happening.

Studies have shown that siblings of some disabled children are more prone to conduct disorders (including aggressive behaviour) and to depression (Breslau *et al.* 1983). There have been no such studies on the twin of a disabled child but it would be surprising if the emotional stress were not at least as great. Indeed these children are likely to feel more complex emotions: the healthy twin may well feel both guilt and jealousy. However, illogically he may feel guilty that he himself was spared – the 'survivor syndrome'. He may feel an especial guilt if his healthy survival was at the expense of his twin – for example, if he received an unfair share of the intra-uterine nourishment. In such cases the healthy twin sometimes tries to make amends by taking on the burden of caring for the disabled one. I met a bright 13-year-old who refused to take part in any extra-curricula activities at school, including a trip to France, because he felt duty-bound to be at home to care for his severely disabled brother, who could neither talk nor participate in physical activities. Such unselfish concern for the disadvantaged twin may seem very welcome but it can go too far. Careful counselling both for the twin and the parents may be appropriate, together with special arrangements to free the healthy twin to pursue his own interests and development. Someone else may be found, for example, to entertain the disabled twin on certain evenings.

A healthy child may well feel jealous of all the time and attention spent on his twin and particularly of the professional visitors he attracts. The mother will often feel that she alone is capable of feeding and caring for the disabled child. Friends may doubt their capacity to do so, whereas any passing friend or neighbour can seem adequate to feed the healthy one. There may be no alternative to the disabled child being carried by his mother for many years, whereas the other one – also capable of being very tired – has to trudge behind as soon as he is able to walk.

The siblings of a disabled child will often welcome their own illness or injury and hence the need for the treatment, attention and nurturing that go with it. Some such children regress in their development and imitate their disabled sibling's behaviour at times of stress. At such times it may be helpful to encourage her or him to undertake independent activities, acquire new skills and develop new friendships.

Friends and neighbours are too rarely encouraged to acquire the special skills required to care for the disabled child, even though they might get great satisfaction themselves from doing so. This would also allow the mother to feel confident that care would be sustained in a crisis, such as her own illness or that of the other child. Such a friend would also be able to give much more ongoing emotional support both to the disabled child and to the parents in normal times. Moreover, relieving the mother sometimes of her care of the disabled child would free her to give the healthy sibling some precious and otherwise rare time alone with his mother.

The disabled twin is likely to receive far more attention from not only the parents, but from professionals and visitors. Visits to doctors and therapists may often be time-consuming and the problems of taking (or leaving) the healthy twin may be considerable. Every consideration should be given to such families and the clinicians or other professionals should be as concerned about arrangements for the care of the healthy twin as for the one with special needs. It is often quite practicable for the healthy twin to join in at least some of the activities of the therapy groups. The mother may then feel more relaxed and more able to concentrate on the disabled child.

Some of the therapists and helpers are likely to become 'special friends' of the disabled child, often effectively ignoring the healthy one. He too, therefore, should have his special friends. It is not unusual in the MBF Twins Clinic for the healthy twin to come on his own so that he too can have some of the paediatrician's personal attention that his brother receives so regularly.

Some children will show their jealousy in aggression, others in negative attention seeking or more complex behaviour patterns. One bright 8-year-old twin became so jealous of all the extra attention and 'treats', such as a taxi journey to school and riding (for the disabled), enjoyed by her sister – who had cerebral palsy – that she became increasingly withdrawn and hostile. She finally reached a crisis when she developed a hysterical paralysis on one side.

A family with a child with special needs will plainly find that some normal family activities such as hiking or museum visiting have to be curtailed. A more subtle cause of curtailment in the healthy twin's social life is his reaction to being seen with his disabled sibling. Some school-age children find it embarrassing to have a twin who does not look normal or who behaves in unexpected ways. He may also be reluctant to invite friends to his home. This is usually less of a problem if the children are not obviously treated as twins.

But there are positive aspects for the healthy twin too. At the MBF a study of twenty-five families who had a twin with a disability was undertaken (Burton and Bryan 1995). Eighteen parents thought there were some benefits for their healthy twin. Many parents thought he or she had become a more caring and responsible child and was more aware of the inequalities in the world and more caring towards disabled people in general. The self-confidence of the healthy twin may also be increased by feeling he has an important role. He may acquire valuable understanding and sensitivity. It is not uncommon for people who have experienced disability in the family to enter one of the caring professions.

But there is also the risk, mentioned above, of the healthy twin developing an exaggerated sense of obligation and thereby fostering some later resentment. Parents will often have to strike a precarious balance between encouraging the child to follow his caring inclinations and seeming to encourage his feelings of guilt.

Reactions of the disabled child

The disabled child must also be helped to understand why, in some ways or areas, he does not have the same abilities as his twin, or indeed of most other children of his age. Many will be keen to understand their disability and also curious as to the cause of it. For those who are born prematurely and very small, there can be a feeling of considerable accomplishment, even triumph, that they have gallantly survived against all the odds.

Sometimes, however, the disabled child may resent receiving what she or he sees as exaggerated praise for achievements. Well-meaning people often overcompensate in praising a disabled child, even where no special tribute is appropriate. The child may often enjoy it more when it is accepted without comment that he can perform some tasks entirely adequately. For example, an intellectually normal child with cerebral palsy but no speech impediment can read a story to the class as well as any other child and does not deserve disproportionate praise. Parents, teachers and others should also beware of depriving themselves of the ability to warn, correct, reprove or indeed discipline a disabled child.

There are of course positive aspects. In his or her healthy twin companion, the disabled child has a constant source of stimulation who in many areas may be more effective in motivating his disabled twin than the parents. His brother's friends will also provide more opportunities to mix with and relate to healthy children. The potentially therapeutic influence of normal siblings on children with disabilities has been clearly demonstrated (Craft *et al.* 1990). For various reasons, not least the extra pressure of any twins on the parents, the disabled twin may be less overprotected than a similarly disabled singleton.

Monozygotic twins

It can be especially hard for both twins when one of MZ twins is disabled. Each twin can see or hear what she or he might have been like. Even in pairs who are close friends, it is inevitably painful to watch the accomplishments of your twin sister or brother when you know that you can never achieve the same. Jealousy, anxiety and anger can easily be precipitated, perhaps sometimes a measure of despair. For the parents the joy in the success of one child is bound to evoke at least sadness for the other.

Healthy discordant twins

Far too often, even DZ twins are compared with each other rather than with their peers. By so doing there is a danger that the child who is slower in acquiring a particular skill will be judged abnormally slow rather than often being a child who is performing well within the normal expectations of a child of his age (or even perhaps better than average). Being slightly slower than his brother should not be the issue.

Even if parents are conscientious in avoiding misleading comparisons, there is still no way that the children themselves can be prevented from comparing each other's performance. The less able child may then become disheartened and therefore reluctant to attempt activities which he will perform less well. In such situations the child should be encouraged to develop a different skill in which he can take pride without being undermined by his brother. Of a pair of 7-year-old dizygotic boys seen at the clinic, one child was excelling in all school activities, both academic and sporting, and his brother, less able and physically smaller, was becoming increasingly demoralised. Being in separate classes at school did not solve the problem, as he was still known as 'X's twin'.

This child was then moved to another school which placed particular emphasis on the arts, including drama. There he flourished, having a natural aptitude for painting and also for acting. His finest moment came when he took the lead in the class play and his brother was in the audience.

This chapter has concentrated on twins discordant for reasons of disability. Clearly, if both children are disabled, some of the problems I have mentioned will not arise. Nevertheless, the physical and emotional burden on the parents can be enormous, not least the guilt – however irrational – they may themselves feel. However, such problems are dealt with thoroughly in general paediatric or specialised books on disabled children. The complexities of caring for a healthy alongside a disabled child/children of the same age are less well understood.

References

Bernabei, P., Levi, G. (1976) 'Psychopathologic problems in twins during childhood', *Acta Geneticae Medicae et Gemellologiae* 25, 381–383.

Breslau, N. (1983) 'The psychological study of chronically ill and disabled children: are healthy siblings appropriate controls?', *Journal of Abnormal Child Psychology* 11, 379–391.

Burton, C., Bryan, E. (1995) 'The healthy twin needs help too', *MBF Newsletter* 27, 2.

Craft, M.J., Lakin, J.A., Opplinger, R.A., Clancy, G.M., Vanderlinden, D.W. (1990) 'Siblings as change agents for promoting the functional status of children with cerebral palsy', *Developmental Medicine and Child Neurology* 32, 1049–1057.

Grether, J.K. (1993) 'A twinning and cerebral palsy: experience in four northern California counties, births 1983 through 1985', *Pediatrics* 92, 854–855.

Little, J., Bryan, E.M. (1988) 'Congenital anomalies in twins', in I. MacGillivray, D.M. Campbell and B. Thompson (eds) *Twinning and Twins*, Chichester, John Wiley, pp. 207–240.

Petterson, B., Stanley, F., Henderson, D. (1990) 'Cerebral palsy in multiple births in Western Australia', *American Journal of Medical Genetics* 37, 346–351.

6 Meeting the educational needs of pre-school and primary aged twins and higher multiples

Pat Preedy

Introduction

It is a common assumption that the needs of twins and higher multiples are no different to those of singletons and all that is required is concern for the development and progress of the individual.

As Head Teacher of Knowle CE Primary School, Solihull, West Midlands, I had my assumptions challenged in 1992 when nine sets of twins were registered to start school. Coincidentally, the Chairman of the Twins and Multiple Births Association (Tamba) was giving a lecture in Solihull about the needs of multiples, and the staff and I attended as a result of the twin phenomenon that they were experiencing.

Tamba revealed that the school was in fact being impacted by the effects of a rapid rise in the number of twins and higher multiples; currently one child in thirty-eight is a twin. The reasons for this rapid rise are linked to the better survival rate of small and premature babies and the tendency for mothers to have their babies when they are older and more likely to have twins. More important than the fact that there are more multiples was the revelation that there are particular issues which affect the development and learning of multiples of which educators should be aware.

Much of the information available regarding the education of twins is based upon Australian research conducted by Professor David Hay. In particular the La Trobe twin studies provide extensive information about twins in school. Inspired by this information and our multiple birth families I began researching the educational needs of twins and higher multiples through the University of Birmingham with the support of Tamba. Professor Hay supported the research, assisting particularly in the development of questionnaires that took into account the Australian findings and the English school system. A major part of the research involved the first national survey of schools in England and interviewing parents of multiples whose children had just started school in Solihull.

I was particularly concerned that apart from the research conducted by Professor Hay (see Chapter 8), much of the research available had a medical and scientific bias focusing upon fertilisation, gestation and birth while neglecting psychological development and educational provision. As an educator, it was of particular concern to me how the social and emotional development of multiples might affect their progress in school and how parents and professionals might be provided with information that would enable multiple children to make the most of their educational opportunities.

One of the major findings from the research was that adults frequently did not discuss with multiple children their feelings and wishes. This led to the production of a book called *Multiple Voices* (Lowe and Preedy 1998), that enables multiples to express their feelings on a range of issues about which they feel strongly. Quotes from *Multiple Voices* are used in this chapter to illustrate the importance of the issues discussed from the point of view of the children themselves.

The national survey 1994

The survey questionnaire was distributed to schools in England using the local education authorities' internal postal systems. The survey produced data from 3,000 schools in seventy-three local education authorities. The sample consisted of 619,633 pupils, of which 11,873 were twin children with 117 sets of triplets and five sets of quads.

The survey confirmed that large numbers of multiples were to be found across the primary school system (see Figure 6.1). At first it appeared that there were far more identical twins than would have been expected – 47 per cent instead of 33 per cent (see Figure 6.2). However, this figure is distorted by the fact that many respondents presumed that same-sex twins were also identical. This may account for educators expecting twins to be similar in personality, performance and progress when in fact if they are fraternal twins they are no more alike than brothers or sisters.

The *Twins In School Study* (Hay and Johnston 1984) recommended that schools should not have a policy with regard to the management of multiples but should adopt a flexible approach, particularly with regard to separating multiples or keeping them together. However, since the 1980s, schools in many countries are required to have policies detailing their philosophy and approach to all aspects of

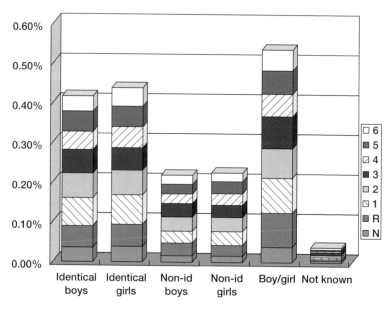

Figure 6.1 Number of twins in each zygosity group present in each school year (including nursery (N) and reception (R)).
Source: © P. Preedy.

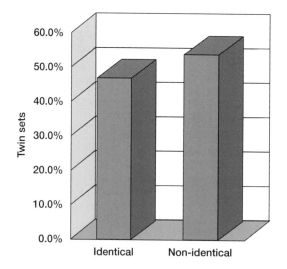

Figure 6.2 Percentage of identical (MZ) and fraternal (DZ) twins in the English school population who took part in the 1994 survey.
Source: © P. Preedy.

school and the curriculum. Thus, the absence of reference to multiples does not indicate flexibility but rather that this issue has not been considered. It was therefore rather worrying when the survey revealed that only 1 per cent of schools had a policy with regard to the education of multiples (see Figure 6.3).

In order to assist schools in developing a policy, an outline policy was drawn up that could be adopted and adapted by schools for their own use (see Appendix I, p. 87).

If schools did not have a policy they were asked what was their common practice. Just over a quarter of schools said that they liaised with parents, 20 per cent having a flexible approach particularly with regard to separating multiples. However, 8 per cent of schools said that they always separated multiples and 21 per cent said they always kept them together (see Figure 6.4).

It was surprising that so many schools kept multiples together, even taking into consideration that 15 per cent were one form entry. When asked why multiples were kept together the main reasons were so that the children could support each other and because of parental request. Where there were no apparent problems, schools kept multiples together rather than separating them. Over 10 per cent said that they organised classes by birth date so the children could not be separated (see Figure 6.5).

It was particularly disturbing that some primary schools had such rigid organisational structures and that there was no option for multiples to be separated, even if there were strong educational reasons for doing so.

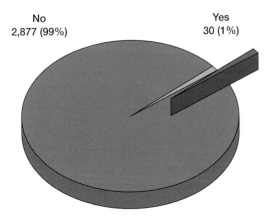

Figure 6.3 Policy with regard to the education of multiples.
Source: © P. Preedy.

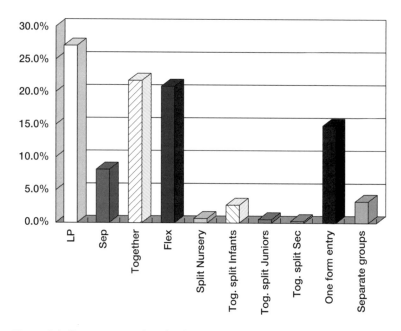

Figure 6.4 Common practices in the schools taking part in the English
         survey.
Source: © P. Preedy.
Notes
LP = Liaison with parents; Sep = Always separate; Together = Do not separate;
Flex = Flexible approach; Split Nursery = Separate start Nursery; Tog. split
Infants = Separate start Infants; Tog. split Juniors = Separate start Juniors;
Tog. split Sec = Separate start Secondary; One form entry = Cannot separate;
Separate groups = Same class different groups.

When asked why schools separated multiples the main reasons were
parental request, to develop independence, dominance of one twin by
the other and restriction of one twin by the other (see Figure 6.6).

Although separating multiples is a major decision, over three-
quarters of schools did not discuss this issue with parents. Many
expressed very firm views about always separating multiples, particularly in order to develop independence, or always keeping them
together in order to support each other. Only one-fifth of schools
stated that the circumstances of each set of multiples varied and they
therefore adopted a flexible approach. It thus appeared that schools
were in a similar position to Knowle CE Primary School, whereby
they were experiencing the impact of higher numbers of multiple
birth children but were unaware of the particular needs and issues

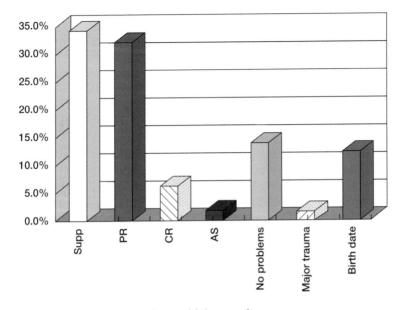

Figure 6.5 Reasons for keeping multiples together.
Source: © P. Preedy.
Notes
Supp = Children support each other; PR = Parental request; CR = Children's request;
AS = Schools always separate; No problems = No reason to separate; Major trauma =
Need to support each other as a result of trauma, e.g. bereavement; Birth date =
Classes organised by birth date.

that needed to be taken into consideration when managing them in an educational setting.

In order to determine the issues of which educators needed to be aware, in-depth interviews were conducted with the parents of multiples who had just started school in Solihull Local Education Authority. These interviews provided the basis for a questionnaire to be completed by parents and teachers prior to school entry (see Appendix II, p. 90). The questionnaire enables parents and teachers to make decisions based upon detailed information about the children both as individuals and as multiples rather than adhering to a rigid strategy applying to all multiples irrespective of their individual needs. The interviews with parents highlighted the main issues of which educators need to be aware:

● the need for pre-school education
● identity, individuality and self-image

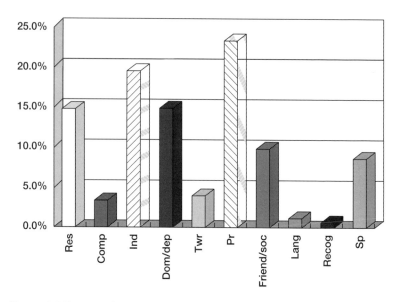

Figure 6.6 Reasons for separating multiples.
Source: © P. Preedy.
Notes
Res = Restriction of one by the other; Comp = Competition; Ind = To develop individuality; Dom/dep = One child dominant the other dependent; Twr = Twin request; Pr = Parental request; Friend/soc = To develop friendships/social skills; Lang = To aid language development; Recog = To aid recognition; Sp = Difference in school progress.

- the nature of the multiple relationship
- relating to others
- fairness
- separate or together in school
- the physical development of the children and particular medical or learning difficulties.

The way the children are managed and treated should depend on how they have developed and how they react, particularly with regard to these issues. Furthermore, the children will grow and change, making it necessary to be flexible and to make changes as and when appropriate.

The need for pre-school education

The national survey indicated that only 22 per cent of schools included twins and higher multiples in their admission criteria for nursery (see Figure 6.7). It appears that many pre-school settings are unaware of the particular needs of multiples and their families. The sheer physical demands of caring for multiples frequently means that they have fewer opportunities for outings and mixing with other children. They particularly need the pre-school setting to develop their language skills and to learn how to establish relationships with their peers in a group setting. Pre-school offers a vital opportunity for individual and separate experiences. It is important that the staff do not treat multiples as a unit in order to ensure that they do not stick together within the setting, thus excluding those around them. If possible, at least one of the sessions should be attended by one child giving the parent or carer the opportunity to relate to the other child as an individual. Thus a flexible approach to placement is helpful and allows individual opportunities for the children.

Parents helping in the pre-school setting should not be put under pressure to give more time helping than others just because they have multiples. Helping within the setting can also be more difficult as they have two or more children making demands upon them simultaneously.

Pre-school offers twins and higher multiples the opportunity to develop their receptive and expressive language in preparation for school. Through structured and role-play situations they can be given the opportunity to explore and develop as an individual. Pre-school is

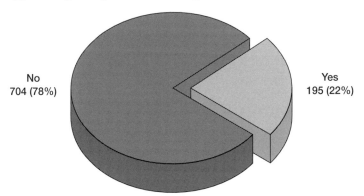

No
704 (78%)

Yes
195 (22%)

Figure 6.7 Percentage of nurseries that had being a multiple as one of the criteria for entry.
Source: © P. Preedy.

important for all children, but for twins and higher multiples it is even more important. The pre-school staff have a vital role in supporting the family and liaising with the feeder schools so that reception teachers can take into account the needs of the children both as individuals and as multiples.

Identity, individuality and self-image

The perception of twins and higher multiples by adults is frequently that of a natural unit. Just knowing that the children are multiples seems to affect the memory, so that identifying them as individuals and calling them by their names becomes an impossibility. If this perception is reinforced by the parents and the children themselves then the teacher is likely to perceive and treat the multiples as one, expecting the same outcomes from each. Even their friends may fail to differentiate, playing with either or both as though they were one.

> Being a twin is hard, because they say both your names, and that's what gets me. It's hard for me when everyone asks me what my name is.
> People kept coming up to me and asking, 'Are you Sarah or the other one?' I would answer, 'The other one!'. One girl had the same shoes as Sarah and she would come up to me and say 'You're not Sarah' and walk off.
>
> (Preedy and Lowe 1998: 13)

Of the parents interviewed, one-fifth made no effort to distinguish between the children. In fact, most of these parents expressed the strong desire to portray their multiples as an identical unit, enjoying the additional attention this brought. This special attention is sometimes referred to as the 'prima donna effect'. Although only 16 per cent of the sample used the fact that they were multiples to gain popularity and attention, most parents felt that the 'cuteness' of being a multiple enhanced their popularity and increased the attention given to them by others. This special attention can result in the children and parents enhancing their identity as multiples rather than as individuals. Being a twin 'is special because you are sometimes counted differently. For example, people sometimes go, "Wow!" when they find out the fact that we are twins' (Preedy and Lowe 1998: 10).

Care has to be taken, as the media tend to promote the idea of multiples being identical by using 'cute' pictures to reinforce the image of multiples as an identical unit. Schools with high numbers of multiples need to consider how the children will be presented in the media and what sort of comments they are going to hear. For example, photographers frequently ask for identical twins, and say to the other children that they are not needed for the photograph!

If multiples look alike and are dressed identically with the same hairstyles, they may not respond to their own name or recognise themselves in photographs or in a mirror. Whether or not the children are in the same class it is essential to regard them as individuals and refer to them by name: 'It's not very nice when people call us the "Tiny Twins" like my tennis teacher does.'

Upon entry to school it is important to assess the entry point of each child and to discuss that child's progress against the peer group, not against their multiple brothers or sisters. Separate appointments, preferably on different days, should be made for parental consultations to enable staff and parents to focus on one child at a time.

Helping the children and others to identify multiples individually takes effort. However, without this effort the children may not be able to function as individuals and become what Keith describes as 'psychological cripples' (Keith *et al.* 1995).

The multiple relationship

Those of us who are singletons cannot truly understand what it is like to have a multiple relationship: 'I think you only really know what it's like to be a twin if you are one!'

Just as our relationships are varied, so are those of multiples. Some multiples, particularly if they are identical, are incredibly alike in looks, personality and achievement, while other multiples seem to be the exact opposite. This special relationship can veer between extreme love and extreme hatred, with some multiples competing, constantly feeling jealous and upset by any attention given to their multiple brothers or sisters:

> 'I like being a twin because you have someone to talk to and when you are lonely your twin will make you happy.'

> 'I really dislike my twin sister, she doesn't show any real kindness for me. . . .'

Where multiples appear to be exact opposites they may have chosen polarisation as a means of establishing their own identities. In the sample, 8 per cent of the children frequently tended to go to opposite extremes of behaviour. This behaviour may result in children being labelled as the 'good twin' or the 'bad twin', with the children growing up fulfilling the roles they have been almost forced to take on. Such children may find themselves opting out of subjects and activities just because their multiple brother or sister has chosen them.

Parents may present their multiples already labelled 'angel' or 'devil', and it is important to separate such children, allowing and helping them to establish a positive self-image outside the stereotype. It can come as a shock to both parents and children when the 'angel' turns out to be human and the 'devil' enjoys success.

Only multiples have the burden of being born together so that every stage of their development can be compared directly with their multiple siblings. Although 40 per cent of parents in the sample tried to discourage others from comparing their multiples, most said that they found it impossible not to make comparisons themselves. For the children, comparison with one's twin can become a major preoccupation, with even a centimetre difference in height becoming a major issue: 'I find it annoying when Margaret plays the violin in front of other people and they say how good she is, while I am sitting there feeling jealous.'

The multiples in the sample mainly compared themselves in terms of physical development, adult approval and achievement. Comparison with regard to achievement by the children and their parents is likely to be even stronger when the children start school. If the children are in separate classes comparisons between teachers are inevitable. Teachers may be unaware that a child may be labelled as a failure at home because they are not making similar progress to their twin who is in another class. Special sensitivity is required with reading particularly if one child is slower to begin reading and writing – a more frequent problem with boy/girl sets. The situation can be particularly sensitive if one of the multiples is identified as having special needs. Parents may find it difficult to support the child with special needs while still giving the other child time and praise for his or her achievements. In the educational setting staff need to be aware of the tendency to make comparisons and avoid comparing one child to the detriment of the other whilst at the same time rewarding the progress and efforts of each child as an individual: 'I don't like it when my brother wins something and I don't, like when he got a trophy in the chess competition and I only got a medal.'

Despite great efforts to enable multiples to develop as individuals, they can combine to form a very powerful unit. When multiples combine to create a unit against the world causing disruption and mayhem, it is essential to separate them in the school system.

The relationship between multiples is greatly affected by which child, if any, is dominant. Although one multiple may always take the lead, dominance may vary according to activities or situations: 'My twin is never organised and his room is always untidy so I am always happy to help and tidy his room, wrap his presents and put his clothes away.'

Special intervention may be required if one child has been constantly speaking for the other. If one multiple is dominating to such a degree that the other is almost totally dependent, it is advisable to separate them in school. However, it is frequently the dependent child who blossoms and grows in confidence whilst the dominant child is left fretting, having lost his or her major role in life (see Figure 6.8). The multiple relationship is unique and complex, varying according to situation and activity. A child who is dominant at home may lose all confidence at school. Educators need to observe the children, particularly in the play situation, to determine the nature of the multiple relationship before making assumptions, particularly regarding dominance. As the children grow and develop, just like any relationship, theirs will grow and change. However, all their friendships and other relationships will be affected by the fact that they are a multiple.

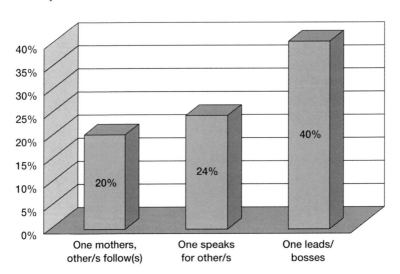

Figure 6.8 Characteristics of dominance in multiples.
Source: © P. Preedy.

Relating with others

From birth, multiples play and interact with each other but, because they are the same age – and it is, in practice, very difficult to arrange separate friends – when they are younger most share the same friends, with many sticking together to the exclusion of others. One-fifth of the multiples in the sample stuck together with few other friends. This situation is likely to make it difficult for the children, particularly when they start school and are faced with large numbers of children without their parents there to support them. When coping with the educational setting, multiples may lack the social skills to develop friendships and be unable to interact with others or join in the play situation and with playground games (see Figure 6.9).

If one multiple does develop a particular friendship, this may result in jealousy and a feeling of great loss in the other child: 'I do not like it when my sister tries to join in with me at school playtime when I am with my friends.'

Invitations to parties can cause particular pain when these are handed out in the classroom and only one of the multiples is invited: 'I don't know if I like going to parties on my own really. I feel left out when my sister goes to a party.'

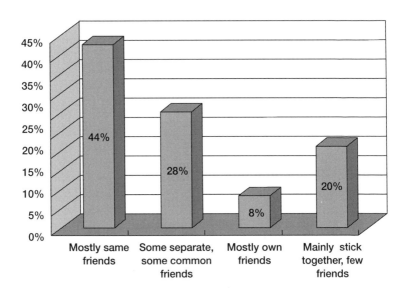

Figure 6.9 Friendships between multiples and other children.
Source: © P. Preedy.

The pain of such situations can be eased if, right from the start, multiples learn to develop their relationships both as individuals and as multiples, understanding that this sometimes involves different experiences for each such as outings and parties.

A teacher presented with one of a multiple set who is unable to relate to others and appears upset and withdrawn may not realise that the behaviour is a result of the nature of the multiple relationship and that the child needs a great deal of support to gain the skills necessary to form friendships, thereby enabling them to learn collaboratively with their peers.

The perception of multiples as a unit, combined with the demands of the children themselves, frequently leads to the conclusion that fairness means treating each child exactly the same. In the sample 72 per cent of children had a heightened sense of what is fair, continually demanding the same: 'Sometimes when there are two things to choose from, and I badly want one and Catherine wants the other, it makes me want the one Catherine wants because it might be better.'

No matter how identical the children are, life cannot provide exactly the same for each child. Multiples have differing needs at different times and it is therefore unfair to try and always treat them in the same way. Even when the children are in the same class they will frequently end up reading different pages from a book, with different parts in a play, with one winning a prize and the other not, and so on. The temptation is to hold back the reward for one multiple in order to save the feelings of the other or to reward both even though only one has achieved. For example, one of identical twin boys at school achieved a swimming certificate and the swimming instructor said, 'What a shame for the other one, we'll wait until they both get one'. She was surprised when it was argued that it would be a shame for the child who had achieved and did not receive his award just because he was a twin. However, life is not straightforward, as frequently the effect of one multiple always perceiving himself or herself to be the loser is for that child to opt out. Of those interviewed, nearly half said that one of their multiples opted out if the other was successful.

As much of a child's learning occurs prior to school entry, one child may enter school having already established the pattern of opting out. If this is the case, it is strongly recommended that such children are separated and that both children experience success in their own right within the peer group. Multiples particularly need support from parents and educators to cope with the feelings associated with the times when life for them simply is not fair.

Separate or together

The issue of whether to separate multiples upon entry to school frequently becomes the main concern for parents. Thirty-two per cent of parents in the sample considered the start of school to be the ideal time for separation. However, this stage is far too late to begin thinking about separation. Most of the multiples in the sample had few opportunities of separation prior to starting school (see Figure 6.10).

Parents found it difficult to arrange separate outings or experiences, and many multiples shared a bedroom even if there were opportunities to sleep separately: 'I would like to have more time and space on my own like my own bedroom. . . .'

Although most of the children had little experience of separation, over 80 per cent of parents felt that the children would not be unhappy if separated at school. Educators need to be aware that parents may express a preference for multiples to be separated but may not be prepared for an adverse reaction from the children. The children themselves may have little experience to draw on in order to cope with the new situation. If the children are going to be separated at the start of school they need to prepare for this. The induction to school needs to be carefully planned so that the children have separate experiences prior to starting school and separate visits to prepare for school.

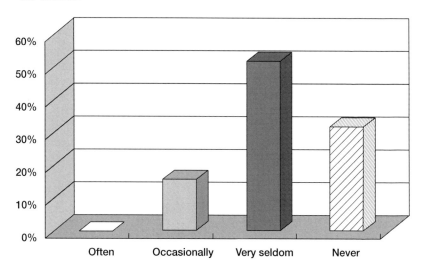

Figure 6.10 Time multiple birth children spend apart.
Source: © P. Preedy.

Parents can use stories and role play to help the children imagine and play through school experience and how they may feel and react to a variety of situations. If the children are upset when separated in school they and their parents may need additional support rather than immediately reversing the decision. Many of the children do not actually need to be together in the same class but like to be able to check what the other is doing.

Whether the children are separated or not over half were upset when the other was ill or upset. If teachers have only one of the multiples they may not appreciate how much the circumstances of the one may affect the other (see Figure 6.11).

For many parents, the option of separation in school is not available as many schools are one form entry. It is important to remember that school is only a part of life and that developing as an individual does not depend solely upon separation in school. The attitude of both parents and educators is much more important than the opportunity to be in separate classes. If right from the start multiples have been encouraged to develop as individuals celebrating their own success and achievements and this is continued by the school, then being in a single form entry school need not be a disadvantage.

Once separated in school it may be difficult to reverse the decision, as one child will have to go into a class leaving behind his or her familiar circumstances and routines. Frequently, the early years of education are less rigid and allow for flexibility of grouping so that

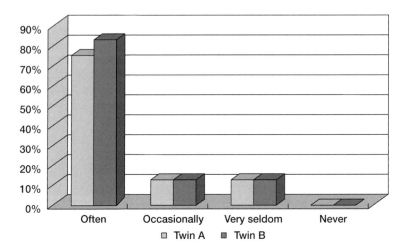

Figure 6.11 The frequency with which twins check on each other.
Source: © P. Preedy.

multiples can have separate experiences whilst still being able to check on each other. It can be very hard having no privacy at school and having to share telling the good and bad: 'When we get home we always argue about who's going to tell our Mum about what happened at school, and we always tell her if the other got a detention or something else like that.'

Separating multiples requires preparation and discussion between staff and parents. The children need to be involved in the process and to be well prepared for separation prior to starting school.

Special needs

Although not all multiples have special needs, many experience learning difficulties, particularly as a result of being premature and of a birthweight that is low for gestational age. The assessment and provision for multiples must be on an individual basis, particularly avoiding the sharing of special support just because the children are multiples.

Particularly noteworthy is the high proportion of children experiencing difficulties with speech and language development. Careful assessment of each child is required to determine if there is a language delay and/or a language disorder. Multiples may experience a delay in language development as a result of reinforcing each other's mistakes

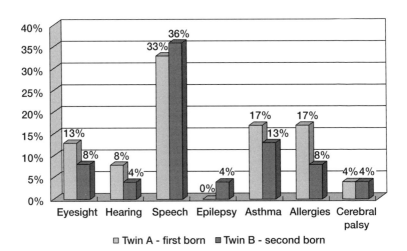

Figure 6.12 Continuing physical difficulties experienced by twins.
Source: © P. Preedy.

and having fewer interactions with adults. One twin may have particular difficulties if the other has been allowed to speak for both. Young multiples particularly need pre-school education where they can develop their oral language alongside their peers in a play situation. Educators who are alert to their needs can then intervene, helping them to extend and enrich their language. Care must be taken not to force the children into formal situations based upon writing before they have developed their oral language and social skills, enabling them to express themselves in a variety of contexts and situations (see Figure 6.12).

Some multiples may have special needs, but being a multiple in itself must not be regarded as a handicap. All multiples will need special consideration so that the issues which impact on them as multiples do not inhibit their educational progress.

Conclusion

Meeting the educational needs of pre-school and primary aged multiples requires schools to acknowledge that multiples and their families have particular requirements which need to be considered as part of school policy. Those in direct contact with the children need to know the development and circumstances of the children both as individuals and as multiples. The parent–teacher questionnaire (Appendix II, p. 90) helps parents and teachers to discuss the needs of the children and to plan flexibly, enabling the children to celebrate the fact that they are a multiple and allowing them to shine as an individual. As one of the children states: 'The most important message I want to put across is that I am an individual and, just as you want to be known for who you are, not what you are, so do I!'

APPENDIX I: SCHOOL POLICY FOR TWINS AND HIGHER MULTIPLES

Introduction

There has been a significant increase in the number of twins and higher multiples with consequent implications for schools and teachers. Twins and higher multiples are not like brothers and sisters born closely together. Their social and emotional development is different because there is always that other person there, and who is exactly the same age, for adults, peers and themselves to compare with. When planning the education of twins/multiples, parents and teachers need to consider:

- prematurity/pre-school development/health problems;
- previous experiences of separation and the reaction of each child;
- relationships with other children;
- the closeness of the bond between the twins/multiples/whether they combine to form a 'fatal combination';
- competitiveness – always striving to 'beat' each other;
- significant difference in ability/one child opting out;
- polarisation where twins choose to go to extremes: quiet/noisy, outgoing/ shy, etc.;
- restriction of one by the other;
- dominance/dependence.

Before starting school, it is advisable for teachers and parents to discuss the pre-school development of the children and how they are to be introduced to school. The 'Twins and multiples starting school. Parent/teacher question-nair' (Appendix II) provides a framework for discussion. The Twins and Multiple Births Association (Tamba) in the UK also provides information for parents and professionals.

Individuality

There is a danger that twins/higher multiples are perceived and treated as a couple or group. Adults and children need to recognise that each child has his or her own personality and emotional needs. Adults and children must ensure that they can identify individuals and call them by name. They should be respected as individuals and never should be referred to as 'the twins', 'twinnie', etc.

Each child must be regarded as an individual and not labelled as 'the clever one', 'the naughty one', etc. It is difficult not to compare twins or multiples but never compare them to their detriment. Generally, identical twins make very similar progress. However, it is important to monitor individual progress against the peer group and national standards. If learning support is required, it must be given to each child on an individual basis. (If both children have special needs they should not share a helper, thus receiving only half of the time given to singletons.)

Arrange separate appointments for parents in the evenings and always discuss children's progress at separate times. Give each child letters to take home. Expect each child to bring replies, money, etc. from home.

Be aware that the children and parents will compare progress whether or not they are in the same class. It is important that one child does not lose confidence, particularly with reading.

Separation/keeping together

Putting twins/higher multiples into separate classes requires careful consideration and consultation with parents. Many twins/multiples have little experience of separation, even sleeping in the same bedroom. Thus the dual separation from parents and twin may be more upsetting than expected.

If the children have experienced a recent trauma such as bereavement, they may need the support of their twin in class.

When twins/multiples are separated it is frequently and surprisingly the dominant child who becomes insecure whilst the other child blossoms.

Parents and teachers need to discuss how they will support the children before reversing a decision too quickly. The longer term implications of changing a decision need to be thought through.

Twins benefit from being apart when there is:

- markedly different ability so that the child sees himself or herself as failing;
- markedly similar progress so that one child is levelling down or up to stay the same as his or her twin;
- disruptive behaviour where twins form a 'fatal combination';
- dependency so that one or both cannot mix with or relate to other children;
- intense competitiveness so that the child's main goal is to keep up with or beat their brother or sister;
- polarisation where twins go to opposite extremes and opt out of activities/subjects just because their brother or sister is doing them;
- lack of privacy where one twin constantly reports to parents about the activities and progress of the other.

Many schools are one form entry; therefore, for many twins and higher multiples the option of separate classes is not available. However, the attitudes of professionals and the willingness to understand the needs of multiples and their families is much more important. Children are not in school twenty-four hours a day and parents and teachers can work together to provide opportunities for individual development through grouping, visits, play, etc.

Language development

The unique environment of twins/multiples means that they receive fewer and shorter interactions with adults. If left together for long periods they reinforce their own mistakes. Such speech is frequently described as a special twin language or cryptophasia. Hay (1991) found that there was a tendency for twins aged between 2 and 4 years and identical twin boys in particular to be six months behind singletons in their articulation and ability to express themselves. Their sentences were shorter and baby talk persisted for longer. Hay also referred to the tendency of twins/multiples to speak loudly and quickly because they are competing for adult attention. The birth date of premature twins may also result in their being pushed into the year above, thus exacerbating the gap between them and the oldest singletons. Teachers need to be aware that the above issues may affect progress, particularly in reading, and that even though phonological problems tend to right themselves there may be a need for specific intervention and learning support.

Attention deficit

The work of Professor Hay has also revealed that there is a greater tendency for twins (especially boys) to have difficulty concentrating and staying on task. Routines, clear rules and self-organisation strategies such as 'plan, do and review' help the children to focus on the learning required.

Nursery admission

Twins and multiples need particular consideration. They should not be labelled as taking up more than one place. Multiples in particular need the nursery opportunity to learn to socialise with children other than their twin, to develop language and to function as an individual in an educational setting.

Be positive

Being a twin or multiple is not a disability. Remember: not all twins and higher multiples have problems.

There are advantages too. Twins and higher multiples have a unique and special relationship which is not available to singletons. There is a companion and friend always available. Twins and higher multiples are frequently independent and have to learn about sharing right from the start.

Twins and higher multiples are special and people give them special attention – so long as this does not go to extremes and the children also develop as individuals, it is a bonus.

With understanding and support where necessary, twins and multiples make good progress at school, developing as individuals with their own strengths, enjoying and celebrating the fact that they are also a multiple.

APPENDIX II: PARENT/TEACHER QUESTIONNAIRE

Twins and multiples starting school: parent/teacher questionnaire

Starting school is a major step for all children. However, for twins and higher multiples there is the added dimension of their multiple relationship and whether they are to be educated separately or together.

There are no easy answers and a flexible approach is best. Questions marked with * indicate that the twins/multiples are probably better separated. Throughout the questionnaire 'twins' also refers to higher multiples.

The information from the questionnaire will enable teachers and parents to discuss educational provision and home support so that the children develop both as individuals and as multiples.

Parents present	
Teacher completing form	
Date	

If possible interview parents together.

1.   Background information

		A First born	B Second born	C Third born	Comments
a	First name				
b	Surname				
c	Date of birth				
d	Age starting school				
e	Sex				
f	Twin type	☐ Identical (1 egg splits) or ☐ Fraternal (2+ eggs)			
g	Siblings' age/sex				
h	Language spoken in home				

Identical twins share the same genetic make-up but are not clones. Fraternal twins are no more alike than brothers and sisters.

2.   Birth history

		A	B	C	Comments
a	Length of pregnancy (weeks)				
b	Type of delivery				
c	Birthweight (lb oz or kg g)				
d	No. days intensive care				
e	No. days special care				
f	Was the child 'difficult' as a baby / toddler?				

a) 37–38 weeks normal for twins. 35 weeks for triplets.

3.   Current physical development (please ✓ where applicable)

		A	B	C	Comments
a	Eyesight problems				
b	Hearing problems				
c	Speech problems / therapy				
d	Epilepsy				
e	Asthma				
f	Eczema				
g	Allergies				
h	Cerebral palsy				
i	Other				
j	Handedness – left / right / uncertain				
k	Fine motor skills, e.g. holding a pencil				
l	Clumsiness				

Social development

4.   Prior to school the twins were apart:

		please ✓	Comments
a	Often		
b	Occasionally		
c	Very seldom		
d	Never		

5.   Separation was in the form of:

		please ✓	Comments
a	Separate bedrooms		
b	Separate childcare		
c	Separate outings		
d	Hospitalisation of one only		
e	Other		

6.   How did your twins attend nursery?:

		please ✓	Comments
a	Did not attend nursery		
b	Nursery same sessions		
c	Nursery different sessions		
d	Other		

7.   Generally do you believe separation is desirable for the individual development of twins?:

		please ✓	Comments / Why is this?
a	Yes		
b	No		
c	Issue not considered		

Some people perceive twins as a couple that should not be separated. Separation does not necessarily develop individuality.

8.   When the twins are separated, how do they react? (✓ only one for each child):

		A	B	C	Comments
a	Very unhappy				
b	A little unhappy				
c	Unaffected				
d	Very happy				
e	Not separated				

If no real previous experience reaction to separation in school may be greater than expected.

9.   Concerning the twins' friendships do they (✓ one only):

		please ✓	Comments
a	Play mostly together / share the same friends		
b	Sometimes play together / some common friends		
c	Rarely play together / mostly have own friends		
d	Don't play together / have their own friends		

The children may not have developed the skills to socialise as individuals.

The twin multiple relationship

10. The twin multiple relationship – does one twin check what the other one is getting or doing:

		A	B	C	Comments
a	Often				
b	Occasionally				
c	Very seldom				
d	Never				

Most twins like to be able to check out the other one – that is why being in separate classrooms can be distressing.

11. If one child is ill or upset is the other affected?:

		A	B	C	Comments
a	Greatly affected				
b	Affected				
c	Hardly affected				
d	Not affected				

Frequently one twin becomes upset if the other is ill – this can result in both being absent at the same time. The effect may be missed if children are in separate classes.

12. Of these phrases which describe the relationship between your twins? (✓ those applicable):

		please ✓	Comments
*a	They compete constantly with each other		
b	They co-operate and have pride in each other		
c	They compete for parental / adult approval		
*d	They are jealous and never praise each other		
e	Other		
f	One twin thinks that the other is always better		

Some twins become obsessive about beating their twin.

13. Do the twins combine forces to be (✓ one in each row):

		Often	Occasionally	Very seldom	Never	Comments
a	Helpful					
*b	Disruptive					
c	Supportive					

Individuality / identification

14. Are your twins very similar? (✓ those applicable):

		please ✓	Comments
a	Physically		
b	Socially		
c	Emotionally		
d	Speech & language		
e	In maturation		

One would expect identical twins to be very similar.

15. If your twins are the same sex / very similar physically do you? (✓ those applicable):

		please ✓	Comments
a	Dress them differently		
b	Have different haircuts / hairstyles		
c	Have name badges		
d	Point out physical differences		
e	Other		

Many twins demand exactly the same.

Emotional development

16. Which of the following is characteristic of dominance in the twins? (✓ one only):

		please ✓	Comments
a	Their dominance changes according to activities		
b	They take turns in dominating		
*c	One twin is always dominant, the other submissive		
d	Neither twin tends to dominate		

With boy / girl twins the girl frequently 'mothers' the boy.

17. Do the twins compare themselves? (✓ those applicable):

		please ✓	Comments
a	In physical appearance		
b	In popularity		
c	In terms of adult approval		
d	Achievement		

One twin may lose confidence with reading if one is, or appears to be, ahead of the other.

18. If one child succeeds does the other(s) opt out?:

		A	B	C	Comments
*a	Often				
b	Occasionally				
c	Seldom				
d	Never				

19. Do the twins show a tendency to go to opposite extremes in behaviour:

		please ✓	Comments
*a	Often		
b	Occasionally		
c	Seldom		
d	Never		

20. Concentration (✓ if any of the following apply):

		A	B	C	Comments
a	Is easily distracted				
b	Cannot follow through instructions without close supervision				
c	Has difficulty keeping attention on tasks or play activities				
d	Often does not seem to listen to what is said to him / her				
e	Often shifts from one uncompleted task to another				
f	Has difficulty playing quietly				
g	Often blurts out answers / interrupts				
h	Often talks excessively				

21. Conduct (✓ if any of the following apply):

		A	B	C	Comments
a	Often argues with parents / adults				
b	Often loses his / her temper / throws tantrums				
c	Often refuses to do things when asked				
d	Often does things on purpose to annoy people				
e	Has been withdrawn from playgroup / nursery				

22. Anxiety (✓ if the child has often and inappropriately complained of):

		A	B	C	Comments
a	Stomach aches				
b	Nausea				
c	Headaches				
d	Vomiting				
e	Dizziness				

23. (✓ if any of the following apply):

		A	B	C	Comments
a	Has he / she routinely been reluctant to go to playgroup / nursery?				
b	Does this child often need a parent or other close person nearby to enable him / her to fall asleep?				
c	Does this child worry about something bad happening?				
d	Does this child worry about death or dying?				
e	Does this child follow you from room to room?				
f	Does he / she feel nervous or uncomfortable around people he / she does not know well?				
g	Does he / she find ways to keep from being around people he / she does not know well?				

24. Have you recently suffered a family trauma such as accident or bereavement? (✓):

		Yes	No	Comments
a				

If yes the twins may need the support of each other in school.

25. At present would your twins prefer to be in: (please ✓)

		A	B	C	Comments
a	Same class				
b	Separate classes				
c	Separate schools				
d	Doesn't mind				
e	Haven't talked to them about separation				

The children will have no experience to draw on. School and separation may be new to them.

26. For your twins when do you believe separation is desirable? (please ✓)
     Beginning of:

				Comments
a	Nursery		Year 4	
b	Reception		Year 5	
c	Year 1		Year 6	
d	Year 2		Secondary school	
e	Year 3		Other	

27. Any further comments

	Comments

28. When will the needs of the twins be reviewed?

Copyright © 1997 P. Preedy – may be reproduced for internal school use only.

References

Hay, D. (1991) *Twins In School: La Trobe Twins Study*, Department of Psychology, La Trobe University, Melbourne, Australia. Australian Multiple Births Association Inc.

Keith, L., Papiernix, E., Keith, D. and Luke, B. (1995) *Multiple Pregnancy: Epidemiology, Gestation & Prenatal Outcome*, London: The Parthenon Publishing Group.

Lowe, M. and Preedy, P. (1998) *Multiple Voices*, Tamworth, Staffs: The Wine Press.

Further reading

Botting, B.J., MacFarlane, A. and Price, F. (1990) *The Three, Four and More*, London: HMSO.

Bryan, E. (1992) *Twins, Triplets and More, their Nature, Development and Care*, Harmondsworth: Penguin.

Cassitt, K. (1982) *Twins, Nature's Amazing Mystery*, London: McClelland & Steward.

Dodd, B. and McEvey, S. (1994) 'Twin language or phonological disorder', *Child Language* 21, 273–289.

Hay, D. and Johnston, C. (1984) *Twins In School – A Survey of South Australian Primary School Teachers*, Melbourne, Australia: La Trobe University.

Hay, D., Prior, M., Cottett, S. and Williams, M. (1987) 'Speech and language development in preschool twins', *Acta Geneticae Medicae et Gemellologiae* 36, 213–223.

Moilanen, I. (1987) 'Dominance and submissiveness between twins, consequences for mental health', *Acta Geneticae Medicae et Gemellologiae* 36, 257–265.

Rutter, M. and Redshaw, J. (1991) 'Growing up as a twin: twin singleton differences in psychological development', *Journal of Child Psychology* 32(26), 885–895.

Sandbank, A. (1991) *Twins and the Family*, South Wirral: Tamba.

Siemon, M. (1980) 'The separation–individuation process in twins,' *American Journal of Psychotherapy* 34, 387–400.

Smilansky, S., Zohar, D. and Snr, R. (1992) *Twins and their Development, the Role of Family and School*, Rockville, USA: BJE Press.

Wright, L. (1997) *Twins, Genes, Environment and the Mystery of Identity*, London: Weidenfeld & Nicolson.

Tamba leaflets (regularly updated)

Parent/Teacher Co-operation to Help Twins at School.
Starting School: Together or Apart.
Twins and Higher Multiples in School (a pamphlet for teachers).
Twins and Language Development.

7   The psychology of triplets

Britta Alin Åkerman

Introduction

I have often come across twins with various problems during visits to
schools in connection with my work at the Department of Special
Education at Stockholm Institute of Education, Sweden. This was the
starting point for my interest in acquiring more knowledge by studying a group of parents and their children who are not very common in
our society. Having studied twins and their psychosocial situation for
a number of years, the question arose: Were there any differences in
expecting triplets or being a triplet when compared with twins?
Obviously, there must be greater and different risks involved in a
triplet pregnancy when compared with a twin pregnancy.

The number of triplet births has increased in Sweden as well as in
other countries (Botting *et al*. 1990, Levine and Wild 1992, Rådestad
1991) mainly due to the increased use of infertility treatment. Triplet
pregnancies are associated with several complications, especially premature births. Despite that, the chances for a happy outcome have
increased, due to early diagnosis, good maternity care and intensive
care during the child's first critical stage; however, triplets are still at risk.

Between 1911 and 1950, 164 triplets were born in Sweden, twenty
of which were stillborn. Between 1951 and 1990, the figure was 223
and nine were stillborn. The significant difference in the number of
triplets born occurred between 1986 and 1990. Between 1991 and
1996, 347 triplets were born and of these only eight were stillborn.

An early diagnosis of a triplet pregnancy is therefore important in
order to try to prevent an early delivery with the risk of complications
for the baby. This also makes it possible to handle the psychological
experience involved in expecting triplets in comparison with one or
two babies, and the parents-to-be can be prepared for the demands
involved after delivery.

Singleton parents or twin parents have many preconceptions about expecting triplets, being a parent of triplets or being a triplet. The concept of triple joys or triple worries is not always accurate. When our two projects were started, one on the rearing and development of twins and the other on triplets' childhood situation, some hypotheses were formed, of which some were proved to be false and others have been confirmed. I followed a group of twins and their parents for sixteen years, in order to shed light on the twins' mental development and relations between them. For nine years I, together with Dr Mia Hovmöller, also followed a group of triplets and their parents. Before starting these studies we had experience of children with normal development as well as children with different functional impairments. This meant that we have been able to make several comparisons of the different developmental stages between singletons, twins and triplets.

To survey triplets as a group is a very different and unique experience. What has been most fascinating is not their likeness or their rarity, but the fact that they have been together for a long time during pregnancy. Recent research has shown that even if genes are the same in identical twins and triplets at the time of the original splitting of the zygote, at least four factors may differentially alter the development of the babies. These factors are chromosome or gene changes, differences in circulation and oxygenation, infectious agents, drugs and chemicals (Fuller Torrey *et al.* 1994, p. 16). My choice of project has been strongly influenced by a wish to learn more about how this time in the womb influences the triplet's start in life and later mental development.

A large number of published studies on the medical, psychiatric and social aspects of pregnancy, delivery and motherhood have mainly focused on the somatic care of pregnant women. There have also been a number of studies of mothers-to-be and of those who have recently become mothers and their psychosocial situation. In the last fifteen years, twinship has been the focus of interest for a number of researchers. Elizabeth Bryan's (1992) main focus has been on medical as well as psychosocial factors with multiple birth parents and their infants. Her experience and ideas have also influenced us to follow a group of triplets with the focus being on both the parents' thoughts and experiences around pregnancy, delivery and parenthood as well as the triplets' mental development and their relationships with each other. Very rarely have fathers been asked to express their thoughts about their psychological situation during the pregnancy and delivery, and these have been illuminating. In this triplet study both of the parents have been given equal space during the interviews.

From a psychodynamically oriented theory, many authors reported that pregnancy, delivery and becoming a parent involve a period of great sensitivity to crisis (Bibring 1961, Bibring and Valenstein 1976). Sensitivity to crisis can be greater in association with triplet pregnancy and triplet parenthood due to the increased risks of complications in delivery and pregnancy. The concept of 'crisis' can be defined in various ways and has a different meaning for different researchers. The theoretical basis for the triplet study is the definition of crisis described by Erikson as a normative life crisis (1994). By this, Erikson means that each step is a potential crisis because of the radical change of perspective. The word 'crisis' in this context becomes a developmental concept and does not represent a threatening catastrophe, but rather a turning point, a critical period of increased vulnerability and increased possibilities and is therefore the ontogenetic source of a productive strength and of maladjustment. Which of these patterns of reactions becomes the dominant one depends, according to psychoanalytic theory, on the person's childhood and is influenced by the way he or she was treated by the parents. The early relationship with the parents in particular is of great importance in how a person functions in his or her own parenthood. If he or she has received help in meeting and solving conflicts in a constructive manner this will enable them to solve an acute crisis in connection with pregnancy in a more positive way. The person in crisis has the possibility, in a new situation and with a mature self, to deal with and find new solutions to infantile unresolved conflicts. If relationships early in life have been negative and difficult, this can prevent the possibility of finding a constructive solution. A triplet pregnancy could in such cases trigger a traumatic crisis, resulting from meeting a life situation of a kind that his or her earlier experiences are insufficient to understand and deal with. The difference between a normative crisis and a traumatic crisis is that the normative crisis is a developmental crisis which all people go through during different stages of their lives, whilst the traumatic crisis arises after an experience which has strongly reduced the person's vitality and ability to act. This could happen if the family is not psychologically prepared or other social prerequisites are unfavourable. An increased vulnerability also makes one's social environment's reaction and attitude more important. The crisis can be reinforced if information on a triplet pregnancy, premature birth or the risks involved in connection with delivery is given in a way that conveys uncertainty about the infant's health or the parents' ability to deal with the situation. Parents can be 'paralysed' in such a way that they are unable to receive their newborn baby (or babies) in a positive way. The way in which parents solve their crises is of considerable importance for the infant's future development.

The study under discussion involved seventeen triplet families living in the middle of Sweden. Only families with complete sets of triplets were invited to participate in the study. Families who had lost one of their babies in connection with the delivery or later are not included in the study. This means that the trauma of losing a child will not be discussed here. The families participating in the study were very positive about taking part. They hoped that they would have not only the opportunity of talking about their hopes and fears but also of sharing the experiences of other families. The study was carried out retrospectively so that parents were able to look back on how they felt about being told that they were expecting triplets, the pregnancy and delivery. The materials and methods are described in Alin Åkerman *et al.* (1995, 1997). Interviews with both parents were carried out when the children were aged 3:9 to 6:2 the first time and 9 years old the second time. On the first examination the ages varied between the triplets of different families, but there has been a correction in the age differences. When the children were examined a second time their difference in age was a maximum of fourteen days. On both these occasions developmental psychological and neurological assessments of the children were carried out. During the developmental psychological assessment, one of the parents was usually present to give emotional support to the child and also to give an opinion on the reliability of the assessment. Occasionally the siblings were also interviewed when the triplets were 9 years old.

The collected data were rather sparse and the question is: Is it representative, as it only involves one part of Sweden? The reliability, however, can be considered to be good, as there has been no drop-out of families between the first and second examinations. We have also had a very positive response from all parents and children which resulted in a high degree of honesty in their replies.

Prenatal and postnatal influences on family relationships

Diagnosis, pregnancy and delivery

In general, but particularly in the case of the mothers, the news of a triplet pregnancy resulted in a a strong sense of shock; see also Spillman, Chapter 3. For most of the families the news was given at 16 weeks of pregnancy, but some were given the information as early as six to eight weeks. Two of the families were told about their twin pregnancy at 16 weeks but were told that they were expecting triplets at 28 weeks. One family received the information at the delivery table. This particular family already had one child and the mother had told the physician, when she had seen him for routine check-ups, that she had felt the baby 'kicking everywhere', but despite that, she did not have an ultrasound scan. The babies were born under very dramatic circumstances prior to the last check-up before delivery. The first baby was born vaginally, a head delivery (vaginal vertex). The staff were not prepared for two more babies and could not turn the next baby, who was born sideways with one arm and one leg emerging first. The third was a breech birth. As was also reported in the UK studies on multiples (see Spillman, Chapter 3), many parents said that staff had told them that they were expecting triplets in a very insensitive way, due to the staff being unaccustomed to diagnosing triplet pregnancies, and the discovery was also a shock for the sonographers. The shock is then transferred to the parents-to-be, who do not know how to handle the information. The feelings of helplessness and separation anxiety or of frustration and aggression that are intimately connected with traumatic crises were not experienced by any of these triplet families. The reactions corresponded rather to what has been described as a life-changing crisis, or normative crisis. As an example of these changing crises, the turning point, also described as a developmental crisis, has three main components in both parents' reactions to the news that they were expecting triplets. All these components are not necessarily found in every parent, but are nevertheless clearly shown by both men and women. The following describes the reactions most commonly experienced by women and men.

The experience of suddenly expecting something other than was originally expected

Expecting a child is in itself a revolutionary situation. The pregnancies were planned by all the couples and the news of the pregnancies was received positively by all of them. Ten of the pregnancies were spontaneous and seven resulted from various types of assisted conception. The news that the woman was pregnant with triplets triggered off new feelings, but as they received the information in advance, the parents-to-be had time to deal with and prepare themselves for the new situation. This applied to all but the three families who received the information late, or not until it was time for delivery.

The *women* experienced a greater shock reaction than the men: 'I cried and laughed alternately.' Becoming a mother is an entirely different process from becoming a father. For a triplet mother-to-be there is a considerable body change in the form of increase in weight. For some this creates a feeling of being 'ugly' and 'not loved' by the husband, even if this is not the real picture. Uncertainty in the role of woman and mother is accentuated by the thought of managing three babies instead of one. The mother also has to form an inner relationship with *three* babies instead of *one,* which in itself is a different experience.

The *man*, on the other hand, can only reflect his experience of the triplet pregnancy through the woman. He has not experienced any body changes that make it different when there are three babies instead of one. None of the men said that they experienced the woman's body changes as ugly. On the other hand, the pregnancy involves bodily risks, pain and strain for the woman. This can activate feelings of guilt that it is the man who has contributed to this pain through his masculine potency.

The problem of obtaining a psychological insight into what it really entails to be a parent of triplets

Many parents have said that they were very positive about expecting triplets once they had had the opportunity of dealing with their first reactions. These positive reactions can be characterised as 'richness', namely something more evident and completely different from having only one baby. But in this too positive experience there could be a risk of denying the possibility of future problems. Many also stated that during pregnancy they 'did not want to face the fact' that it would be difficult to have three children.

On the *woman's* part there were some fears about how they would have time for the other children in the family, which were expressed as feelings of anxiety and guilt. Six of the families already had children aged 2 to 10 and two other families had children in the upper teens or older.

For many of the women the husband's positive reactions were experienced as very important. This positive experience had strengthened their self-esteem and their identity as a woman and mother. This self-esteem had increased over time as the children had grown up and they had found that they had actually succeeded in taking care of all the children.

The *men* were not as worried as the women. However, one of the men who was told that they were expecting twins tells of his reaction at the birth:

> 'When the staff told me that there were three babies, I said "No, that's not true. There are two." I never understood why there was such a lot of activity during the delivery. The time just disappeared. Then I sat in front of three boxes with three babies and did not understand that they were mine. Newspaper and television reporters just stormed in. It was very unpleasant. Not until we brought the babies home could I really grasp that there were three of them.'

The women as well as the men told us that the men were more positive about the news that they were expecting triplets. From the beginning the men understood that they would be needed in a very different way. The mother can handle twins all by herself, but with triplets much more help is needed from the father. Because a triplet pregnancy is much more unusual and remarkable than an ordinary pregnancy or even a twin pregnancy, the community also reacts differently. Could it be that the triplet father-to-be is met with more understanding, tolerance and support from the community? He receives more attention and has a more important role during pregnancy. This in itself creates feelings in him of inner strength and security, which is not as apparent in an ordinary pregnancy.

The uncertainty syndrome

All the families had planned to have children, but very few had counted on having three, or even two. For the families with spontaneous pregnancies (n=10) the triplet diagnosis was completely unexpected. Those pregnancies which had resulted from assisted conceptions (n=7) were intellectually aware that there was a risk of more than one baby. However, *none* were prepared emotionally. Several claimed they had not been properly informed that the hormone treatment could result in more than one baby (see also Spillman, Chapter 3).

The concept of the 'uncertainty syndrome' has been given to the effect on the parents-to-be who had been informed of the possible risks of the pregnancy and complications during delivery after the triplet diagnosis. All had been informed that there would be a premature delivery, that the babies would be smaller than singletons, and that the delivery itself would be more complicated than the birth of singletons and twins. 'The syndrome' was, however, specific to the women and has only occasionally been seen in the men. One man said: 'I never had any thought that there was any risk or that something could happen to the babies.'

One woman said: 'When I was told at the ultrasound examination about all the heads and legs, I thought I had Siamese twins in my womb, possibly a monster with two heads, I never thought I would wake up with three healthy babies.'

The feelings of anxiety and fear which had been present prior to the delivery also concerned what delivery method would be used. Three women delivered vaginally and thirteen by Caesarean section. For several women it was uncertain until the last moment what delivery method would be used. Some were informed about the Caesarean section, but not that they would be under a general anaesthetic. One mother said:

> 'When it was time for the operation I got very frightened. I was about to faint and could not breathe. I had to sit up during the epidural and it did not have any effect. I just screamed and screamed. Then I was given the anaesthetic. The whole delivery was dramatic, I felt cheated.'

There are doctors who are of the opinion that it is just as efficient to deliver triplets the normal way as by Caesarean section, but not all doctors agree on this point. Most triplets are delivered by Caesarean section, usually because the mothers are feeling anxious and scared. Sometimes the delivery starts in the normal way and then ends up with Caesarean section, which occurred in this study. When several fetuses are crowded together some can be in the wrong position. Considerable experience is needed to be able to turn the babies before delivery if at all possible, which happened in the case of one of the families in this project. Some babies can also suffer from lack of oxygen, in which case a Caesarean section is the only option.

The most usual experience was that the delivery was more of an occasion for the staff than for the family. Lots of doctors, nurses, midwifes, photographers and other staff invaded the delivery room or the adjacent room with a window, and there were often between fifteen and twenty people present. A couple of families had noticed that there was a priest outside the delivery room. This frightened them enormously. They were not informed of the reason for the priest being present and were therefore convinced that their babies would not survive. At these hospitals it was common for a priest to be present at multiple births. Five of the women had acute Caesarean sections, due to complications in the mother or a risk of triplet collision. These women felt 'cheated' of the delivery, as it happened under general anaesthetic. In many of the planned Caesarean section deliveries, the mothers were totally unprepared for the procedure. All had different ideas which did not always correspond to what actually happened.

Triplet and family relationships

Zygosity

The zygosity in triplets arises in the same way as in twins. Triplets are often trizygotic, i.e. the result of three different eggs fertilised by three different sperm. This was usually the case when conception took place after the woman had received treatment. Without hormone stimulation or other types of assisted conception the chances of having triplets are one in 7,000 births. In some cases two of the triplets are monozygotic and the third is a singleton. In very rare cases all three babies can be monozygotic, i.e. one fertilised egg splits in two and then yet another split takes place of one of these two eggs. There are different reports of the relative frequency of these three types of triplets. MacGillivray *et al.* (1988) assumed that the most common variation is two separate eggs with one egg splitting. In this case two will be identical and the other fraternal.

In our study seven sets of triplets were trizygotic (all fraternal); for all except one of them, the mother had undergone ovulation induction and/or assisted conception procedures. Nine were dizygotic (two identical and one fraternal) and one was monozygotic (all identical). The zygosity was assessed by histological examinations of the fetal membranes and/or comparison of physical features between triplets of the same set.

Infancy

The triplets in the study were born between four and seven weeks early and weighed between 1,290 and 2,670 grams. Three infants had a birthweight of less than 1,500 grams, twenty weighed between 1,500 and 2,000 grams, twenty-four weighed between 2,001 and 2,500 grams and four weighed more than 2,500 grams. The average weight for the girls was 1,882 grams and for the boys 2,104 grams. These considerably high weights may have been the result of very careful prenatal care, with continuous check-ups and the mothers being on sick leave. The women were on sick leave after the triplet diagnosis from approximately the sixteenth week of pregnancy. Several women were hospitalised from six to eight weeks before delivery. The babies were then in a neonatal clinic for approximately as many weeks as they were prematurely born. In the cases where there were no complications they would leave the hospital earlier. This means that many of the families spent a long time at the hospital; first the mothers and then the babies were in hospital. This put a lot of strain on all of them. Seven sets of triplets were of the same sex. None of the infants showed any significant differences in birthweight according to birth order.

The triplet's parents' experience of their situation during the first years were that 'the sum of two plus one is different to three'. Their lives were turned upside down and everything revolved around the children. If one of the babies was not crying one or two others were. If one of them had a clean nappy the two others had dirtied theirs. When the parents had just changed one baby's nappy, it was time for the next one to have a nappy change. In between all the nappy changes there was the feeding to take care of. This went on day and night and there was hardly any time for the parents to sleep or relax. It was particularly difficult at the beginning when everything was new. Many of the infants were sick when they were small and they would catch diseases from each other. Gastric disorders were very common and this meant that the nappies had to be changed more often. Several of the infants got ear infections and had breathing problems. Nineteen of the triplets have had recurring ear infections.

In other words, the initial time at home was chaotic for most of the families, with very few continuous periods of rest. Feeding and nappy changes went on for more or less twenty-four hours. Breastfeeding was unthinkable for most of them as the babies were so small and did not suck very well. Only three mothers breastfed their babies and they only fed one baby at each feeding time. Some mothers expressed their milk, but gave up in the end. Feeding was difficult and hectic at first.

All the families realised from the beginning that the only way to deal with the situation of feeding and nappy changing was to have a routine. For practical reasons it was impossible to meet the individual child's need for a certain rhythm. All the parents knew this and felt unhappy about it. This was most noticeable when the husband was at work and the domestic helper, which most of the families had to have, had left the home (Alin Åkerman *et al.* 1997).

Looking back, what the triplet parents remembered most was lack of sleep and all the attention they got from everyone. The triplet pram is rather conspicuous. When they were out walking, most of the families had been stopped by curious people who thought it must be fantastic to have triplets. One mother said:

> 'One becomes public property. People think they know me just because they once asked me how the triplets were. Sometimes this feels hard, but one has to get used to it. All of a sudden I understand how famous people live.'

When the triplets were aged between 1.5 and 3 years there was another problem. The triplets learned to walk and climb and run around everywhere, exploring their environment. What does a mother do when all three toddlers run in different directions? Several families living in houses had solved the problem by putting up a fence around the house so that the infants were secluded when outdoors. Although this resembled a kennel run it was very convenient, as the parents did not have to worry about their triplets disappearing.

During the first year the families usually received help with child-minding and domestic work from their local authorities. During the second year the help was not always available, but despite that the triplet families very seldom complained, particularly those who had got pregnant as the result of an assisted conception. They did not feel that they had the right to complain, as they had waited for such a long time before they had their children. When we met the parents and their children after three years, the parents reported that everything was much easier. They could talk to their children and make them understand what the rules were, so that the parents were able to manage the situation. One would expect that there would be more divorces, considering the pressures these triplet families were under during the children's first years. However, this has not been the case except for one family, where the parents divorced when the triplets were between 2 and 3 years of age.

Growing up as a triplet

The most interesting result from this triplet study is the difference in mental development at the first meeting of the triplets in the same set who are born small for gestational age. Eight triplet girls and three boys were born small for gestational age. The mental development of these children was compared with the development of their siblings from the same set of triplets (five girls and eight boys) who were not born small for gestational age. The scale used at pre-school age is Griffiths' Mental Development Scales, which covers 2 to 8 years of age. There are six different subscales: the locomotor scale, the personal-social scale, the hearing and speech scale, the hand and eye co-ordination scale, the practical reasoning scale and the performance scale. The triplets born small for gestational age had significantly lower scores on the C-D-E-F-subscales, which are the more cognitive-related subscales and also on the total Griffiths' score. When comparing triplets with twins of the same birthweight there were no differences in total mental development. However, some differences between the two groups were found in language, speech and social development. My theory about these differences is that language and speech is, to a high degree, dependent on optimal surroundings as compared with locomotor and eye and hand co-ordination, which is much more dependent on organic, biological factors. It is a different psychological situation for triplets who must constantly compete for the attention, stimulation and love of their mother (parents) to a greater degree than twins and, of course, singletons. The early dialogue between mother and triplets must naturally be organised in a different way from that between mother and singletons and even mother and twins.

When the triplets were 9 years old they were interviewed individually and were able to talk about their experiences of being a triplet. Remarkably enough, very few of them knew what 'triplet' meant. They were only aware of being a sibling in a family. On the other hand, they could clearly indicate what the advantages and disadvantages were of being a triplet. However, the children all agreed:

- 'We're never alone'
- 'When we're afraid there is always someone there'
- 'We always have someone to play with'
- 'If somebody quarrels with me at school there is always someone there to defend me'
- 'It's not difficult being at home without our parents as there are always three of us'
- 'We never have a dull moment, because one of us always finds something to do'.

The triplets were equally agreed on the negative issues:

- 'It's always very noisy, we often fight'
- 'It's always the others who make the decisions'.

Many of the triplets in the study were dizygotic. Two sets were only girls and two sets only boys, two sets were two girls and one boy and three sets were two boys and one girl. These monozygotic sets of triplets were much more dependent on each other when compared to the trizygotic triplets. This applied mostly to the monozygotic girls. In one set with only girls, the third girl was completely excluded from the two monozygotic girls' very intimate closeness. They had each other as best friends while the third girl had to find friends elsewhere. When the boy was the third in a set of monozygotic girls the feeling of being the outsider was not experienced as strongly, as he looked for friends among other boys. The significant difficulty for the odd triplet girl was compensated for when she started school and made friends among her classmates. The triplets were extremely popular and there was no difficulty for any of them in making friends. They were never bullied or excluded by any group of children. If any of the triplets in a set got into trouble at school, the other two would always come to the rescue. This always happened, even if they had had a disagreement immediately before the incident. They were completely loyal and supportive to each other on such occasions, which means that together triplets form a very strong team and no one dares to tease them or be unkind to them – a common occurrence among children of this age.

Siblings

Ten sets of triplets had older siblings. One family also had a younger child and two of the mothers were pregnant again at the first interview. The parents were aware of the difficult situation that the siblings experienced after the birth of the triplets. They were used to getting their mother's attention, which they now had to manage without. The older siblings not only lost the attention of their parents but also that of some of their friends. They were ashamed to bring their friends home as it was always very messy. Their smaller siblings never left them alone, and when adults came to visit the triplets got all the attention and they felt left out.

Sometimes the older siblings' jealousy and feelings of being left out could be relieved by involving them in the daily care of the babies. However, this could also create problems, as triplets are extremely small when they arrive home. Parents might prevent older siblings from being too active in handling the triplets for fear that they would harm them.

Older boy siblings seem to find it more difficult to create emotional contact with the new babies compared to older girls (see also

Sandbank, Chapter 10). There could be several reasons for this. A girl of 4 to 6 years of age (as some of the siblings were at the birth of the triplets) has often formed a close relationship with her father, and the father might not spend the same amount of time with the triplets as the mother. Girls often like to play the role of extra mother and they often feel more important than boys.

Grandparents play a very important role for siblings. They can relieve the parents by taking care of the siblings and inviting them to visit more often. Through this contact the older siblings can feel important. It might be easier for the older generation to take care of the siblings who are not in need of the same type of care as the triplets. This gives the parents the opportunity to give more time to their triplets. The problems which can occur should not overshadow the fact that older siblings in a triplet family can get a great deal of pleasure from the babies. In one of the families in the study an older sibling of the same sex as one of the triplets showed intense warmth and closeness to that particular triplet, while the other two triplets of the same sex shared the same interests. In this family they formed two pairs and could thus eliminate some of the feelings of being the outsider which can sometimes occur if triplets are dizygotic and thus two of them are monozygotic.

Naturally parents questioned themselves about how their children would get on in life, even before they were told that they were expecting triplets. One family expressed themselves as follows:

> 'Our daughter was 5 when we were told that we were expecting triplets and we involved her from the start of the pregnancy. She came with us to the ultrasound scan and looked at books on how babies develop in the womb. She also looked at books on premature babies. During the triplets' stay at the neonatal clinic she came with us as much as she was allowed. Sometimes she got tired and was able to stay at the hospital's play therapy department, when both of us needed to be with the triplets. When the triplets arrived home they occupied all our time. We constantly felt guilty about only spending time with her when the babies were asleep. She has been able to help us change the nappies and this has made her feel grown up and helpful.
>
> Now that the triplets are older (9 years) she behaves like a little mother to them and she feels very responsible.'

This sibling, who was 14 years old at the last interview, mentioned that she was both proud and happy about her three siblings, one girl and two boys. The triplets were often with her even when friends of her own age came to visit. Her close relationship with her triplet siblings is probably the result of her parents involving her from the very beginning, not pushing her away but helping her to take part in the care of the triplets when they were small.

However, triplets can be a problem to older siblings if they are still very young when the triplets are born. They cannot understand why the triplets take up such a lot of the parents' time. Very young siblings should also get to see the triplets as much as possible during the time they are in hospital. However, young children often become quickly bored and it is very difficult to take care of them in a neonatal clinic without jeopardising their own and other patients' safety. It is therefore best if someone can take them home to their familiar surroundings when they are tired of – in their view – rather boring small siblings who take up all their mother's time.

Triplets at school

Same class or different class

Special problems occur when triplets start school. There are so few triplets that knowledge of what is best for them is minimal, so decision-making is more difficult than for twins. At some schools, during certain periods the policy has been to place all twins and triplets in separate classes from the start.

When there are three children, additional problems around class placement occur. Sometimes a set of triplets includes one monozygotic twin pair and the third dizygotic. Should the two be placed together and the third in a separate class? Should children of the same sex be placed together and the one of a different sex in another class? Should the ones who are emotionally close be placed together and the others in different classes?

Due to possible complications at birth, one child in a set of triplets could be delayed and perform less well than the others. This can be very difficult for the teachers to handle when they start comparing them with each other. Sometimes the monozygotic pair of a triplet set is placed together in the hope that it will be easier for the third triplet to be alone. This is usually a bad solution as the third triplet feels left out. In such cases it is much better either to let all three be together or to separate all of them if there are several parallel classes at the school. The greatest problem has been for the schools in small Swedish communities which do not have three parallel classes, which makes it impossible to place them in separate classes. In such cases they should be placed in different schools, which would be practically impossible for the families. If the children are placed in the same class they should not sit near each other and preferably not at the same table. A girl from a triplet set with a monozygotic pair of girls could already feel left out of the sibling relationship and usually finds it more difficult at the beginning of school.

Consequences for teachers and parents

At the time of this study when the children were 9 years old they were in the last term of the second form. The teachers had therefore known the children for nearly two years. During this study, teachers have expressed the more or less unanimous opinion that it is best for triplets to be placed in separate classes. This has been explained as necessary for the triplets in order to help them separate from each other and enable them to become individuals. This has very seldom been the parents' wish. For practical reasons the parents have usually chosen to place the triplets in the same class. In Sweden the parents have the right to choose the school and whether their children should be in the same or in separate classes. In our triplet study only five of the seventeen families chose separate classes for their triplets. Out of these, two families placed two children in one class and the third in another. In all of these families there have been considerable differences in achievement between the children, and the reason for their choice of class has been those differences. The teachers are very pleased, as the triplets attend the same school and are able to meet each other at breaktimes. The children have, according to the teachers, been able to develop their identity and have also gained self-esteem. They are less dependent on their triplet siblings and have made friends of their own. The parents who chose different classes for their triplets are also very pleased, as they have noticed less comparison between the triplets. The education is usually designed differently, as teachers are free to teach the different subjects in the most suitable way for their particular class. Due to this, one child might have become more advanced in reading, while another has worked more on learning to write and the third knows more about maths.

The twelve families who put their triplets in the same class have also been pleased with their choice. They have experienced this as positive both for themselves and for the children, but they have often had to cope with advice from others on how wrong they have been in their choice. For the uncertain and insecure parent, this feeling of having made the wrong decision for their children can be more negative than the consequences for the children of being in the same class. The teachers have not always had a positive attitude and have often pointed out that there is competition between the children, that they are always comparing themselves with each other, and that they are too dependent on each other. They are also of the opinion that many conflicts start at home and then continue at school. One of the children in a set of triplets is often better at school work as well as socially. This means that the child becomes the spokesman for the others, who more or less stop listening to what the teacher is telling them. The teachers also point out that the children are always watching what the others are doing or saying and in this way 'have nothing to say of their own'.

However, some teachers have been able to see the advantages of having triplets in the same class. They have seen the situation more from the parents' perspective and understood that if the parents believe the choice of having their children in the same class is a good one, this positive attitude is transferred to the children. The teachers have seen that it is more convenient to have one teacher contact, the same routines and homework. They have also responded as teachers to the demand to discover each child's individual needs and to stimulate their interests. Whether or not the triplets have been very different in performance ability, this is no easy task. In the latter case it was easy to get them mixed up, and the teachers have not been able to see the children as separate individuals. Some teachers are fascinated by triplets and feel that it is an exciting challenge to have triplets in their class and follow their development. One teacher explains:

> 'As the girls function very well together and like each other's company and they are not dependent on each other, it is good for them to be in the same class. It's exciting for me to follow their development.'

For the teachers who are negative about having triplets in the same class because they feel that the triplets do not see themselves as separate individuals, the problem often lies in the teacher's own inability to see them as individuals.

Consequences for the triplets themselves

Some children in the study who are in the same class consider the placement to be good. They are not aware of the competition between them or that their siblings could make the learning situation difficult. On the contrary they feel secure having siblings at the same school. However, one triplet boy of a family, who had chosen different classes for all three boys, said: 'I would like us to go to the same class. I miss the others.'

To the question, Were you able to make your own choice of class? they reply 'No', but many mean 'mother and father wanted us to be in the same class and that is good'. Here the parents' positive feelings were transferred to the children, who find this choice the best.

Epilogue

What hypotheses about being parents of triplets and being a triplet have been confirmed and what hypotheses do not correspond with the ongoing study? What is the difference between twins and triplets? First, it is not possible to compare parenthood for twins and triplets. The fact that all triplets are born prematurely and placed in the premature ward often results in the important early dialogue between the mother and baby being prevented. The fear that one of the babies will not survive has an impact on parenthood and the intimacy between the parents and their infants. The constant round-the-clock care which *all* triplet parents give influences both their psychological well-being and their opportunity to socialise with friends. To carry twins, one on each arm, is difficult, but to carry triplets around is impossible for the mother. The feeling of loneliness and isolation is much stronger for triplet mothers when compared to twin mothers.

Triplet development is somewhat delayed when compared to twins, particularly in the area of language. There are several factors involved in this. It is partly due to an increased frequency of triplets being born small for gestational age (SGA) compared to twins and this has proved to be decisive for the development of the children's mental ability. Furthermore, the contact is considerably less between parents and triplets, as the time for contact and intimacy is limited due to lack of time.

Triplets always play with each other. They always have a close friend. If two in a set fall out, there is always a third in the triplet set. Despite this, many triplet sets expressed a strong dependence on each other. In my experience this is not as strong as in twins, perhaps due to the fact that they are three. Twins only have each other while triunity gives more choices.

Like many others, I believed that triplets should not be in the same class at school. However, the results of this study have shown that it works better than might be expected. Both parents and children feel happy about it. Only in the cases where either the parents, or the children themselves, wish them to be in separate classes, which is often the case, for example, during illness or wide differences in performance, has it been a good thing to separate them. It is an advantage for them to have the security of each other so that the first days and years at school can be a positive experience. As a parent, it is easier to help the teachers get to know the children so that they can learn to separate them early.

References

Alin Åkerman, B., Hovmöller, M., Rådestad, A. and Thomassen, P.A. (1995) 'Physical and mental development in 4–6 year-old triplets', *Acta Paediatrica Scandinavica* 84, 661–666.

Alin Åkerman, B., Hovmöller, M. and Thomassen, P.A. (1997) 'The challenges of expecting, delivering and rearing triplets', *Acta Geneticae Medicae et Gemellologiae* 46, 81–86.

Bibring, G.L. (1961) 'A study of the psychological processes in pregnancy and of the earliest mother–child relationship', *Psychoanalytic Study of the Child* 16, 9–72.

Bibring, G.L. and Valenstein, A.F. (1976) 'Psychological aspects of pregnancy', *Clinic Obstetrics and Gynaecology* 19, 357–371.

Botting, B.J., MacFarlane, A.J. and Price, F.V. (1990) *Three, Four and More: A study of Triplets and Higher Order Births*, London: HMSO.

Bryan, E. (1992) *Twins and Higher Multiple Births*, London: Edward Arnold.

Erikson, E.H. (1994) *Identity: Youth and Crisis*, New York: W.W. Norton & Co.

Fuller Torrey, E., Bowler, A.E., Taylor, E.H. and Gottesman, I.I. (1994) *Schizophrenia and Manic-Depressive Disorder*, New York: Basic Books, HarperCollins.

Levine, M. and Wild, J. (1992) 'Higher multiple births and the modern management of infertility in Britain', *British Journal of Obstetrics and Gynaecology* 99, 607–613.

MacGillivray, I., Campbell, D.M. and Thompson, B. (eds) (1988) *Twinning and Twins*, New York: John Wiley.

Rådestad, A. (1991) 'Trilling- och Fyrlingsfödslar i Sverige' (Triplet and quadruplet births in Sweden), *Nordiske medicin* 106, 297–298.

8   Adolescent twins and secondary schooling

David A. Hay

Introduction

The title of this chapter has been chosen deliberately, even though it may seem redundant to refer to both adolescence and 'secondary school' since the two overlap so much. However, it is important to distinguish that there are two separate but interrelated sets of potential pressures on twins and their parents at this age. One concerns adolescence and the need to develop independence not just from one's parents but also from one's co-twin. It is not just puberty that changes the twin situation, but also the transition from primary to secondary school. There is a growing body of information on twins in primary school (Gleeson *et al.* 1990), with such issues as separation into different classes and comparisons of achievement. The secondary school situation is very different, with subject options that reflect preference, aptitude and career ambitions. The primary school question about whether twins should be in the same class is replaced by such questions as whether twins should do the same subjects, attend the same school (if their career plans are very different) or even leave school at different year levels.

It is clear that this chapter draws upon many of the issues raised in the other chapters. The early speech and language problems discussed by Mogford-Bevan in Chapter 4 might be of less consequence if these were only transient developmental difficulties of multiples rather than having *sequelae* in adolescent academic and behavioural problems. Spillman emphasises the stereotyping that parents and others may make of infant twins based on minor (as distinct from medically significant) differences in birthweight and similar variables. The work of student Ann Bruce (discussed below) shows how such stereotyping actually gets worse rather than better as twins move into adolescence and that it is often independent of actual differences in behaviour or in how the twins are perceived by others such as teachers. Preedy (Chapter 6) reviews questions around achievement and separation of twins in primary school. What becomes clear is that separation is not a one-off decision about the placement of multiples but an ongoing dilemma, made even worse by the multiplicity of options that increase throughout secondary schooling. When Preedy discusses her own as well as the Australian work on issues around primary school separation, it may be worth remembering that twins need to learn that separation should be seen as something flexible rather than a permanent decision. Some aspects of the situation in secondary school may require the twins to be back together again; for example, if both were desperate to do a specialised subject for which only a single class is available.

The initial focus of this chapter is on the essential point that all twins are different and that there is no simple or single remedy for all twins. In more than twenty years of work with multiple birth families, I have had contact in some way or another with perhaps over 10,000 sets of twins of all ages. While trying to generalise about what is most likely to be the situation, it must be remembered that there are many families where exactly the opposite will occur and this is something of which all professionals need to be aware. There is no faster way to lose rapport with an individual family or with an audience than for someone to say, 'But my twins are exactly the opposite of what you are saying . . .'.

This chapter continues to question just how difficult is adolescence, and reconsiders the old pessimistic view of this stage of the life cycle, as well as introducing the topic of whether adolescence may be 'better' or 'worse' for twins. It then moves on to consider evidence at adolescence of differences between twins and singletons in academic achievement and behavioural problems, with particular emphasis on Attention Deficit Hyperactivity Disorder.

The following section deals with the factors contributing to differences within the twin pair, focusing on achievement, stereotyping and the role of genetics, contributing both to similarities and differences. After summarising research on how adolescent twins develop autonomy from their parents as well as each other, the chapter moves on to the related question of how to balance competition and co-operation. The final section deals with a neglected topic: the needs of the parents and siblings of adolescent multiples.

The terminology used for different levels of secondary schooling may not be the same as that in the reader's own locality. Even within Australia there are major differences between various states in how secondary education is organised and named, with the last two years being 'forms 5 and 6' or 'years 11 and 12' or the 'post-compulsory years', etc., and there is the development of senior high schools, community colleges and other approaches to best handling the last few years of schooling. Readers will need to translate these ideas into what happens in their own locality.

All twins are different

It is essential to begin this chapter with a caveat. One cannot think of adolescent twins as a homogeneous group. There are a variety of influences which make it clear that six subgroups should be identified, the first four being identical (MZ) and non-identical (DZ) girl–girl and boy–boy pairs, and the last two girls and boys from opposite-sex pairs. I deliberately use the term MZ and DZ rather than 'identical' and 'non-identical' throughout this chapter for a very simple but key reason: MZ twins only share their genes in common and there may be many other influences that contribute to similarities or differences between twins. For example, Koch (1966) identified what she termed the 'prima donna' reaction in MZ girls (the use of their unusual degree of resemblance as the key to their social success). Here they are building upon their identical characteristics, making them even more similar than their genes would suggest.

It is important to appreciate that genes are not everything. This is not the venue to discuss the classic nature–nurture argument (Hay 1985), but there are many aspects of our appearance and behaviour where genes play only a modest role. Thus there are some characteristics where MZ twins may not be very similar, and others where their shared environment may make DZ twins quite similar. Genetic studies are based on the accumulation of data from many sets of MZ and DZ twins and one cannot take a single set of MZ or DZ twins and say they should or should not be similar in their behaviour as a consequence of their zygosity.

The reason for making the potential distinction among the six groups will become obvious throughout this chapter. Even though there may be more variation within than between these groups, this approach seems more helpful than treating adolescent twins as a single group with the same needs and facing the same issues. Unfortunately there is a shortage of recent studies of possible differences among these groups. Koch's (1966) study and especially her thumbnail sketches of the six groups in her Chapter 8 should give anyone working with adolescent twins food for thought. But of course it is derived from US twins in the early 1960s and its relevance to young people from other countries more than thirty years later needs to be considered.

Is adolescence different for twins?

It is surprisingly difficult to answer the question of whether twins as a group experience the same stressors and triggers as other young adults or whether there are extra pressures and benefits. The old 'storm and stress' view of adolescence that emphasised what could go wrong during adolescence has fortunately been replaced with one that focuses much more on the ability of young people and their families to cope with stressors.

It is important to consider the context in which the 'storm and stress' view of adolescence developed, since this is fundamental to appreciating how best to intervene with families. This very negative view came from psychoanalytic approaches such as that of Anna Freud, who viewed disruption and conflict within the family as fundamental to the development of independence in the adolescent and even a healthy way of resolving earlier Oedipal and other complexes. However, most recent research (reviewed by Hill and Holmbeck 1986) indicates that independence occurs most effectively when there is a supportive family environment. There is no doubt that there is more conflict within the family when there are adolescent offspring, but such conflict is more often minor than major and is usually resolved quickly in the effective family. To put it another way; look at the family with adolescents at any one point in time and conflict will often be found (and this has been the basis for the negative view of 'storm'). *But* go back later to that same family, and the conflict has been resolved and there is some other issue, hopefully equally as transient, that is causing difficulty within the family.

In working with families, I find it useful to extend one aspect of the old 'storm and stress' analogy to make the whole situation seem more positive and more practical. Swimming in the ocean, one can cope with successive waves. What one cannot cope with is the giant wave that comes all at once. The successfully developing adolescent (or adolescent twins) and their family can cope with small conflicts as long as they are successive rather than simultaneous. When parents place demands on their adolescents, there may be pressure coming at the same time from school and from peers. What makes the twin situation different and potentially more difficult is that there is an additional source of pressure associated with the co-twin. Such pressure may not come directly from the twin him or herself but may arise from comparisons between the twins by peers, by teachers or by parents. Thus there is more of a potential for the giant wave that overwhelms everyone.

There have been few adequate studies of adolescent twins that address the question of whether this period of development is more difficult for twins than for singletons. Rosambeau's (1987) book does recount the experiences of the many families that chose to reply to her request for information about how twins grow up. Of course that does mean it is selective. However, her book is very important, as every family with multiples or every professional working with multiple birth families will find some example of the situation they are currently experiencing. While she does speak of many families' experience of twins at adolescence as 'open conflict if not actual war', two points need to be emphasised that make this statement seem much less negative.

First is the issue already discussed where conflicts do occur and occur frequently, but the transitory and often trivial nature of these conflicts does make it easier to view them positively rather than as some permanent difficulty within the family. Second is the fact that most families seem to resolve these issues by late adolescence, emphasising that any problems are only a transient part of development. One question which no one has yet been able to answer is whether adolescence in twins may actually be easier in some ways than for singletons. Although they do have the constant presence of the co-twin, there are some situations where this may be useful. In new social situations there is always someone to talk to. The co-twin can function as an essential buffer in some of the social dilemmas which adolescents can find devastating. On the other hand, there is the question of whether twins at adolescence can be too close and this is discussed later in this chapter and also by Sandbank in Chapter 10.

Are adolescent twins different in academic achievement and behaviour?

There have been many reports of twins as a group having difficulties in academic performance but, as mentioned before, not all twins are the same. The classic remains Mittler's (1971) book where he discusses his analysis of the old 11+ examination, which was fundamental to UK education for many years. While the ideas behind the 11+ can be questioned in so many ways, the essential point is that Mittler found twins as a group were significantly behind single-born children, except where the co-twin had died. This implies that there is something about growing up with a co-twin that may impede the adequate development of literacy skills.

Since 1971 there have been a significant number of studies of speech and reading ability which indicate that some problems are more common in multiples. Ironically some of the studies that could have contributed so much to this area failed to identify twin difficulties specifically, because they were twin approaches to genetic analyses, and all that can be found in their reports are the data on the similarities in MZ and DZ twin pairs. For example, the famous Loehlin and Nichols (1976) study of twins who sat the National Merit Scholarship Qualifying Test (a US system for providing tertiary scholarships) focuses on the MZ and DZ similarities in a whole range of academic and personality variables. As an aside it is mentioned that only one-third as many twin boys as singletons were deemed to have the ability that would warrant them sitting this test.

There have been a whole range of smaller scale studies crucial to identifying twin–singleton differences and especially the relationship between earlier speech language differences and later reading problems, for example, in Canada by Lytton (1980) and in Australia by Johnston *et al.* (1984). It can be easy to dismiss such studies because they were small and intensive and because of possible biases in whom they recruited and studied. The Australian study was fortunate in also having access to the 1975 National Survey of Literacy and Numeracy, conducted on very large (13,000-plus children) and very representative samples of 10 and 13 to 14-year-old Australian children. (The main results are discussed in Hay *et al.* 1984, 1986.) There is a twin-by-gender-by-age interaction, which showed that any problems in twin girls generally diminish by adolescence while those in twin boys stay the same or even get worse. At age 10, both girl and boy twins were behind their singleton peers. By age 13 to 14, the twin girls had essentially caught up. Over 70 per cent of these girls and of the male and female singletons had adequate mastery of literacy and numeracy. For the twin boys it was a very different matter, with only 42 per cent having adequate skills. A frequent criticism of these conclusions has been that twins are no different from children in closely spaced families. Fortunately, data on family size were available and it could be shown that children from families with seven or more children had few of the same problems as the twins.

With the general move now in many countries to frequent and

large-scale assessment of academic performance at different levels of the school system such as the PIPS study discussed by Preedy in Chapter 6, more attention is going to be drawn to such assessment and the question of how best to express such issues to twins (especially boys) and their families. While there is much discussion of the gender differences in ability in the general single-born population, the fact that this difference seems so much larger in twins does raise a potential problem for boy–girl pairs. The girl may be the one who is more likely to get a scholarship to a selective entry school, to be placed in groups for accelerated education and to be identified as more academically skilled than her twin brother in many other ways. When this is compounded by the Attention Deficit Hyperactivity Disorder (discussed below) and some of its behavioural consequences in adolescence, then there is no doubt that differences in ability in the boy–girl pair need to be handled carefully.

It is important to emphasise that any problems are simply more frequent for twins and are by no means universal. Twins, parents and teachers need the message that most twins will manage adequately and there must be no suggestion that being a twin is a reason, an excuse or a prediction of less than adequate academic success. It is very hard to achieve an adequate balance between creating awareness of such issues and the possibility of appropriate intervention, and the defeatist view that twins are doomed to academic poor performance. We have been fortunate in Australia that in the last few years there have been well-publicised cases of twin boys (often both members of a pair) doing exceptionally well at senior school examinations and such cases have been vital in putting the twin situation in perspective. Emphasising the success of some twins is crucial to achieving the right balance between awareness of the risk of problems in the twin situation and the fact that the majority will succeed adequately.

However, the school system does need to be aware of what may go wrong and why, so that there can be appropriate and targeted intervention. It was found, in a detailed analysis of errors on the Australian National Survey (Hay *et al.* 1986), that the real problem of multiples was associated more with paying attention than with academic performance. That is, many of the errors on achievement tests were related to failing to attend sufficiently to the problem. For example, twins made more mistakes on simple arithmetic problems and even something as easy as telling the time on a clock face, which hardly demands enormous intellectual effort for a 14-year-old.

Attention Deficit Hyperactivity Disorder

This leads on to consideration of the attentional problems of multiples. Closely associated with school achievement is Attention Deficit Hyperactivity Disorder (ADHD). ADHD is now being increasingly identified in young people and we have shown that this problem is more common in twins than in their singleton siblings (Levy *et al.* 1996), but no other behavioural problems are more common. In a complementary approach, Siminoff (1992) examined case records for young people referred to a London clinic and found both truancy and relationships with other children to be the key differences in why twins were referred, compared with singletons. This does raise the issue of how ADHD is seen in the UK compared with the rest of the world.

It is important to recognise what ADHD actually is, especially because definitions have been changing rapidly in the last few years and do differ between countries. Australia has gone with the American Psychiatric Association set of guidelines, the Diagnostic and Statistical Manual for Mental Disorders (DSM). When DSM-IIIR (the Third Edition Revised) came out in 1987, it recognised one global ADHD disorder, where the young person had to have eight out of a list of fourteen symptoms of inattention and hyperactivity. In 1994 this was superseded by DSM-IV which recognised three disorders: an inattentive type (with six out of nine symptoms of inattention), a hyperactive type (with six out of nine hyperactive and impulsive symptoms) and a combined type that met both sets of criteria. In addition, this number of symptoms had to be recognised by two individuals (for example, parent and teacher) and most significantly had to cause significant disruption to aspects of the person's life. It is worth noting that this change was based on feedback from field trials and clinical experience to identify the best strategy.

Why do nuances of psychiatric definition matter to adolescent twins and their families? DSM-IV did great service by recognising the inattentive type and turning attention away from the traditional focus on hyperactivity. The United Kingdom and many European countries have long emphasised the Hyperkinetic Disorder which is a rigorously defined and thus reasonably rare disorder just of the symptoms of activity. Views are now changing to a classification much more like DSM-IV. It transpires that the inattentive type is by far the most common form of ADHD, being found in up to 10 per cent of twin boys, while the purely hyperactive form is the rarest. This information comes from the Australian Twin ADHD Project (ATAP) which has been following almost 2,000 sets of 4 to 12-year-old twins and their brothers and sisters over an eight-year period, but some other studies are finding the same, if they are actually identifying ADHD. This is a key issue for clinics which use child behaviour check-lists, such as that developed by Achenbach, at their intake. Their measure of externalising behaviours or even the specific sub-scales concerning activity and attention really do not isolate the key features of ADHD and so differences between twins and singletons are less likely to be found. Apart from this, consistent differences between boys and girls and between twins and their singleton siblings are being identified. Twins have more problems and boys have more problems than girls, so twin boys are worse-off (on average but not universally), while singleton girls have the fewest problems.

There is no doubt that rigid diagnostic classifications such as DSM-IV are less than perfect (Hay and Levy 1996), but the main point is clear. There are many twins who have a problem with attention that is sufficiently significant as to impede their performance at school and these twins may have none of the signs of hyperactivity that would have led to their identification by other definitions of ADHD. Even more significant is co-morbidity; that is, the presence of other disorders associated with specific subtypes of ADHD. The Australian study showed that twins with the purely hyperactive type have no higher rates of speech and reading problems than do twins in general, but both the inattentive and the combined type have much higher rates of learning problems. About half of them have or are still receiving formal therapy for their reading difficulties and many of these had previously experienced delays in speech and language development that warranted intervention.

The issue of ADHD at adolescence does need to be considered from several aspects. One is a purely clinical one, where the effect of the stimulant medication often prescribed for ADHD may suppress appetite and have effects on growth at adolescence. In most Australian states, stimulant medication can only be prescribed by paediatricians or child psychiatrists and so families can be assured that the medical implications of ADHD are being catered for by those with particular expertise in issues related to child and adolescent development.

A more significant question is what happens to young people with ADHD at adolescence. This literature has been reviewed elsewhere (Hay and Levy 1996) and unfortunately for many families the situation is not good. The data on twins are only now being collected, but there is extensive information on single-born young adults that identifies much higher rates of substance abuse and conduct problems, including criminal convictions. Without trying to over-simplify a complex issue hotly debated within psychology and psychiatry, the key problems seem to be impulsivity and risk-taking behaviours – you may choose to try drugs that you are offered or to steal a car to get home after the last bus, without thinking seriously of the consequences of your behaviour. Twins are no different from other young people in such situations, except that they may have more of the behaviours which put them at risk.

Why is this so? The answer does not seem to lie in biology. While there have been some suggestions that pre-term birth and associated complications are a major contributor, this study and many others have not found this to be the case. Even when those twins born before 30 weeks' gestation and thus at the highest risk of biological insult were specifically identified, the rates of ADHD and other problems were found to be little higher than in twins overall. There was found to be a high rate of language problems in twin boys who experienced intra-uterine growth retardation and a failure to develop adequately in the last few weeks of the pregnancy, but this is a very extreme situation not experienced by the majority of twins. There does appear to be a strong association with early difficulties in speech and language development (Levy *et al.* 1996) and one can see why some aspects of the twin situation may contribute to problems in both areas. Rushing to get words in before the co-twin encourages impulsive behaviour and the constant presence of the co-twin and the distraction of their activities not only limits the need to develop good communication skills but may also adversely affect the twin's ability to focus attention.

Why do adolescent twins differ, or appear to differ, in behaviour?

The traditional quote about 'the child being the father of the man' may be sexist, but accurately reflects one aspect of the situation with twins and one which Sandbank explores from the psychodynamic point of view in Chapter 10. What has gone before will partly if not largely determine the twins' behaviour at adolescence. But there is one fundamental and positive message for multiples, their families and professionals, associated with the quotation above. Differences may lie not in the young people but rather in the perceptions of those around them. Adolescence is a time to break these patterns with a possible shift in schools, a wider choice of subjects and even the contemporary view discussed later that adolescence is a time when new genes are switched on, so that patterns of similarities and differences may change biologically as well as socially.

It is important to remember that not all twins start off the same at secondary school and three specific areas where twins may be different and where support may need to be focused will be considered. The three areas covered are as follows.

Academic achievement

The issue that more twins than singletons may not achieve adequately at school has already been discussed. Young people who are not achieving academically may feel less adequate about themselves and may seek attention in other less socially desirable ways. In one of our studies of adolescent twins, this turned out to be a major contributor to their self-esteem. If you do well at school, you feel better about yourself. Parental concern about differences between twins in their school achievement accentuates the feeling of inadequacy and differences between twins. There is no doubt that this is more of an issue for twins than for singletons, since academic achievement is not being compared with the whole school but simply with the twin. The question is how to get across to the twins, their peers, the teachers and the parents that one twin is not 'dumb' (and that is the sort of derogatory term the adolescent uses) just because he or she does not do as well as the co-twin. This will apply even if the twins are first and second in the class, as one will be 'inferior' to the other. Sympathy has to be given to the twins in this case, as the problem is not in them. It is partly in the school system of assessment that allows such obvious comparisons to be made between co-twins and also in the need to educate teachers, parents and peers to regard both twins as individuals, rather than perceiving them as a pair. The nature of the secondary school system is that twins may 'vote with their feet' and leave school altogether or move to another school, or at least to another group of school subjects, in order to make comparisons between them more difficult.

One question that has deliberately not been addressed here is that of the separation of adolescent twins in secondary school. The rationale for this is the same as when considering twins in primary school (Gleeson *et al.* 1990), in that there is no evidence that separating twins will 'fix' a problem. Apart from the fact that twins spend much more time out of school than within, it should be clear from the topics discussed in this chapter that questions such as school ability, behavioural problems and stereotyping will not be resolved by separation. It is a solution that is easiest for everyone, but it is really only a short-term means of avoiding what may be much more major issues for the multiple-birth family. Certainly there are families where this may be the appropriate solution if conflict is so intense or if differences in ability are so marked, but for the vast majority of multiple-birth families the answer is not so simple.

Education can help, especially where people may not be aware of the fact that their behaviour is contributing to feelings of difference and concern within the twin pair. One example which I often use to illustrate this is that of a pair of elderly twin women. When they were children their grandparents had been in the habit of giving ten shillings (a considerable amount in those days) to the twin who achieved higher marks at school that year. It was always the same one, and sixty years on the other twin has never forgotten it. The grandparents had done this with the best of intentions, to foster academic achievement, little realising how long term the consequences could be. But every time parents promise their children some reward for a particular achievement, parents of twins need to consider what will happen if only one twin reaches this goal.

However, being a twin should not be the basis for inappropriate preferment. I have been approached so often by parents when one twin but not the other has received some academic recognition, such as a scholarship to a selective entry school, and the parents are seeking support for the other twin to receive the same. Of course there may be valid reasons for some reconsideration of what has happened. For example, the second twin may have been ill or otherwise distressed at the time of the scholarship examination. But if there have long been such differences in school performance, it is quite unfair for the less able twin to achieve preferential treatment just because they are a twin. It is unfair to the singleton young people who missed out and it is unfair to both twins, giving them the message that twins should be treated the same and rules should be 'bent' to achieve this. Differences in achievement and success are a fact of life for everyone and parents need to help their twins to recognise this, rather than shielding them. There is an even worse solution that some families have considered, namely to deny the award to the twin who has achieved it. One cannot think of anything more capable of leading to ongoing resentment within the family. Yet parents do constantly seek to find ways to ameliorate the impact of differences between twins in academic ability, in sporting performance and many other aspects of behaviour. The reality is that there

may well be significant differences. Trying to hide these or to mini-
mise their impact is a disservice to everyone. The time will come at
tertiary entrance or employment interviews that these differences will
become obvious and totally beyond the control of the family.

Stereotyping

In the Australian Twins in School publication available through most
of the multiple-birth associations, the point is made that the main
problem for twins is that there are two of them. This may seem
trivially obvious, but it is a key issue. It is easy to compare twins in
so many ways. Right from birth, parents and relatives are often
identifying who is the most able, the most outgoing and so on.

We live in a society which encourages individuality and thus it is no
surprise that parents and others seek to find something that distin-
guishes their twins. If there is nothing obvious, they may focus on
minor and otherwise irrelevant features. Thus we have found that
there are much more likely to be consistent ratings in favour of the
first-born twin in MZ pairs (Hay and O'Brien 1984). There is less of a
distinction based on birth order in same-sex DZ pairs (where there
may well be other differences that distinguish the twins) and there are
no birth order differences in boy–girl pairs. While there certainly used
to be medical advantages in being the first-born, the changes in
obstetric practices mean that this is no longer universally the case.
Yet even nowadays every parent of twins is used to being asked who
was the first-born and one wonders what use is being made by the
questioners of this distinction. Is it likely that such distinctions persist
into adolescence? One of my students, Ann Bruce, studied twenty-
seven pairs of MZ girls aged 12 to 18 years. These girls had been part
of longitudinal research for many years and there were data on
parental ratings from the time when the twins were toddlers. In
addition, in primary school there were both parent and teacher ratings, as well as formal psychometric assessment of ability. So what
happened at adolescence when Ann followed them up for the third
time? The answer was disturbing in two quite different ways.

First, there was a growing bias in favour of one twin. Looking at
the various questions about preferences across a whole range of
aspects of the twin situation, at the first assessment, in the toddler
pre-school years, there were 63 per cent of the parents who rated one
twin more favourably than the other. In the primary school years, this
figure had risen to 78 per cent and in the adolescent years to 85 per
cent. One way of viewing this is that parents were coming to recognise

the increasingly different personalities that were developing and that this difference in preference by parents is thus just what one would expect of parents clued into changes in their developing twins.

Unfortunately, the second aspect of the study made it clear that this was *not* the case. The parental differences in the perception of which twin was 'better' had no association either with the twins' performance on ability measures or on the assessment of their behaviour by their teacher (or teachers, in the cases where they were in different classes for the majority of their schoolwork).

The advantage for the analysis, if not for the actual families, was that the longitudinal data meant that it was possible to identify which aspects of the parental evaluation of differences between their twins continued throughout development, irrespective of the actual differences in the twins' ability or the perceptions of them by their teachers. Apart from some association with birth order and birthweight, the one variable that really mattered was which twin had left hospital first after the birth (remembering that this could have been as long ago as eighteen years before the evaluation at adolescence). Of course, differences in when twins left hospital could have been associated with major differences in medical status, but in previous analyses (Hay and O'Brien 1987) it has been shown that this was less of an issue than such simplistic views as 'Take one home and get used to this child, before you start trying to cope with the second one'. We are sure that the perinatal staff of the 1970s were well-meaning in giving this advice but it is worrying to see the impact of this strategy so many years later. Modern medical practice may mean that twins are less likely to come home from hospital at different times, given the instructive work of Klaus and Kennell (1976), showing the long-term potential of this variable. On the other hand, the growing emphasis on managed healthcare and on economic efficiency may well mean that the decision when to release one new-born twin has less to do with the needs of the multiple-birth family and more to do with hospital or medical insurance economics.

Within child psychology and psychiatry, we rely extensively on parental reports of symptoms of behavioural problems. For example, as already noted, DSM-IV does require information from at least two sources in making a diagnosis of specific behavioural disorders. But Ann's study indicates that we may have to question the adequacy of such information coming from parents, especially if it is prefaced with such comments as 'He was always the more difficult baby and we have found the same throughout childhood'. The question must be whether such continuity is in that twin or in the parent and any professional working with the family needs to explore this issue thoroughly and sensitively. Of course it also influences the views of the twin and the twin pair, especially as regards their potential for education beyond the school situation. What are your realistic aspirations if you have always been identified as the 'less able' twin?

This can be an especially difficult area to consider in adolescent counselling. When parent–child relationships are already tenuous, the last thing one needs is to address the issue that your parents have always found you to be the 'less able' twin. It also means that when parents are being 'helpful' and describing the differences between their twins, it is important to consider whether these are the real distinctions between the twins. As the professional relies ever more on parent, teacher and youth self-report information in deciding the best course of intervention with a family, the potential contribution of such biases needs to be considered more closely. Just how much is in the young person and how much in the emotional perceptions of differences from their twin that they have accumulated since birth, or even earlier, given the work by Piontelli on prenatal experiences? (Piontelli 1996).

Biological factors

DZ twins have only half their genes in common and thus there may well be an expectation that some differences in behaviour will occur. But this is not necessarily the case. It does depend upon the extent to which that behaviour is genetically determined. Three points about contemporary behaviour genetics (Hay 1985) should be emphasised.

First, not all behaviours are inherited to the same extent. The old question of whether nature or nurture determines our behaviour is being replaced by the much more realistic (if not so simple) one of the relative contributions of nature and nurture to specific behaviours. For example, ADHD has a much stronger genetic component than most other childhood behavioural problems (Levy *et al.* 1997). At the same time there is also an appreciation that the extent of genetic effects may change during the lifespan (Hay 1999). This is much more than the simplistic view that one's genetic endowment is expressed more in childhood but that its effects diminish with the impact of one's environment. From medical genetics, it is now known that there are many disorders where the genes remain inactive until being 'switched on' later in development. The complexities of measuring behaviour mean that we are a long way from having such clear examples but there are some cases which are best explained in this way. Several studies of adopted children show them at adolescence as becoming more similar to their biological parents in personality, but no more similar to their adoptive parents with whom they have spent all their formative years. Given the difficulty of interpreting this environmentally, one plausible explanation is that genes affecting aspects of adult personality only become active in adolescence. Although the mechanisms underlying such developmental processes are unknown, this is something for both families and professionals to bear in mind. Changes in adolescence and particularly changing patterns of difference between DZ twins may not just reflect puberty or environmental influences.

Second, behaviour genetics now identify two distinct types of environmental influence: that which makes siblings more similar and that which makes them more different. While the classical view of the environment and particularly the influence of parents upon their offspring has been that growing up together makes children more similar, this is not necessarily the case. For example, in our own longitudinal studies of ADHD, twins do not become more similar in their symptoms of inattention, whereas they do become more similar in their hyperactivity. When the more internal nature of attention compared with the more overt expression of hyperactivity is considered, this distinction makes sense. There is now a growing use of questionnaires such as the Sibling Inventory of Differential Experience (SIDE), designed to highlight the specific factors which make children from the same family different from each other (Dunn and Plomin 1990).

Third, there is growing discussion in behaviour genetics of genetically based contrast effects (Nadder *et al.* 1998). In real terms, what this means is that DZ twins are less similar in some behaviours than would be expected and sometimes even less similar than single-born brothers and sisters. The genetic differences between DZ twins and their constant proximity leads to an exaggeration of behavioural differences. How this actually happens is another matter (McDonald *et al.* 1993). It may be that DZ twins do actively compete with each other in what has been called the 'couple effect' (discussed by Sandbank in Chapter 10) or the answer may lie in the rest of the family. Twins may be treated more differently than possibly modest differences in their behaviour would initially suggest, or parents and others may rate them as very different when they are really quite similar. Thus when one twin is described as the 'active' one, we do need to identify if they are both very active but one is slightly more so than the other, or if there really is a major difference in their activity.

The key point about the role of genetics is that one cannot simply assume that MZ twins will necessarily be more similar than DZ twins. It all depends upon the particular characteristic. To give an example. One of our students, Michelle Holian, asked twins aged 11 to 15 to complete a questionnaire covering thirteen aspects of attitudes and personality. There was clear evidence of genetic effects for only a few of these aspects. On others both MZ and DZ twins were equally alike, indicating that simply growing up together mattered, rather than genes. On the scale dealing with vocational ambitions, there was evidence of the 'contrast' effect discussed above, with DZ twins being very different from each other while MZ were very similar.

Developing autonomy

A fundamental part of adolescence for every young person whether they be twins or singletons is the development of autonomy. This really means two different but closely related issues; namely, the ability to function as an independent individual, and to replace childhood dependency upon parents with a more mature and equal relationship. As such the achievement of autonomy depends both on individual development and on changes in the family structure, emphases and expectations. In other words, while the young person has to change so also has the parent, letting go and recognising the growing autonomy of their offspring from parental influences. What makes the situation potentially different for twins is the additional need to achieve at least some degree of autonomy from the co-twin.

In adolescent research it has become customary to identify two major dimensions of autonomy, namely emotional and behavioural (Michelle Houghton, a student at Deakin University in Victoria, studied this distinction in adolescent female twins from the LaTrobe Twin Study and the information in her Honours thesis is gratefully acknowledged). Emotional autonomy refers to the development of a sense of independence from one's parents. This covers such things as not relying on one's parents when there is a problem ('I depend on my parents to straighten things out when I've done something wrong') and having one's privacy ('there are things about me my parents do not know'), as well as recognising that parents have a life outside their role as parents and the fact that parents are not always right. While such emotional autonomy is a complex of many different aspects of growing up and becoming independent, behavioural autonomy is easier to define as who makes decisions about what the adolescent does. 'Who makes the decisions about your friends, your leisure, your education, your clothes and your time (how much time you spend on homework, when you should be home from a party and so on)?'

Of course, this is the area where twins are most likely to be different from other adolescents, since decisions may be made not just by the adolescent or his or her parents, but also by the co-twin or in the context of what the co-twin does (for example, 'You can only go to the party if your twin is going as well'). Probably the most corrosive aspect of the twin situation is where parents rely on one twin as the informant about the other and their peer relationships. For example, such a casual remark to the co-twin as 'Has Jenny had another row with her boyfriend?' is such an easy, intuitive and apparently caring thing to do. On the other hand, it is one specific way of invading privacy that is much less likely with single-born adolescents.

As well as asking the twins aged 12 to 18 years to complete a questionnaire, in Michelle's study each twin was also asked to pass on a set of corresponding questionnaires to a single-born friend, which is a particularly useful way of matching families. What emerged was that emotional autonomy was no different between twins and single-born adolescents, whereas MZ twins were identified as having much less behavioural autonomy. This distinction is consistent with the fact that emotional autonomy is more an internal process and one can 'do one's own thing'. In contrast, behavioural autonomy is more overt and there can be pressures from parents and peers as well as from the twins themselves. The MZ twins did report their relationship as generally being more positive and thus they felt there was some-thing to be gained by sharing decision making.

Competition and co-operation

The most difficult aspect of being an adolescent twin or their parent is how to cope with the conflicting demands of being twins and individuals at the same time. Twins can benefit from being close and supporting each other through the experiences of adolescence, but can they be too close? Unfortunately, there has been extensive publicity of sets of twins where the bond has been too close, leaving both families and professionals with the impression that a close bond may result in disaster. The Gibbons twins are a good case in point (Wallace 1987). The bizarre life-style of these MZ twin girls at home and at school, where their fanatically close relationship excluded everyone else, does raise concerns for everyone about the possibility of this happening within their own family or multiple-birth family. While we know little about the formal psychiatric diagnosis of this twin pair (or of others who have achieved similar publicity), it is clear that they were vulnerable individuals in the first place. As twins, they chose to base the expression of their problems around the twin situation. Thus when one died, the other was able to function at a much higher level. But this is not a twin-specific situation. If they had not been twins, there may well have been some other focus for expressing their problems. While the publicity surrounding their situation has been so extensive, it is not appropriate to consider their unique situation as the basis for deciding what is best for the vast majority of twins who do not start off with such a vulnerability. Unfortunately, cases such as this do form the basis for a rationale for the regular separation of twins, despite the lack of empirical evidence for this practice (Koch 1966, Gleeson *et al.* 1990).

One area where the twin situation can intrude is that of boy/girlfriends and their effect on the relationship between the twins. In practical terms and given my experience of such families, there is a difference between the situation where one twin is making such comments as 'Why is he/she (namely, the boy/girlfriend) at the dinner table yet again?', and the much more disturbing situation when a serious and possibly permanent relationship has developed and the other twin is constantly trying to infiltrate. Competition to have the first serious boy- or girlfriend is not the same as coping after one's twin has entered into a serious relationship (see Sandbank, Chapter 10) and professionally there is much to be done to help the other twin in this situation.

I have found that many difficulties occur when the relationship is homosexual. While the wider community does now accept relationships within the same gender, there seem to be particular reactions when this happens in a twin pair. Accepting homosexuality in the community is so different from that in your co-twin.

But beyond the boy/girlfriend experience, are there situations where being a twin can contribute to problems in adolescence? One of the most debated scenarios is that of eating disorders. The twin issue is that the focus is not just on what the media says is 'best', but rather on how one compares with one's co-twin, as Sandbank points out in Chapter 10. When adolescent twin girls count the number of peas on their dinner plate and decide that the one with the most is destined by the family to be the 'fat' one, obviously something needs to be done to help this family. While such a situation is not good for the family, it is a prime example of where the professional can focus on the twin situation and its ramifications for the entire family in developing appropriate intervention.

Three common problem scenarios

It seems appropriate to summarise the previous discussion with three examples of situations specific to the multiple-birth family where help may be sought.

1   *Dislike or denial of being a twin.* I have encountered a few sets of adolescent twins where conflict has developed to the extent that separation to different accommodation became necessary, one going to stay with relatives or to boarding-school. Obviously such twins are not the norm – one climbed on a roof and tried to drop a boulder onto his twin's head – but their experiences do reflect many of the issues discussed so far: competition, perceived preference for the other twin and sometimes poor verbal skills that limit the ability to talk things through. It is interesting that there is some indication that DZ twins may become more similar in personality when they leave home and establish separate lives, since there is no longer the pressure from the other twin.

2   *The situation where one twin is positive about their twinship and the other negative.* This is a classic 'no win' experience, as whatever happens, it is going to hurt one twin or the other. A key question here is whether this is just a developmental difference in the acquisition of individuality or something much more. Does one twin have Koch's 'prima donna' condition, where focusing on the twin situation and the attention it brings is one way of compensating for poor social skills? Is this a case of one MZ twin seeking behavioural autonomy and the ability to make decisions without the involvement of the co-twin?

3   *Expressing individuality by doing the same as one's twin.* The most common example of this is the situation where one twin chooses 'the' school subject or 'the' career. The well-publicised cases of twins whose closeness was pathological have already been mentioned and one must wonder whether concern over twins making the decision to do the same thing is being viewed in the same way. Is it not natural that young people who share some if not all the same genes (depending on zygosity) and who have grown up in the same environment with similar experiences may have similar preferences at school or for vocation? While one may question whether there is some ulterior motive to do with attracting

attention in choosing the same, it is equally appropriate to consider the opposite and why they are *not* choosing to do the same. Michelle Holian's finding of such differences in career aspirations of DZ twins exemplifies this issue. With their genetic and environmental similarities, why are they not more alike and is there something in the twin situation that forces them away from their natural preferences?

The rest of the family

Being a parent of adolescent twins does raise a whole new range of issues, the crucial being 'the power of two' and the ability not only to answer the demands of two adolescents, but also to cope with differences in how they are treated (or perceived to be treated). Our experience of instruments such as Abidin's Parental Stress Index is that stress is associated with the failure of the community to recognise that the experience is particularly stressful. Thus in a recent Honours study by Roisin Reid, parents reported less stress in caring for a child with cerebral palsy where there is a formal medical diagnosis, than for one with ADHD where both differences from normality and causation are complex. Parents of multiples experience this latter situation with comments or implications such as 'Are you any different from other parents with children similar in age?'

There has been a fundamental role for Multiple Birth Associations in dealing with this and associated needs in the first few years of life, but there have been few resources that identify the particular needs of these families when the multiples are in primary, far less in secondary school. One issue that does arise is the development of 'focus groups' separately for parents and for their adolescent multiples. There is no clinical implication here with the involvement of only families with problems. It is simply that sharing experiences of this particular situation is the best way of realising that the experience of any one family is by no means unique.

There is a need for a more family-focused approach to siblings of twins. Previously we have shown (Hay *et al.* 1988) that there can be major problems for siblings in the first few years after the twins arrive. One would hope that in most families any such effects would diminish and one would worry if this were not the case. While this does seem to be true when the twins are DZ and not so obviously similar, the situation at adolescence is different, especially when the twins are not so dissimilar in age from their single-born brother or sister. For example, 'Why should they get more attention, just because they are twins?'

This is clearly the crux of the family situation with adolescent multiples with so much of the impact on the family depending upon the multiples themselves. MZ twins who rely on their similarities for attention are so different from boy–girl pairs, both in themselves and in their impact on the rest of the family. Adolescence should be seen as the time for reconciliation. There is no doubt that the arrival of twins has meant so much disruption and focus for the family, but now there is scope to treat every child equally.

Conclusion

This chapter has emphasised some of the things that can go wrong when multiples reach adolescence. However, it is important that twins and higher multiples as well as parents and teachers adopt a positive approach to adolescence. A distinction needs to be made between those families where professional help is essential and the vast majority of multiple-birth families who only need reassurance that things will work out in the end. Yes, there may be problems, but these are often typical rather than clinical. It is vital to make this differentiation. It is challenging but accurate to say that from the time of the diagnosis of a multiple pregnancy, both parents and professionals need to be conscious of what can be done to advance a satisfactory outcome into adolescence and adulthood.

Acknowledgements

Our own research discussed in this chapter comes mainly from the twenty years of the LaTrobe Twin Study in Victoria and more recently from the nationwide Australian Twin ADHD Project run jointly with Associate Professor Florence Levy of Sydney, which uses the resources of the Australian Twin Registry. The support of both LaTrobe University, Victoria, and more recently Curtin University of Technology, Western Australia, is much appreciated, as is the continued co-operation of so many multiple-birth families. These studies have been funded by the National Health and Medical Research Council of Australia, the Australian Research Council and by many charitable foundations. The Australian Council for Educational Research provided access to data from their 1975 National Survey of Literacy and Numeracy. Over my twenty years of research with multiple-birth families, too many staff and students have been involved for them to be recognised individually here. Special appreciation must go to the Australian Multiple Birth Association for its ongoing support of and enthusiasm for our efforts.

References

Dunn, J. and Plomin, R. (1990) *Separate Lives: Why Siblings are so Different*, New York: Basic Books.

Gleeson, C., Hay, D.A., Johnston, C.J. and Theobald, T.M. (1990) 'Twins in School', an Australia-wide programme, *Acta Geneticae Medicae et Gemellologiae* 39, 231–244.

Hay, D.A. (1985) *Essentials of Behaviour Genetics*, Oxford: Blackwell Scientific.

Hay, D.A. (1999) 'The developmental genetics of intelligence', in M. Anderson (ed.) *The Development of Intelligence*, Hove: Psychology Press.

Hay, D.A. and Levy, F. (1996) 'Differential diagnosis of ADHD', *Australian Educational and Developmental Psychologist* 13, 69–78.

Hay, D.A. and O'Brien, P.J. (1984) 'The role of parental attitudes in the development of temperament in twins at home, school and in test situation', *Acta Geneticae Medicae et Gemellologiae* 33, 191–204.

Hay, D.A. and O'Brien, P.J. (1987) 'Early influences on the school social adjustment of twins', *Acta Geneticae Medicae et Gemellologiae* 36, 239–248.

Hay, D.A., MacIndoe, R. and O'Brien, P.J. (1988) 'The older sibling of twins', *Australian Journal of Early Childhood* 13, 25–28.

Hay, D.A., O'Brien, P.J., Johnston, C.J. and Prior, M. (1984) 'The high incidence of reading disability in twin boys and its implications for genetic analyses', *Acta Geneticae Medicae et Gemellologiae* 33, 223–236.

Hay, D.A., Collett, S.M., Johnston, C.J., O'Brien, P.J. and Prior, M. (1986) 'Do twins and singletons have the same language and reading problems?', in C. Pratt, A.F. Garton, W.E. Turner and A.R. Nesdale (eds) *Research Issues in Child Development*, pp. 125–134, Sydney: Allen & Unwin.

Hill, J.P. and Hombeck, G.N. (1986) 'Attachment and autonomy during adolescence', in G.J. Whitehurst (ed.) *Annals of Child Development*, Vol 3, London: JAI Press.

Johnston, C., Prior, M. and Hay, D.A. (1984) 'Prediction of reading disability in twin boys', *Developmental Medicine and Child Neurology* 26, 558–595.

Klaus, M.H. and Kennell, J.H. (1976) *Maternal–Infant Bonding*, St Louis, MO: Mosby.

Koch, H.L. (1966) *Twins and Twin Relations*, Chicago, IL: University of Chicago Press.

Levy, F., Hay, D., McLauglin, M., Wood, C. and Waldman, I. (1996) 'Twin–sibling differences in parental reports of ADHD, speech, reading and behaviour problems', *Journal of Child Psychology and Psychiatry* 37, 569–578.

Levy, F., Hay, D., McStephen, M., Wood, C. and Waldman, I. (1997) 'Attention Deficit Hyperactivity Disorder (ADHD): a category or a continuum?

Genetic analysis of a large scale twin study', *Journal of the American Academy of Child and Adolescent Psychiatry* 36, 737–744.

Loehlin, J.C. and Nichols, R.C. (1976) *Heredity, Environment and Personality. A Study of 850 Sets of Twins*, Austin, TX, and London: University of Texas Press.

Lytton, H. (1980) *Parent–Child Interaction: The Socialisation Process Observed in Twin and Singleton Families*, New York: Plenum.

McDonald, A.M., Bryan, E.M., Derom, R., Hay, D.A., Hebebrand, J., Kirschbaum, C., Kracke, B., Pauls, D.L., Rowe, D.C. and Rutter, M. (1993) 'Group report: What can twin studies contribute to the understanding of childhood behavioural disorders', in T.J. Bouchard and P. Propping (eds) *Twins as a Tool of Behavioural Genetics*, Chichester: John Wiley, pp. 227–42.

Mittler, P. (1971) *The Study of Twins*, Harmondsworth: Penguin.

Nadder, T.S., Sulberg, J.L., Eaves, L.J., Maes, H.H. and Meyer, J.M. (1998) 'Genetic effects on ADHD symptomatology in 7- to 13-year-old twins: results from a telephone survey', *Behaviour Genetics* 28, 83–99.

Piontelli, A. (1996) *From Fetus to Child*, London and New York: Routledge.

Rosambeau, M. (1987) *How Twins Grow Up*, London: The Bodley Head.

Siminoff, E. (1992) 'A comparison of twins and singletons with child psychiatric disorders: an item sheet analysis', *Journal of Child Psychology and Psychiatry* 33, 1319–1332.

Wallace, M. (1987) *The Silent Twins*, Harmondsworth: Penguin.

9   Growth and development of twins

John M.H. Buckler

Introduction

Although this chapter essentially focuses on growth of twins, the implications overlap with other aspects of twin development and psychology and, of course, what is valid for twins will also be valid for higher multiples with appropriate adjustment.

Fundamentally, all the problems and variations that occur in the singleton population are also relevant to twins, and these have been considered in depth in previous publications (Buckler 1987, 1990, 1994). However, the impact and significance of these growth variations are greater when considering twins, not only because they show more common incidence and severity of low birthweight but also because of the inevitability of comparison of their growth with that of singletons, and notably siblings, and most obviously of all between the two of a pair.

In order to evaluate the growth of any particular twin, it is important to be aware of the pattern of normal growth in twins. The following discussion presents what is known of twins' growth from many publications, but adds to it from my own recent observations which will subsequently be published more fully. In reporting on these, many of the twin data are presented in terms of standard deviation scores (SDS) using the recent British singleton data (Freeman *et al.* 1995) as the baseline for comparison.

$SDS=(X-X_1)/S_x$, where X is the child's measurement, X_1 is the mean height or weight (based on singleton standards as indicated) and S_x is the standard deviation at that particular age. The score indicates how far from this average the relevant values fall, an SDS of 0 corresponding to the average of singleton values. Twin birthweight and skull circumference data have already been published based on information from thirty-six maternity units in Britain (Buckler and

Green 1994). The centile distributions have been obtained using the LMS method of Cole (1990). Birth lengths in addition are presented here which are much smaller in number and derived from information from three of these maternity units and from a questionnaire. Longitudinal observations on height, weight and head circumference over the first four years of life are largely based on information obtained retrospectively from health visitor or clinic records in response to a questionnaire and from personal measurements on a cohort of twins followed from birth.

Although a few pairs of twins have been followed longitudinally for more than four years, most of the data on older twins have been obtained by cross-sectional observations in which each individual pair has been seen only once. The description of this work and preliminary results have already been published (Buckler and Buckler 1987) but the numbers have subsequently been considerably increased. Where twins have been measured repeatedly, their data are only included once in any age group (usually the observations at the oldest age seen). The SDS values have been combined for individuals of different ages as they have a similar significance whatever the age.

Intra-uterine growth

It has long been recognised that twins are smaller at birth than singletons. This is partly due to the differing duration of the pregnancy, the average twin gestation being a little over two weeks shorter than that of singletons, but also because twins are smaller than singletons for the same length of gestation. About 30 per cent of twins are light for dates by singleton standards (-1.5 SD). Numerous publications have presented centiles for twins' birthweights according to length of gestation (Naeye *et al.* 1966, Leroy *et al.* 1982, Scottish Livebirths Data 1992, Rydhström 1992), and birth lengths/heights (Leroy *et al.* 1982, Wilson 1986, Scottish Livebirths Data 1992). On average, twins are about 0.9 kg lighter and 3.5 cm shorter than singletons at birth. However, this is partly due to their shorter duration of gestation. The deficit in *weight* at comparable lengths of gestation increases progressively with longer gestation. Before 30 weeks' gestation the weight difference between singletons and twins is insignificant, but at 32 weeks is of the order of 100 g, at 36 weeks 300 g, at 38 weeks 450 g, and at 40 weeks 600 g. The differences in *birth lengths* between twins and singletons is proportionately not so marked as weight and is not evident until a later stage of gestation, various reports suggesting about 1 cm difference at 36 weeks and 2 cm at 38 weeks.

Figure 9.1 shows the intra-uterine growth of English twins compared with the singleton data derived from the Scottish Livebirths Data (1992) as described in a previous publication (Buckler and Green 1994). The comparisons are based on median values and largely confirm the observations of previous reports, though the twin deficit in birth length is rather less. A deficit in skull circumference is only evident after 35 weeks' gestation, being about 1 cm at 40 weeks.

Throughout the course of gestation, as with singletons, boy fetuses are slightly bigger than girls, about 50 g on average before 31 weeks, increasing to about 100 g from 36 weeks onwards, and about 1 cm longer at 37 weeks (Boomsma *et al.* 1992).

Dizygotic (DZ) twins are slightly heavier and longer than monozygotic (MZ) twins from about 33 weeks' gestation. At 36 to 38 weeks this difference is about 150 g and 0.8 cm respectively, and mixed-sex twins tend to have higher birthweights than same-sex twins (Naeye *et al.* 1966, Boomsma *et al.* 1992). As with singletons, twins born to mothers with other children (multipara) are on average 250 g heavier than those born to first-time mothers (primips) (Bleker *et al.* 1988, Rydhström 1992). There is little difference in the weights or lengths of first-born compared with second-born twins. Intrapair discordance increases with gestational age, especially for mixed-sex twins (averaging >400 g at 38 to 40 weeks' gestation). Differences in birthweight are slightly less for DZ than MZ twin pairs. The current data showed mean birthweight differences of 0.301 kg for DZ same-sex twins, 0.335 kg for mixed-sex twins and 0.335 kg for MZ twins. Wilson (1979) suggested that this difference was even more evident for birth length than for birthweight. This implies that certain conditions of intra-uterine growth – especially placental anastomoses or eccentric insertion of one of the two umbilical cords into the placenta – may favour the growth of one MZ twin at the expense of the other.

Data on birthweights of a small number of English triplets (about 400 male and 400 female) have been obtained as part of the report already referred to (Buckler and Green 1994). The smaller weights of twins compared with singletons is even more marked with triplets, particularly after about 33 weeks' gestation. Most triplets are born before 36 weeks' gestation and in this report, with pregnancies of between 33 to 36 weeks, triplet girls are about 150 g lighter than twin girls and triplet boys showed a progressive deficit from 150 g to 250 g compared with twin boys.

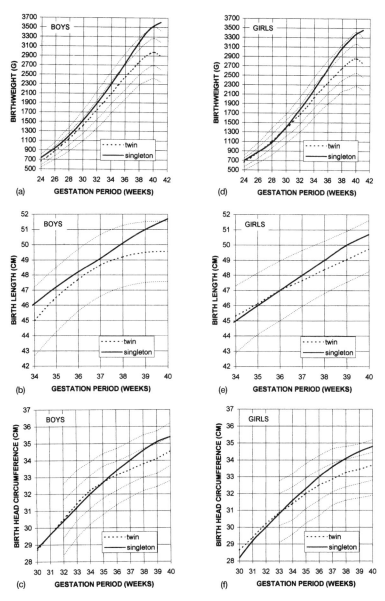

Figure 9.1 Birth measurements of English twins compared with fiftieth centile Scottish singleton values. (a) Boys' weight, (c) Boy's head circumference, (d) Girl's weight, (f) Girls' head circumference, show tenth, twenty-fifth, fiftieth, seventy-fifth and ninetieth centiles, (b) Boy's length and (e) Girls' length show twenty-fifth, fiftieth and seventy-fifth centiles.

In a review of the literature, Bryan (1992) commented that for a long time it has been recognised that the greater the number of babies the lower their individual birthweights, triplets averaging 1.8 kg and quadruplets 1.4 kg. However, whatever the number of fetuses, growth rate of each individual is similar until about 28 weeks' gestation, after which it falls off in direct relation to the number of fetuses.

Several reports suggest that the smaller proportionate placental size in multiple pregnancies compared with singletons is an important factor responsible for fetal growth retardation in twins (Bleker *et al.* 1988, 1995). From about 24 weeks, placental weights for individual twins are less than those of singletons and this retardation of placental growth precedes the retardation of fetal growth.

Summary

At birth, twins are markedly smaller than singletons in terms of weight, length and head circumference, not only because they are more commonly born prematurely but also because their growth becomes progressively slower than singletons in the later weeks of the pregnancy. This is even more marked with higher multiples.

Growth of twins through childhood

After birth, twins show a remarkable catch-up in growth (Bryan 1992) and over the first three months they gain weight faster than singletons, so that an average 0.9 kg deficit at birth is reduced to 0.45 kg (Wilson 1974). This early catch-up in weight may largely be compensation for the underweight due to prematurity, for further weight catch-up is subsequently slower. Wilson (1979) showed that the average 30 per cent deficit in birthweight of twins compared with singletons is reduced to 10 per cent by 3 months, but only to 8 per cent at 1 year and by 1 per cent per year to 4 per cent at the age of 5. His studies indicated that by the age of 8 there was no longer any significant weight deficit, though other reports suggest that twins remain mildly underweight compared with singletons throughout (Ooki and Asaka 1993).

Catch-up in length/height is more gradual, but continues steadily so that an average 17 per cent deficit in length at birth compared to singletons, which is proportionately much less deficit than weight, is reduced to only 16 per cent at 3 months, to 9 per cent at 1 year, to 3 per cent at 5 years and 1 per cent at 8 years (Wilson 1979).

Subsequently (before puberty) there is no significant difference between the heights of twins and singletons (Ooki and Asaka 1993).

The catch-up shown by twins is much greater than that shown by 'light for dates' singletons. Chamberlain and Simpson (1977) compared the growth of twins, postmature and small for dates singletons with a random 'normal' sample. The gestation duration for all groups was the same: 38 to 41 weeks (except the postmature singletons born at or later than 42 weeks' gestation, who showed no growth deficit at birth or subsequently). All the light for dates singletons were below the fifth centile for gestational age – which was somewhat lower than the twin equivalent – but these small singletons had a deficit in weight and height which persisted through the duration of the study to age 3, by which time the twins had mostly caught up (and these twins did not have the benefit of catch-up due to prematurity). As Gedda *et al.* (1981) suggested, 'low birth weight in twins is a different condition from low birth weight in singletons and should be dealt with independently especially for the different implications for child growth and survival.'

Figure 9.2 shows recent longitudinal data on the early postnatal growth of twins, largely acquired retrospectively from a questionnaire, with weight and length/height from birth to 4 years and head circumference from birth to 3 years. These are compared to the median (fiftieth centile) values for singletons from the British standards of Freeman *et al.* (1995). These graphs all include a correction for prematurity up to the age of 2 years, so that the ages are not 'real' ages but aligned so that age 0 corresponds to the values forty weeks from conception. These initial values have therefore allowed for the marked early catch-up dependent on birth being pre-term. The error otherwise introduced for measurements over the first two years would be considerable, for Elliman *et al.* (1991) have shown that even at 7 years children born markedly pre-term are shorter and lighter than the normal population, but when corrected for prematurity the difference is insignificant, particularly for height. However, except for those born extremely prematurely, this correction becomes relatively trivial after the age of 2, and for practical convenience has been omitted from that age. Figure 9.2 demonstrates that having corrected in this way for prematurity, at age 0 twins are slightly underweight but by 1 year this deficit no longer exists. However, from about age 3 years twins fall back compared with singletons and by the age of 4 are on average about 0.5 kg lighter. There appears to be a sex difference in relation to height, for at age 0 female twins are of similar length to singletons and from 6 months become slightly taller and remain so, so

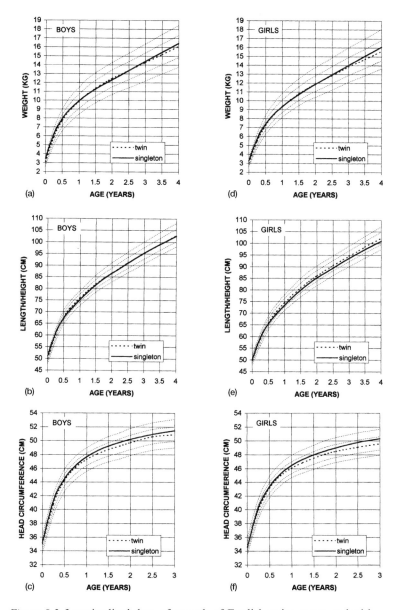

Figure 9.2 Longitudinal data of growth of English twins compared with median English singleton values. (a) and (d) Weight, (b) and (e) Length/height from birth to 4 years, (c) and (f) Head circumference from birth to 3 years. Values corrected for length of gestation up to 2 years. Twin centile values tenth, twenty-fifth, fiftieth, seventy-fifth and ninetieth.

that the average 4-year-old twin girl is about 1 cm taller than her singleton counterpart. Boys at age 0 are an average of 1 cm shorter than singletons, which deficit is caught up by age 6 months. For a few months twin boys are slightly taller than singletons but subsequently, at least until age 4, the median height values are superimposed. Boy and girl twins both have smaller skull circumferences than singletons. Although this deficit is negligible at the corrected age of 0, it gradually increases and averages about 0.5 cm at age 3.

Preliminary results of another twin growth study which has been cross-sectional have already been reported (Buckler and Buckler 1987). The number of twins now seen has greatly increased to provide the data for Figures 9.3 to 9.5 and 9.7 and 9.8. Most of these twins have been seen once only at any age from 2 years to maturity and the measurements of height, weight and head circumference have been translated into standard deviation scores (SDS) and pooled together for comparison with a comparable British singleton population (Freeman *et al.* 1995). Each SDS value relates to the singleton norm at that age, and pooling the data gives an overview but without showing the trends at any particular age. For convenience and consistency in these older age groups corrections for prematurity have not been made despite the associated error already referred to.

Figure 9.3 shows the SDS values for height and weight for the total group of 1,200 twin children over 2 years of age, presented as histograms. These are compared with 'target' height SDS which indicate

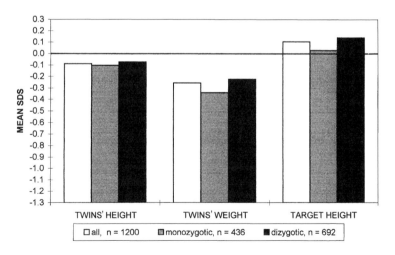

Figure 9.3 SDS pooled values for height and weight of twins compared with target (mid-parental) height values.

the relationship to parental heights – the target value being the average of the mothers' and fathers' height SDS. The total twin height SDS is -0.09 – only slightly below zero, which is the mean for a comparable singleton population. However, when compared with the parental 'target height', DZ twins are about 0.21 SD below target (the parents of DZ twins tending to be taller than average) and MZ twins about 0.13 SD below target.

The overall weight SDS is at a lower level however, averaging -0.26 SD, and this difference between weight and height confirms the observations of Figure 9.2.

Figure 9.4 compares these twin SDS data with those of their own siblings, who provide the most appropriate group for comparison. The number of twins represented is smaller than in Figure 9.3, as only those twins who had siblings for whom measurements could be obtained were included. It is noteworthy that twins with siblings were smaller than the overall group of twins with height SDS of -0.21 (compared with -0.09 for the total group) and weight SDS of -0.37 (compared with -0.26). The siblings, whose overall height and weight SDS corresponded well, as would be expected, were bigger than their matching twins, but this was more evident for DZ than for MZ subjects. The overall sibling height SDS of 0.06 was 0.27 SD greater than the twins, and the weight SDS of 0.03 was 0.40 greater than the twins.

Figure 9.5 compares the height SDS and weight SDS of boy twins

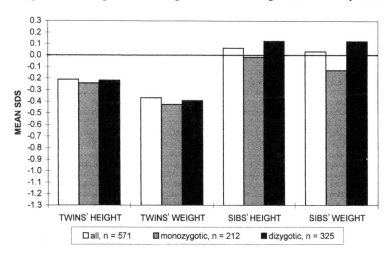

Figure 9.4 SDS pooled values for height and weight of twins compared with values for their siblings.

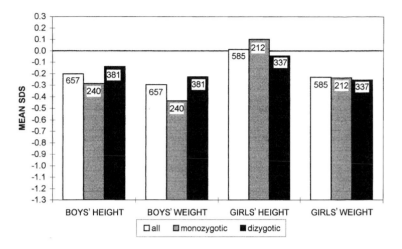

Figure 9.5 Comparison of SDS pooled values for height and weight of boy and girl twins.

with the values for girls. This shows the girls overall to have greater height SDS than boys, and to be underweight (relative to their height) to a greater extent than boys. The height SDS for the total group of boys is −0.2 compared with +0.01 for girls, and the boys' weight SDS of −0.30 compares with that of the girls of −0.23. This suggests that girl twins' heights approximate to those of their siblings or parents whereas boy twins are smaller. However, these observations are more evident with MZ than DZ twins, MZ twin boys being smaller than MZ girls and their siblings whereas DZ boy twins have heights which are closer to those of the girl twins.

Skull circumference SDS scores for the total group confirm that the deficit compared with singletons shown in Figure 9.2 is subsequently maintained – the overall mean SDS being −0.41 (see as part of Figure 9.8).

The differing pattern of early growth of boys and girls was previously reported by Wilson (1974, 1979) and confirmed by Ooki and Asaka (1993). Wilson showed that weight and length of boy twins and girl twins were similar at birth, but over the first six months males grew more rapidly, and at 18 months boy twins were on average 0.75 kg heavier and 2.0 cm taller than girl twins. From the age of 2, however, girls grew more rapidly, so that by the age of 5 for height and age 6 for weight the values for boys and girls were similar. The reported slightly greater weight of DZ twins compared to MZ was not evident from three months onwards, according to these authors. Sex differences are similar in their trend in the present report, though less in magnitude, as shown in Figure 9.6 derived from the values in Figure 9.2.

The similarity between MZ pairs increases with age and decreases between DZ twins (Furuscho 1968, Wilson 1979, Ooki and Asaka 1993). At birth, Wilson (1979) cited correlation coefficients for MZ twins' height 0.62, which by the age of 3 had risen to 0.93 where they remained subsequently. Corresponding values for DZ same-sex twins were 0.79 falling at age 3 to 0.56 and at age 8 to 0.49 (for mixed-sex twins these values were 0.67, 0.60 and 0.65). The correlations for

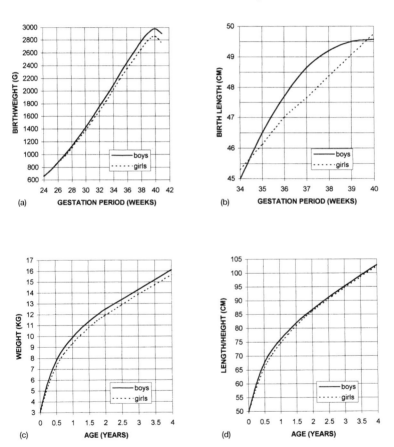

Figure 9.6 Comparison of the growth of boy and girl twins – median values. (a) Birthweight, (b) Birth length plotted against gestation period, (c) Weight, (d) Length/height for first four years of life.

height for MZ twins were higher than for weight, whereas for DZ twins height and weight correlations were similar. At birth, MZ interpair weight correlations were 0.63 rising by 1 year to 0.88 where they subsequently remained. DZ same-sex twin weight correlations were 0.68 at birth, 0.52 at 3 years and 0.49 at 8 years (the values for mixed-sex twins being 0.64, 0.54 and 0.46). The poorer correlation of weight than height in MZ twins may be due to a persisting effect of unequal prenatal nutrition or to the increased susceptibility to idiosyncrasies of food preferences and appetite within pairs (Wilson 1979).

To indicate the long-term effect of the degree of intra-uterine stunting on subsequent growth, the twins in the present cross-sectional study have been arbitrarily divided into three groups on the basis of the appropriateness of their weight at birth in terms of singleton standards. This is not categorising according to *actual* birthweight – Group 1 had birthweights above the tenth centile for singletons (considered appropriate birthweight for gestational age), Group 2 had birthweights between the fifth and tenth centiles (moderately growth retarded) and Group 3 had birthweights below the fifth centile of singleton standards (severely growth retarded). The results shown in Figure 9.7 indicate, as with growth retarded singleton babies, the severe long-term adverse effect of intra-uterine growth retardation on subsequent growth. Excluding these growth retarded babies of Groups 2 and 3, Group 1 values would be comparable to those of parents and siblings. It must be acknowledged that an element of the poor growth of some babies of Groups 2 and 3, both before and after birth, would be familial – the overall target heights of these groups being less than those of Group 1. Figure 9.7(a) confirms in all these groups the lower weight SDS than height SDS. Figures 9.7(b)and (c) compare the values for boys and girls for height and weight respectively. In all groups it is shown that the growth in height of the boy twins is poorer than that of the girls and this is particularly evident with those with severe intra-uterine growth retardation. Girls show a greater degree of underweight in relation to height than do boys.

Figure 9.8 shows that the lesser growth of the heads of twins is also

---

Figure 9.7 (opposite) SDS pooled values for twins' height and weight, related
to zygosity and appropriateness of weight at birth (Groups 1, 2
and 3 – see text), numbers of twins indicated at the tops of the
columns. (a) Height compared with weight, (b) Height comparing
boys and girls, (c) Weight comparing boys and girls.

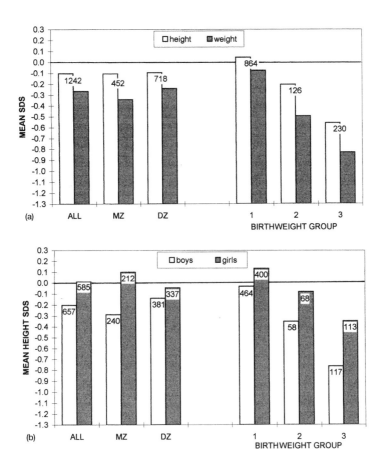

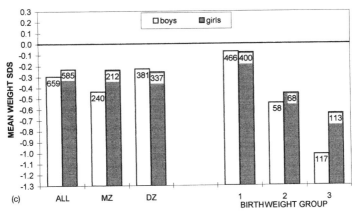

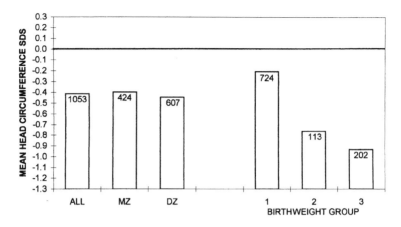

Figure 9.8 SDS pooled values for twins' head circumferences related to zygosity and appropriateness of birthweight.

related to the degree of antenatal growth retardation, but even with twins of Group 1 head growth is less than that of singletons. (Despite this, the intelligence of twins is only slightly less than comparable singletons (Bryan 1992).)

There are many reports in the literature about the growth of twins and though they do not all agree in every respect, there is general consensus about the adverse effect on subsequent growth of severe intra-uterine growth retardation and that those twins with appropriate birthweight for gestational age grew well subsequently (Babson and Phillips 1973, Wilson 1979, 1986, Henrichsen *et al.* 1986, Keet *et al.* 1986, Blickstein *et al.* 1988, Luke *et al.* 1995).

Bryan (1992) has suggested that the duration of intra-uterine malnutrition may be a crucial factor, for if growth up to a certain stage of pregnancy has been satisfactory, the full cellular complement may have been achieved and there is a greater likelihood of normal growth potential. Adverse influences slowing down growth from an early stage of pregnancy (with greater evidence of bony growth suppression as indicated by length and head circumference) are likely to have a more permanent effect (see also Wilson 1979).

Summary

Twins grow faster than singletons in the neonatal period and rapidly reduce the deficit in length and weight, though tending to remain mildly underweight for height and with slightly smaller head circumferences than singletons through their growing years. Those twins who are severely underweight for gestational age at birth continue to be short of stature, but the remainder grow well and achieve heights close to those expected on the basis of their parents' heights. Though often differing considerably in their measurements at birth, MZ twins become progressively more alike as they grow up, particularly in height, but in contrast DZ twins diverge in their measurements.

Growth of higher multiples

Measurements of a small number of triplets (114) and quadruplets and quintuplets (thirty-three) have been documented at some stage in childhood in a similar way to that described for twins (see p. 148) and reported previously (Buckler and Buckler 1987). The effects on growth were similar for higher multiples to those for twins but were more marked (Table 9.1).

These values are as reported in that paper and show the overall deficit in height SDS to have been greater for triplets than for twins, and greater still for quads and quins. The more marked effect on weight than height is evident similarly for all groups. The parents of triplets were above average stature to a similar degree to those of twins. Relating height SDS of triplets to the appropriateness of their birthweights to gestational age showed that a greater proportion of triplets were light for dates (by the criteria described), 29 per cent only having had what was termed appropriate birthweight for gestation (i.e. above the tenth centile for singletons). However, this minority subsequently in later childhood had much better height SDS values (+0.18) than those whose birthweights had been light for dates (−0.24), as has been shown for twins.

Table 9.1 Comparison of growth parameters in twins and higher multiples

	Height SDS	*Weight SDS*	*Target height SDS*
Twins	+0.06	−0.25	+0.31
Triplets	−0.12	−0.47	+0.35
Quads and quins	−0.29	−0.56	..

Twin growth at puberty and to adult life

The results from the cross-sectional study so far reported have shown values resulting from the pooling of data of all ages of twins. There may however be differences in growth at different ages of childhood and notably at puberty. The total group has been divided to show the pooled values from ages 2–5, from 5–10, and over 10 (which will include almost all pubertal subjects). After age 5 there appeared to be a falling off more marked for weight than for height and more evident in the group of over-tens. In view of the relevance of pubertal status in the group over the age of 10, review of the data suggested that those not yet in puberty and those in puberty had retarded growth – possibly due to being delayed in their pubertal development, whereas those fully mature boys who were presumably completely or almost fully grown had heights comparable with singletons, and girls were taller than their singleton counterparts. The minority of twins who were definitely fully grown had heights which compared favourably with the values of their parents. These observations show that the overall deficient stature indicated for twins over 10 years of age was misleading, being dependent on the high proportion still in puberty and probably developmentally delayed. The mean age for menarche in sixty-one twin girls who had passed that stage of maturity was 13.16 years, which was slightly delayed compared with comparable singleton values which averaged 13 years. Ultimately, adult stature compared well with singletons, girls doing rather better than boys, but all groups throughout were underweight. It is of interest to compare these results with those reported by Ljung *et al.* (1977) and Fischbein (1977), who followed 323 pairs of Swedish twins (born 1954–1955) longitudinally from age 10 until they were fully grown (16 years in girls, 18 years in boys). They also found a different pattern of growth between boy and girl twins when compared with a group of control singletons, but throughout the course of puberty the growth of the twin boys was closer to that of the singletons than was the case with twin girls, except ultimately. Up to the age of 16 the heights of the twin and control boys were almost identical and the twins' weights were between 0.6 and 0.9 kg less than singletons. However, the twins accelerated their growth 0.2 years earlier than singletons with a slightly lower velocity, and in consequence slowed down and stopped growing earlier so that by 18 years of age twins were on average 1.5 cm shorter and 1.4 kg lighter than singletons. Twin girls, in contrast, were slightly delayed in changes of puberty compared with singletons by about 0.2 years, and their growth fell off from the start, stature having a deficit of 1.9 cm and weight 2.0 kg by 13 years. However, stature did not fall off any more and ended up 1.4 cm on average less, but rather more underweight by 2.6 kg. Thus ultimately the small deficit between adult twins and singletons was similar for boys and girls, though the girls were rather more underweight.

This study agreed with the findings of others (Furuscho 1968, Sharma 1983, Hauspie *et al*. 1994, Koziel 1998) that correlations in growth were much closer for MZ than DZ twins in all respects through puberty and as adults, i.e. height, weight, timing of the stages of puberty, and magnitude of the peaks of height and weight velocity. Hauspie *et al*. (1994) also noted that short-term variations in growth velocity were more similar in MZ twin pairs than DZ.

Summary

After the age of 10 there is often a slight falling off in twin height centiles based on singleton age standards, probably due to delay in puberty, but if the growth of twins is followed to full adult stature many reach their target heights or approximate closely to them, though continuing to be moderately underweight. MZ twins showed a much closer parallelism than DZ twins in their growth through puberty and the observations indicate a predominantly genetic element in the regulation of growth, and particularly at puberty, but also imply a significant role for environmental factors.

Concerns and problems related to the growth of twins

Many parents are anxious that their twin children will be shorter in stature and underweight compared with their peers and that they will be small as adults. This fear is often fuelled by comparisons with the growth of siblings of the twins – or by differences between the pair of twins. As indicated in the introduction, the commonest causes of atypical growth of twins are the same as those found among singletons, and it is often the case that such occurrences are attributed to the fact that such children are *twins*, when in reality this may not be the explanation at all. Concern might not even have arisen had the child not been a twin. Such causes reflect the huge variation in normal measurements of the overall childhood population, as indicated by centile charts for height, weight, head circumference, etc., which are usually genetically determined. This genetic aetiology would be indicated by measurements of the parents which should always be taken into consideration in evaluating any child's growth. In addition, the different timing of growth spurts, notably at puberty with all the implications for early and late developers, are just as evident among singletons as they are among twins (Buckler 1987, 1990, 1994). Ignorance of what should be considered normal in children's growth and particularly in the changes associated with puberty is the basis of much unnecessary anxiety for children and their parents.

There are, however, several other aspects which *are* specific to twins that may be the basis for concern. It has been shown that the normal distribution of measurement of twin growth does show differences from that of singletons, and twin centiles (for weight, length/height and head circumference) should be used as the basis for evaluation at birth and over the neonatal and early childhood period (applying a correction for prematurity for at least two years), and probably for weight throughout the full growing years. Basing conclusions or impressions on singleton standards may be misleading at these ages.

Comparison with other twins may be reassuring, though deviation from the typical twin growth range is just as likely to be of no significance, as such deviation would be for a singleton among a singleton population.

Those twins who are markedly underweight at birth for the duration of gestation may indeed have an ongoing growth problem, but that is comparable to the picture of singletons with intra-uterine growth retardation. The fact that twins are often underweight when compared to singletons does not usually imply that there is any underlying problem, for this is a common finding and not a cause for concern if health and activity are normal. In a similar way the head circumferences of twins are slightly smaller on average than those of singletons, without the implication of associated developmental delay, but in both these situations reference to standards of growth that are normal for twins is a useful aid.

Being one of a twin pair provides, in the co-twin, more dramatic and convincing grounds for comparison than that with other children, and perhaps the commonest cause for concern is dependent on disparity in growth between the two twins of a pair. The previous discussion has shown that differences between a pair of twins are not uncommon but to draw the conclusion that they are not a cause for concern requires careful evaluation. This depends on a knowledge of the variation that can be expected in twin growth patterns dependent on zygosity, sex and the particular stage in childhood.

It has been documented that MZ twins can be expected to be

similar in height, weight, physique and timing of development, and though their size at birth may be disparate they become progressively more similar in growth as time progresses. Marked difference in growth of MZ twins, if zygosity is confidently known, *is* a cause for concern and warrants investigation. Sometimes, if stunting of the growth of one of MZ twins in utero is sufficiently severe, this can be the explanation for subsequent retardation of growth. With DZ twins there is no more reason to expect their growth to be alike than that of siblings brought up together (at comparable ages). If there are wide differences in parental size, twins need not both take after the same parent, and though their environment is usually the same their genetic make-up is not. These differences become particularly important at puberty, and the different timing of puberty in the pair will often result in one having a growth spurt months or even years before the other. Growth at such a time must be interpreted in the light of the evidence of other changes of puberty – and ultimately the late developer should catch up by continuing to grow for longer.

Psychological implications of growth problems of twins

Parents may be concerned about the growth of one or both of their twins from the start, either because of their own observations and interpretations or as the result of comments made by other groups of people such as relatives, close friends, schoolteachers, medical and paramedical personnel or the twins themselves or their schoolmates. As they grow older, the twins become aware of differences between themselves and other children at school, or their co-twins, partly from *their* comments. These concerns are the same as those of any children who are taller or shorter, fatter or thinner, of different physique or physical maturity than the majority of other children, and this is most likely in the teenage years. Such differences may be a worry whatever the cause, but there is often an underlying fear that there is something fundamentally wrong, with implications for general health, development and ultimate outcome as an adult. Such fears may be increased if there are associated secondary symptoms which could be truly organic or psychosomatic, such as aches and pains, appetite changes, bowel upsets, recurrent low grade illnesses, etc.

The level of upset to a child is greatly influenced by the attitude and reaction of others – particularly at school, where the child may be aware of or imagine the unkind comments of others, or be teased, bullied, isolated or have few friends. Of course, twins are different from singletons in having the support and friendship of the co-twin, whether or not they share a growth problem, though if only one suffers or if there are further differences in terms of intelligence, physical ability, temperament, etc., these may be detrimental.

Psycho-emotional effects are particularly likely to occur in those who develop early or late in puberty. The short stature which is already evident in many who prove to be developmentally delayed becomes increasingly evident with delay in puberty, with the added embarrassment of physical immaturity.

Within a twin pair, not only will there be marked difference in stature, but the delayed twin will also be less strong physically and will be left behind in sporting activities, and will be less mature both physically and emotionally. If development previously had been relatively similar, this deviation will inevitably create anxiety and embarrassment. This difference in growth is very frequent and particularly striking with mixed-sex twins, as girls normally go through puberty with its component growth spurt earlier than boys by between one and two years. Boys will thus be temporarily left behind, but subsequently usually dramatically overtake their twin sisters, ending up on average 12 cm taller.

The growth differences commonly result in lack of confidence, low self-esteem, frustration and even depression. Behavioural disturbances such as aggression, violent temper outbursts, negativism, rudeness and moodiness may be very difficult to cope with. Such features are not uncommon in 'normal' puberty and are nearly always transient, but the additional burden of the effects of atypical timing of puberty cause them to be of much greater concern, particularly when experienced by one of a pair of twins.

Management of growth problems

It is essential in the evaluation of growth in twins to have a knowledge of what is 'normal' and what to expect, and of the differences in their growth from that of singletons or between two twins of a pair in relation to zygosity and sex. As with the assessment of growth of any child, this involves the use of correct centiles for weight, height and head circumference, and monitoring of growth over time to see whether or not there is a deviation from a centile line, and relating this at the appropriate age to pubertal status. Parental and preferably sibling centile positions for height and weight provide essential information in interpreting the appropriateness of twins' measurements.

The heights of a child's classmates may differ from the national average, perhaps due to the social setting, which may give a misleading impression of the degree of smallness of an individual.

Confident reassurance of 'normality' and prediction of ultimate satisfactory outcome of growth and development is of great value, for much anxiety may be due to fear about these aspects, but the basis for such reassurance must be well founded. Concerns about disparate growth with DZ twins must therefore be directed to determining whether the problem is more than can be accounted for by variation within the normal population (Buckler 1994).

Major difference either in growth measurements or in the timing of puberty is a much greater cause for concern in MZ than DZ twins. If there is doubt whether there is some underlying pathological cause, whether treatable or not, this justifies investigation – and the grounds for such conclusions have been discussed extensively elsewhere (Buckler 1994).

In all cases, communication with and explanation to the parents and, if old enough, the twins themselves are of great value. Involvement and discussion with the school staff may also be helpful. Such children need psychological support, particularly from the family, through encouragement and showing interest in them and an understanding of their problems, and through nurturing a sense of the child's worth, potential and self-esteem which may be helped by identifying and promoting any particular skill, ability or interest that nearly all children possess. At adolescence the balance between love, discipline and a degree of continuing dependence on the one hand, and in contrast the appropriateness of encouraging breakaway and independence on the other, is important but not easy. The relationship between the two twins themselves is unique and presents a different aspect in these considerations, which will be particularly relevant when there are major differences in the growth and timing of development of the two. It is appropriate that they should grow apart in the sense of developing their own individual personalities, interests and independence, yet retaining a bond and the knowledge of each other's support and involvement. This latter aspect will be of great importance in those dizygotic twin pairs who are drawn apart in physical terms through disparity in timing of puberty.

Fortunately, the majority of concerns related to growth of twins, which often reach their greatest level in teens, are transient, for ultimately adult physical size and performance prove satisfactory. These intervening years, however, require an awareness and commitment in support and explanation to alleviate the emotional stress and to avoid the occasional permanent psychological sequelae.

References

Babson, S.G. and Phillips, D.S (1973) 'Growth and development of twins of dissimilar size at birth', *New England Journal of Medicine* 289: 937–940.

Bleker, O.P., Oosting, J. and Hemrika, D.J. (1988) 'On the cause of the retardation of fetal growth in multiple gestations', *Acta Geneticae Medicae et Gemellologiae* 37: 41–46.

Bleker, O.P., Wolf, H. and Oosting, J. (1995) 'The placental cause of fetal growth retardation in twin gestations', *Acta Geneticae Medicae et Gemellologiae* 44: 103–106.

Blickstein, I., Schwartz, Z. and Lancet, M. (1988) 'Growth discordancy in appropriate for gestational age term twins', *Obstetrics and Gynecology* 72: 582–584.

Boomsma, D.I., Orlebeke, J.F. and Van-Baal, G.C.M. (1992) 'The Dutch Twin Register: growth data on weight and height', *Behavior Genetica* 22: 247–251.

Bryan, E.M. (1992) 'The growth and development of twins', in *Twins and Higher Multiple Births: A Guide to their Nature and Nurture*, London: Edward Arnold, Chapter 12, pp. 153–164.

Buckler, J.M.H. (1987) *The Adolescent Years: The Ups and Downs of Growing Up*, Ware: Castlemead Publications.

Buckler, J.M.H. (1990) *A Longitudinal Study of Adolescent Growth*, London: Springer Verlag.

Buckler, J.M.H. (1994) *Growth Disorders in Children*, London: BMJ Publishing Group.

Buckler, J.M.H. and Buckler, J.B. (1987) 'Growth characteristics in twins and higher order multiple births', *Acta Geneticae Medicae et Gemellologiae* 36: 197–208.

Buckler, J.M.H. and Green, M. (1994) 'Birth weights and head circumference standards for English twins', *Archives of Disease in Childhood* 71: 516–521.

Chamberlain, R.N. and Simpson, R.N. (1977) 'Cross-sectional studies of physical growth in twins, postmature and small for dates children', *Acta Paediatrica Scandinavica* 66: 457–463.

Cole, T.J. (1990) 'The LMS method for constructing normalised growth standards', *European Journal of Clinical Nutrition* 44: 45–60.

Elliman, A.M., Bryan, E.M., Elliman, A.D. and Harvey, D.R. (1991) 'Gestational age correction for height in preterm children to seven years of age', *Acta Paediatrica Scandinavica* 81: 836–839.

Fischbein, S. (1977) 'Intra-pair similarity in physical growth of monozygotic and of dizygotic twins during puberty', *Annals of Human Biology* 4: 417–430.

Freeman, J.V., Cole, T.J., Chinn, S., Jones, P.R.M., White, E.M. and Preece, M.A. (1995) 'Cross sectional stature and weight reference curves for the UK, 1990', *Archives of Disease in Childhood* 73: 17–24.

Furuscho, T. (1968) 'On the manifestation of genotypes responsible for stature', *Human Biology* 40: 437–455.

Gedda, L., Brenci, G. and Gatti, I. (1981) 'Low birth weight in twins versus singletons: separate entities and different implications for child growth and survival', *Acta Geneticae Medicae et Gemellologiae* 30: 1–8.

Hauspie, R.C., Bergman, P., Bielicki, T. and Susanne, C. (1994) 'Genetic variance in the pattern of the growth curve for height: a longitudinal analysis of male twins', *Annals of Human Biology* 21: 347–362.

Henrichsen, L., Skinhøj, K. and Andersen, G.E. (1986) 'Delayed growth and reduced intelligence in 9–17 year old intrauterine growth retarded children compared with their monozygous co-twins,' *Acta Paediatrica Scandinavica* 75: 31–35.

Keet, M.P., Jaroszewicz, A.M. and Lombard, C.J. (1986) 'Follow-up study of physical growth of monozygous twins with discordant within-pair birth weights', *Pediatrics* 77: 336–344.

Koziel, S.M. (1998) 'Effect of disparities in birthweight on differences in postnatal growth of monozygotic and dizygotic twins', *Annals of Human Biology* 25: 159–168.

Leroy, B., Lefort, F., Neveu, P., Risse, R.J., Trevise, P. and Jeny, R. (1982) 'Intrauterine growth charts for twin fetuses', *Acta Geneticae Medicae et Gemellologiae* 31: 199–206.

Ljung, B.-O., Fischbein, S. and Lindgren, G. (1977) 'A comparison of growth in twins and singleton controls of matched age followed longitudinally from 10 to 18 years', *Annals of Human Biology* 4: 405–415.

Luke, B., Leurgans, S., Keith, L. and Keith, D. (1995) 'The childhood growth of twin children', *Acta Geneticae Medicae et Gemellologiae* 44: 169–178.

Naeye, R.L., Benirschke, K., Hagstrom, J.W.C. and Marcus, C.C. (1966) 'Intrauterine growth of twins as estimated from liveborn birthweight data', *Pediatrics* 37: 409–416.

Ooki, S. and Asaka, A. (1993) 'Physical growth of Japanese twins', *Acta Geneticae Medicae et Gemellologiae* 42: 275–287.

Rydhström, H. (1992) 'A birthweight-for-gestation standard based on 4737 twins born in Sweden between 1983 and 1985', *Acta Obstetrics Gynecology Scandinavia* 71: 506–511.

Scottish Livebirths Data (1992) *Birthweight, Head Circumference and Length for Gestational Age (1975–1989)*, Information and Statistics Division, National Health Service in Scotland.

Sharma, J.C. (1983) 'The genetic contribution to pubertal growth and development studied by longitudinal growth data on twins', *Annals of Human Biology* 10: 163–171.

Tanner, J.M. (1962) *Growth at Adolescence* (2nd edn), Oxford: Blackwell Scientific Publications.

Wilson, R.S. (1974) 'Growth standards for twins from birth to four years', *Annals of Human Biology* 1: 175–188.

Wilson, R.S. (1979) 'Twin growth: initial deficit recovery and trends in concordance from birth to nine years', *Annals of Human Biology* 6: 205–220.

Wilson, R.S. (1986) 'Growth and development of human twins', in F. Falkner and J.M. Tanner (eds) *Human Growth, A Comprehensive Treatise* (2nd edn), New York and London: Plenum Press, Vol. 3, Chapter 9, pp. 197–211.

10 Personality, identity and family relationships

Audrey C. Sandbank

The early years

Twinship is a unique relationship which can also be a very positive one.

As we have seen in Chapter 2, the relationship between twins may be laid down before birth. The children's individual personalities develop alongside their awareness of the mother who is carrying them – the beginning of a triangular relationship which continues after birth.

The twin's relationship with his mother is different in quality from that of the singleton. There is rivalry for the mother's breast, though 'breast' for twins is more frequently replaced by 'bottle' (Sandbank 1988).

Carers' cuddles usually have to be shared; sometimes one or both twins will reject being cuddled as the carer may often be unavailable when needed, either because there is little time for relaxing or because the co-twin is already in possession. There has to be an acceptance of sharing. Turn-taking for twins is a triangular affair which may have a long-term effect on language development as discussed in Chapter 4, as well as for triplets (see Åkerman, Chapter 7). The projection, introjection and identification with the mother by the twin may be blurred in the absence of a consistent 'mirror' and instead the twin may become an additional mirror, though one that is unable to contain and reframe the child's emotions.

> Where the twin is the primary object, the projective and intro-jective identifications between the two set up powerful inter-penetrating forces creating a confusion of identities that is not adequately resolved by such processing because neither twin has yet developed the capacity to do so . . . the skin is round the pair rather than the individual.
>
> (Lewin 1994, p. 501)

This can result in the twin remaining a dangerous as well as a 'safe' object, one that is life-threatening as well as life-giving, and the infant feeling of omnipotence may continue inappropriately because the 'object' – the twin – has become a part of his or her own identity. The mother may remain outside because she is seen to have failed to supply what has been obtained from the twin.

When the mother, or carer, bonds with only one of a pair and finds it difficult to relate to the other (see Spillman, Chapter 3 and Hay, Chapter 8), or one twin opts out of the relationship in order to avoid rivalry, the twin on the outside may form a parasitic relationship with the co-twin in order to have a proxy relationship with the mother (Athanassiou 1986). This desire for emotional sustenance from the co-twin can become a lifelong dependency, as letters and telephone calls received by Tamba from desperate adult twins who can no longer cope with the emotional stress from their twin demonstrate. However, the parasitic twin may view the other twin as parasitic by reciprocity. This can lead to the later experience of the twin as life-threatening as well as life-giving, giving rise to the disturbing aspect of physical conflict between twins. Parents of twins and higher multiples usually need to accept help from relatives, friends, etc., when available, in order to promote the health of the family. When there is an increase in the number of carers (Robin *et al.* 1988), the secure base (Bowlby 1988) may be less secure. The twin, as a 'transitional object', in place of the teddy bear or comfort blanket, may become an alternative base with the danger (particularly in the case of the girl in boy/girl pairs) of one twin, and sometimes both, attempting to take on the mantle of mother at an early age.

A base that has a tendency to move with you may inhibit exploration by the individual twin, and twins can become stuck and feel 'unsafe' when separated. However, a secure base which is provided for both of them plus regular periods of one-to-one time with the main carer, alternating with regular solo time away from the carer, will not only introduce twins to 'safe' separation but will also enhance language development, social skills and a sense of individual identity (see Preedy, Chapter 6). When neither twin has had the security of being able to command his mother's entire attention, he may be less willing to let her go unless his twin is with him. Not only does this give each twin an extra sense of security, it also ensures that the co-twin is not getting the attention that he himself is missing.

Jealousy is an emotion that twins probably experience earlier than other children, and for this reason it may be particularly strong. The twin may become a dangerous rival as well as a loved companion.

Twins usually try to find ways of avoiding situations that can create jealousy. Identical twins, because of their strong identification with each other, find it particularly difficult to tolerate such feelings. To avoid jealousy, each twin may attach themselves to a different parent and often play out that parent's role within their own partnership (Sandbank 1988). This can be seen in the under-fives when one takes on the maternal, caring role in their relationship, tucking the other one into bed perhaps, or making sure that he puts his coat on before they go out to play. The other twin may act as his twin's protector, fighting their joint battles – particularly if one twin is bigger or stronger than the other. There may be other more subtle differences between parents which may show themselves in the twin relationship. Choice of roles may be influenced by the children's early environment and their emotional and physical make-up. Other ways of avoiding jealousy are always to have the same as each other and to be as alike as possible.

'Siblings in a family exaggerate their differences for the same reason that species in an ecosystem evolve into different forms: each niche supports a single occupant' (Pinker 1997, p. 454). However, it may be in the interest of identical twins to emphasise their similarity, in order that each may be equally cared for and thus protect their mutual genes. This throws a different light on twin demands for fairness and equality.

Clearly identity is a much greater problem for the identical twin. He recognises his twin in the mirror before he recognises himself and is several months behind the non-identical twin in recognising his own mirror image (Bernabei 1976). He takes longer to say 'I' and 'me' and more often answers to his twin's name. It is probable that 'look-alike' non-identical twins have the same problem.

Parents sometimes lose the original hospital name-tags and may reallocate names when consistent small differences enable them to be sure which one is which. In one of the early studies of twin children the reaction of other small children to the twins was observed; they often behaved as if the children were interchangeable. One child got very cross when twin Peter refused to answer when called 'other Paul' and triplets suffered from the same treatment (Burlingham 1952).

The relationship is such a close one in the early years that a toddler who is separated from his twin, perhaps by a period in hospital, may react in a similar way to that of a child separated from his mother. His feelings are so strong that he cuts himself off from emotion and rejects the loved object that he feels has rejected him. Visits by the twin will help to reassure him, even if he appears to react badly to them. On his return, allowances may need to be made for anger directed towards the twin as well as towards the parent. This is also a way of testing out the relationship and the twin will often show a great deal of understanding.

Because they spend so much time together, because they may look alike, because they are often treated as interchangeable, or as two parts of a whole, and because the separation from the mother may be incomplete, twins do not go through the same steps as most singletons in acquiring a sense of personal identity and self-sufficiency.

Once having learned to recognise his mirror image, the identical twin may still make mistakes. Many identical twins have told of their sense of confusion when they have looked in the mirror and for a moment believed that it was their twin who was staring back (Zazzo 1960).

Birth order

My own research into family relationships, using the Bene Anthony Family Relations Test and an analysis of personality inventories filled in by parents based on a sample of fifty-three pairs of twins and thirty older siblings, has indicated that though the position that twins occupy in the family is important, the effect on self-image and family relationships is not the same as it is for singletons (Sandbank 1988). This is primarily because the birth order of the twins themselves may offer them another choice of position (see Table 10.1); also

Table 10.1 Personality by birth order and zygosity

	All twins p	MZ p	DZss p	DZos p
1 Tends to be the leader	.05 Oldest	..	.05 Oldest	..
3 Shy	..	..	..	.05 Oldest
4 Prefers to stay at home	.05 Oldest	..	..	..
5 Bossy	..	..	.05 Oldest	..
8 Tidy	..	.05 Youngest	..	..
20 Mummy's child	.05 Oldest	..	..	..
25 Laughs a lot	..	..	.01 Youngest	..
26 Independent	..	.05 Oldest	..	..
27 Sense of humour	..	..	.05 Youngest	..
29 Serious	..	.05 Youngest	..	..
47 Giggles	..	..	.05 Youngest	..
48 Likes music	.01 Youngest	..	.05 Youngest	..

their place in the family is shared by the co-twin. Other variables include birthweight, sex of the twins and task sharing as a result of the 'couple effect' (Zazzo 1976). Prenatal and perinatal factors will also intervene.

Birthweight

The relationship between birthweight and maternal preference has already been referred to by Spillman in Chapter 3 and this may lead to persistent differences in personality and family interaction. However, as Hay points out in Chapter 8, these differences may be more in other people's perception of the twins and such stereotyping may 'get worse rather than better' as the twins move through childhood into adolescence.

My research showed that mothers tended to be more protective of their lighter birthweight sons, particularly DZss, but closer to the heavier of MZ and DZss daughters. The older of DZss males seemed to feel more secure in their relationship with both parents than their 'younger' brother. There was evidence that where one of a pair of twins was closer to the mother the other moved closer to the father. Most twins felt that the parent to whom they were closest did not love them enough and/or was too busy to have time for them. Closeness to one parent was often accompanied by strong negative feelings towards the other.

Sex differences

Table 10.2 shows the closeness of MZ and DZss twin girls and MZ boys as quantified by parents. DZos twins are shown as either very close or going their different ways. MZ and often DZss girls become used to attention and interest from an early age and often make being a twin work for them (see also Hay (Chapter 8) on the 'prima donna effect', p. 138). MZ girls were generally found to have an easy relationship with both adults and other children. However, for all twins the 'close twosome' can sometimes be too close for comfort, particularly when they are 'only' twins, and may lead to arguments and feelings of resentment. The 'couple effect' (see p. 177) will generally have a stronger influence on 'only' twins and those for whom twinness has been emphasised by parents; they may find separation as injurious to the self as remaining together.

DZss girls often become each other's best friend but are more likely to compete with each other. However, the research showed that they

Table 10.2 Twin intra-pair relationships

	MZ	DZ	DZos	MZ		DZ		Controls	Only twins
				Girls	Boys	Girls	Boys		
Number of pairs	34	34	9	19	14	17	17	26	8
Inseparable (%)	11.8	0	0	15.8	7.1	0	0	0	0
Closer than most brothers and sisters (%)	52.9	54.5	66.7	47.4	64.3	62.5	47.1	38.5	75.0
Just like any two brothers or sisters (%)	29.4	42.4	11.1	31.6	21.4	31.3	52.9	57.7	12.5
Tend to go their own way (%)	2.9	0	22.2	0	7.1	0	0	3.8	0
Don't like each other's company very much (%)	2.9	3.0	0	5.3	0	6.3	0	0	12.5

felt their twin had a duty to supply their need for help and companionship and this may be reinforced by parents. The twin can feel badly let down when this is not forthcoming. Preedy (Chapter 6) quotes one twin as saying, 'I really dislike my twin sister, she doesn't show any real kindness for me . . .' That is where they differ from MZ girls who frequently give each other support without any outside encouragement. Quoting again from *Multiple Voices* (Preedy and Lowe 1998), 'I like being a twin because . . . your twin will make you happy'. Most twin girls had an easier relationship with their father than did their singleton counterparts.

Parents experienced twin boys as more stressful than girls; MZ boys tended to make both parents feel inadequate. When fathers found their traditional father–son relationship unavailable they tended to opt out or to adopt a more maternal stance, thus sometimes usurping the mother's role (Sandbank and Brown 1990). Of all boys, whether twins or singletons, MZ boys experienced the greatest lack of competitiveness with the father and felt generally closer to him than to the mother. Conversely, DZss boys tended to be closer to the mother and more wary of the father. Fathers were generally firmer with these twins than with MZ boys and, though aware of personality differences, tended to treat them in much the same way (Cohen and Dibble 1977). In my clinical experience same-sex twin boys are more likely to be mischievous both at home and at school, which could be an attention-deficit problem (see Hay, Chapter 8). DZss boys can sometimes lack confidence and the close relationship with the mother may not always be a positive one. My research also shows them to be more home-loving, while the MZ boys were more interested in activities outside the home.

The girls of the DZos twins often enjoyed a good relationship with their father which was similar to that of identical girls. However, they were sometimes in competition with him, which could lead to arguments. Generally they also had a good relationship with their mother and in my professional experience the girl is often the dominant partner in the pair (although the weight, height, rate of maturity – both physical and mental – of the boy can alter this pattern), and this can make the boy over-reliant on his sister and more easily led. However, in some families sons are more valued than daughters, resulting in the boy being dominant (Woodward 1998). Both brother and sister may borrow from each other's roles. Although this can be an advantage it may not always be seen in this light by parents who may have more traditional expectations of the boy.

The confusion of roles and role models for these twins, coupled with a relationship that in closeness appears to be more similar to female same-sex twins than to male same-sex twins, may be a contributory factor to their apparently being at greater risk of being admitted to hospital as adults for a psychiatric disorder compared with singletons and twins of other types – the next most at risk being all-female twins (Klaning *et al.* 1996). This may indicate over-closeness as being a risk factor for twins.

Earlier onset of illness was also found for twins in the above research. Given the vulnerability of twins to separation anxiety, it would not be surprising to find that adolescent twins and young adults are more likely to show signs of distress. The twin relationship needs to be taken seriously in any therapeutic intervention and therapists are likely to find that the twin is reflected in the transference relationship (Lewin 1994).

Older siblings

According to my research, where there was an older child in the family, birth order seemed to increase in importance so that the first-born MZ boy became closest to the mother and the youngest MZ girl became closest to the father (Sandbank 1988). Those children who are born before twins have to make a greater adjustment to the birth of two babies rather than one, and often find it more difficult to cope with the greater reduction in available time from parents and to deal with the 'film star' attention the twins attract (Sandbank 1991).

Tables 10.3 and 10.4 show that the older sibling of twins tended to be more self-sufficient and found it difficult to cope with the new arrivals, but that parents were generally sympathetic towards him or her. All twins preferred an older sister to an older brother and, not surprisingly, older brothers had a greater dislike of their younger twin siblings, feeling overshadowed and pushed out, than did older sisters who were more likely to enjoy being the twins' big sister and to use them as a way of getting extra attention for themselves. Parents are more likely to find an older sister a useful extra pair of hands and eyes. See also Hay, Chapter 8.

My research also showed that when there were more children in the family the older child was better able to deal with the situation. If there was another sibling close in age they would often form another pair within the family. A single older child tended to look outside the family for companionship or attempted to join the twin group either by becoming its leader or by seeking to form an alliance with one

Table 10.3 Items on parent–child interaction where the older sibling of twins scored significantly higher than the older sibling controls

	p
Was the older child difficult after the birth of the twins?	.05
Do the twins receive more attention than the older child?	.03
Do parents avoid making the older child jealous and treat him differently?	.05
Is mother closer to the older child?	.03
Is father closer to the older child?	.03
Does the older child have a different bedtime from the twins?	.05

Table 10.4 Personality items for older siblings of twins showing a significant difference when compared with older sibling controls

	p
Older siblings of twins are more likely to get on with adults	.05
Older siblings of twins are less likely to be good at games	.05
Older siblings of twins are more likely to be independent	.05
Older siblings of twins are less likely to want a cuddle	.01
Older siblings of twins are less likely to bring their problems to their parents	.05

twin in order to split the pair. In spite of the difficulties, the older sibling proved to be more involved with younger twins than would have been the case if there had been only one younger child. Older and younger siblings often felt deprived because they were not one of twins. This could result in a closer relationship with their parents (Woodward 1998).

The twin group

Within a family there are two main subgroups: the parental dyad and the children's group. When the family includes twins there is a second dyad. The twin dyad usually has a strong effect on the rest of the family. Twins may support each other in the face of opposition from others. They may also exert pressure on members of the family to join their group. Being outside a twin group can create a feeling of isolation and impotence. If the parent group is strong enough this can act as a counterbalance, but there are many situations where one parent may be absent, either permanently or temporarily. Frequently the solo parent may seek help for themselves in their struggle to parent, when what is needed is help for the family to change their interaction with the twins. Twins who are encouraged to have individual friends and activities and their own personal possessions, and who are treated as individuals by the family and others, without labelling, and praised when it is deserved, will grow up with a sense of individual identity and self-worth which should enable them to have a good relationship with their twin as well as enjoying close relationships with family and friends. Hay (Chapter 8) reports that labelling – or stereotyping – may continue to be a problem in adolescence and 'that it is often independent of actual differences in behaviour'.

Children can become emotionally disturbed because of changes and loss that occur within or outside the family, but twins, particularly identical twins, may find support and safety by withdrawing into their own little group. If they are separated at such times, the loss is compounded and the trauma magnified. One of a pair of twins, who had experienced many losses during their young lifetimes, was triggered by a further loss at the age of 12 to regress to the age of 6 – the age at which the loss of a loved grandparent had been followed by first-time separation from her twin in school; she was the more dependent twin of the pair. Preedy (Chapter 6) also recommends that twins should not be separated at times of loss.

Occasionally the very closeness of the twin couple can create a pressure between the two that can feel very uncomfortable. By forming a united front, feelings of rivalry or resentment may be suppressed. When these feelings are released there can be quite an explosion. These feelings can also be directed against the self, or others around them, as can occur with singletons.

When the family breaks down the twin dyad may be the only group to remain intact. Rather like two plants in a pot, the pair may have become mentally intertwined because of their mutual interdependence so that any attempt at separation can be injurious to both, while together they inhibit individual activity. Workers with twins 'in care' have reported this phenomenon, also mentioned by Hay in Chapter 8. June and Jennifer Gibbons, 'the silent twins', are an extreme example of this relationship (Wallace 1986) which was exacerbated when they were removed from their family.

The greatest priority for twins who are uprooted together is to receive early and sensitive help in creating a sense of individuality and personal identity, and to assist them to cope with their anger which may become focused on their twin. This may well be met with resistance from the twins but those involved should persevere, enlisting their co-operation in a very gradual tailor-made programme.

If parents join the twin group their influence can be weakened.

Group support for group rules may lead parents to have self-doubts and this can affect their ability to parent; they can also lose their own identity as an adult. The parent who is outside the twin group may become depressed and isolated. Under these circumstances the parental dyad may break down. However, many parents find that twins in the family keep them on their toes and provide a challenge that is always changing and that can be very rewarding.

The couple effect

This term was coined by Professor Zazzo, who observed that being part of a twin group affected twins in a variety of ways.

The first, as we have seen in Chapter 4, is through language. Twins who spend their early life together may develop a private language. These and others may also develop a private shorthand containing words and gestures that convey instant messages to their twin. These messages, based on their joint experience of the world, serve to confirm the way they see their world, and together they build up their twin group culture, which may be different, in some ways, from that of family or friends. This bond which is expressed in language has been termed by Zazzo their 'Secret Garden' – a place which only they can enter.

The second way in which twins are affected is in the allocation of tasks. For example one takes care of the finances, the other the catering. At school, as we have seen in Chapters 6, 7 and 8, one may specialise in one subject, the other in another. Tasks can be emotional as well as practical. One partner may make friends and bring them home, while the other may be more cautious. They may inhibit such skills developing in the other twin. Each has been allocated certain duties, often from an early age. The more closely coupled their lives have been, the more likely they are to specialise. Twins who have older or younger siblings have more opportunity to dilute the twinship, though younger siblings often find they are left out, and 'only' twins tend to have a more intense relationship (see Table 10.2). They become like two pieces of a jigsaw puzzle, each needing the other to become complete. One may lead, the other follow like a shadow. If the balance in the relationship alters, tasks may be reallocated.

Although such twins may appear to be very different in personality, they may be closer than twins who appear to be more similar. Twins who have been separated in early childhood, particularly DZ twins, are often more alike than those who have been brought up together.

They have been able to develop all their skills free from the 'couple effect'. If twins are treated as two separate individuals and encouraged to have their own friends and activities, as well as shared ones, they will learn to develop the skills that are needed when their twin is not available. Though there may still be some specialisation, it will be within acceptable limits and they will not be tied together.

Adolescence and separation

The identical twin's sense of self is inextricably bound up in the partnership, both mentally and physically. Once having learned to recognise his mirror image the identical twin may still make mistakes. Many identical twins have told of their sense of confusion when they have looked in the mirror and, for a moment, believed that it was their twin who was staring back. Identical twins often try to reinforce the similarity in hair and dress, sometimes unwittingly. On the other hand, they may make a deliberate attempt to individuate by putting greater emphasis on, or artificially creating, differences.

If twins go to different schools, or follow separate interests, they may not admit to being one of twins. If friends meet the co-twin there will often be a case of mistaken identity. Twins may accept the false identity rather than bother with explanations or they may make a joke of it. The mistake suggests that they are interchangeable, that they have made no permanent mark of their own, that they have not got an individual identity (Rosambeau 1987). One twin told me of having received a birthday card addressed to 'Marjorie's sister'!

When the body image is intertwined with that of the reflection seen in the twin, any change or disturbance in one affects the body concept of the other. For example, it was reported that one of a pair of identical twins said that she could only be free of anorexia if her sister were also free (Crisp *et al.* 1985). However, more than body image would be involved here. For example, an identical twin's identity is often dependent on very slight differences between the pair, perhaps being the thinner one, then if the co-twin diets, she has to become even thinner to maintain the difference – this can become a dangerous spiral. On a more basic level, if the twin has a spot or untidy hair it is likely that the other will believe that she has the same and may be seen to comb her own hair rather than suggest that the twin combs hers. Problems around unequal changes at puberty are discussed by Buckler in Chapter 9. Adolescence is a time when we rework the experiences of infancy, particularly those of separation. For many twins this is 'unfinished business'. The early triangulated relationship with the mother and the bonding difficulties that may have been experienced with one or both can not only leave the children feeling as if they have never been fully satisfied by the mother, but the mother may also feel that she has not been able to give enough to her twins. Her guilt feelings, and those of the father, coupled with the constant demands of the twins, may sometimes persuade the parents to 'give' at an inappropriate level, thus making it difficult for the whole family to move on.

The time when separation threatens the twinship is usually in adolescence, when most children begin to expect to have a life of their own. Girlfriends and boyfriends appear on the scene, or perhaps there is a need to move away from home to college or a new job. While most children are excited by this prospect, for some twins it may seem fraught with danger.

Twins may not be ready for the thrust towards separation until much later than their physical maturity would suggest. My research showed that twins remained closer to their parents in adolescence than the singleton controls (Sandbank 1988). There appears to be a need for some rejection of parents and their values during adolescence to enable the adolescent to successfully move on and separate – although these values may be re-espoused in adulthood. Hay (Chapter 8) points out that a supportive family may be more important; however, if one twin has been preferred, the other twin may not see the parent/s as supportive. Twins may have greater difficulty in rejecting their parents' values because these have been reinforced within the culture of the twinship. If they reject their parents they have to reject each other. But perhaps some distance from each other may be necessary in order to develop into a separate individual, and for some this may be geographical distance rather than emotional.

The most frightening prospect for many twins is the loss of the co-twin. Elizabeth Bryan (Chapter 11) shows how the death of a twin is probably the most traumatic event in the surviving twin's life, often greater than that of the death of a spouse. In one case known to the author, the death from anorexia of an adolescent twin could be linked to the unresolved loss of the co-twin in early childhood. The death of a twin can also be the means by which one twin can become whole – taking on the lost parts of themselves which have been buried with their twin (Wallace 1986).

However, separation rather than death may seem to be preventable. When the partnership is threatened by the budding independence of one then steps may be taken to protect the organism and restore homeostasis. If there has been little or no opportunity for separation or individuality either at home or at school, this will reinforce the twins' belief that they cannot exist as separate individuals or that they are safer when together. Like a tortoise retreating into its shell, the twin or twins take shelter in their twinship or one may put pressure on the other who is trying to separate by creating a problem that can only be solved by the pair. Research has shown that identical twins usually prefer to pace themselves on each other rather than compete (Segal 1982). They may sometimes jointly compete with others and can achieve great success on the sports field or in business. Ways of avoiding competition can be by the allocation of tasks within the twinship and may also include identifying with a different parent where both are available. What may sometimes appear to be competition can be the pendulum effect; an attempt to restore whatever specialisation or differentiation pre-existed in the twin partnership. Sometimes dominance may alternate or change more or less permanently in response to new requirements from outside the twinship, or to new skills acquired by one of the twin pair. However, non-identical twins are more often competitive, particularly if this is the family pattern or if they are in a 'too close for comfort' relationship.

Impending separation may lead to a crisis of identity. If the dominant twin in a partnership is the first one to seek to become independent then the dependent twin may take flight from adolescence and the threat of separation by increasing his dependence and his hold on the twin. If it is the dependent twin who is beginning to stretch his new-found wings, then the dominant twin, who is threatened with the loss of his caring role, may use his dominant position to 'ground' his twin and maintain the close bond of twinship. The finding that where MZ twins are discordant for anorexia it is usually the dependent twin who is the anorexic would support this view of the twin relationship (Crisp *et al.* 1985). Certainly, in my clinical experience the twins who are the most disturbed by separation from their twin are usually those who are the dominant partner in the relationship (see also Preedy, Chapter 6).

When one twin has succeeded in forming a new partnership or decides to continue life on their own, the remaining twin may suffer from a severe lack of confidence because they have lost in the twin a part of themselves, someone who helped to make the decisions and who fulfilled some of the roles that the other preferred not to take (see the 'couple effect', p. 177). However, like a tree growing back when it has been pruned, they may gradually regain the missing parts over time. Adult twins who live apart often grow more alike in personality because of this.

Having a pair, or more (see Åckerman, Chapter 7) children who move on at the same time can also create problems for parents, particularly if they are the only or the youngest children in the family. The impending loss is even greater if the mother's identity and status are dependent on her being 'the mother of multiples' or if she has joined a twin or triplet group. She may attempt to sabotage any separation by the children either from herself or each other. The children may then find themselves unable to move forward into puberty. Involvement in a multiple births association may help the mother to feel that she still has a useful role as a parent of multiples, passing on her knowledge and experience to others. Fathers too, of course.

Identical twins have a unique culture built on their shared experience and reinforced by their close companionship. This may result in negative as well as positive attitudes becoming entrenched. When a twin pair find that they can be more assertive and more powerful when they act in concert, parenting may be undermined, and this will in turn reinforce the twins' need to take control – particularly in times of stress. Control exercised inappropriately, either together or on each other, may lead to 'folie a deux'. An extreme example is that of the 'silent twins' Jennifer and Jane Gibbons for whom fire-raising became their only way of expressing their anger and frustration. Escape from the constricting bonds of twinship came only through the death of Jane (Wallace 1986).

Some twins, particularly identical twins, may decide that they prefer not to be separated and find that the relationship is a positive one and will continue to work and/or live together. Others may separate some of the time while still maintaining a close bond. Twins must do what is right for them and possibly the happiest twins are those who are able to allow each other freedom to develop independently while continuing a lifelong friendship. There is no doubt that the relationship between identical twins can be a special one – and a friend who intuitively knows how the other feels and thinks can be a marvellous companion. Friendships between non-identical twins can also have this quality. Some DZos twins are more similar to identical twins than to non-identical twins in their relationships and may have a natural sympathy and understanding that can survive separation.

Marriage and partnerships

It has been reported that twins tend to marry rather later than singles, which may be partly due to the special relationship that some twins have with each other (Zazzo 1960). There is often a feeling of resentment against outsiders who threaten this intimacy and they may, in various ways, try to prevent it from happening. Having been in a couple relationship all their lives may also disincline them from forming a new partnership.

Identical twins who have been very close may find it difficult to walk out of their 'Secret Garden' to find happiness with someone else. It can seem disloyal to abandon a childhood partner and they may identify with their twin's feelings of loneliness, of being left behind. It may be made a condition of the new partnership that the old one continues alongside, while others can only tolerate breaking away by putting considerable geographical distance between themselves and their twin. The feelings of the twin who is left can be a mixture of jealousy and loss, while the twin who is forming the new partnership may experience a strong sense of guilt. After the first twin marries, or forms a new partnership, the second may find a partner quite quickly, even too quickly, but some may need time to work through their feelings and find a new identity.

A threatened twin from a close pair may deliberately sabotage the other's relationships, but sometimes adult friendships are shared, as childhood friendships have been, in order to maintain the balance of the twin couple. This is sometimes an acceptable solution, but can lead to complications and upsets between the twins and be confusing for friends. A rare solution, but one that seems to work extremely well, is for twins to marry twins. An alternative is to marry a pair of brothers or sisters or a pair of close friends.

Twins who have been encouraged to tolerate each other's friendships in childhood will find it easier to accept each other's boyfriends and girlfriends and will be happy, as well as sad, when their twin falls in love. Rather than attempting to destroy that relationship they may try to find one of their own, or may feel free to pursue a career of their choice. However, as Hay points out in Chapter 8, when the new relationship is a homosexual one this may be even harder to take – the twin is literally replaced by another. For the same reason twins from mixed-sex pairs may have similar feelings.

Twins tend to marry someone with a personality similar to their twin (Byng-Hall 1995), although parents and brothers and sisters are sometimes also used as models. Relationships may be influenced not just by family patterns but also by the pattern of the twinship; for example, DZos men may find themselves attracted to strong women. Expectations that are brought to a marriage can be high. Most of us are hoping to find a soul mate, but may be prepared to settle for less.

Twins, who for many years have lived with someone who understood their moods and feelings and who may have intuitively known what they were thinking or what they would like to do, may feel disappointed and cheated if their new partner fails to live up to such standards.

The fear of being alone can be greater for twins and help to prevent an early breakup of a marriage. This may give time for a greater understanding to develop. On the other hand, they may return, disillusioned, to the old partnership or continue looking for the ideal partner. If twins maintain the tie with their co-twin, where it is a strong one, alongside the marriage, there may be fewer inappropriate emotional demands made on the marriage partner.

However, in my professional experience and as letters and calls to Tamba have shown, some partners can find it difficult to accept a close relationship between a partner and their twin and try to separate them, or at least place limitations on the amount of contact between them. Twins need to be aware of their new partner's needs as well as that of their twin. Partners who feel confident that they come first may feel happier about the twin coming second.

Twins who have been used to sharing each other's friends may sometimes find it difficult to tolerate a wife's girlfriends or a husband's pals. There may be attempts to undermine a friendship or else to share in it and turn it into a threesome. The relationship between partners of a DZos pair can vary a great deal. If the relationship has been a close one there may be difficulty in finding a marriage partner who can replace the twin. If the pair has been a rejecting one, this could make future relationships hard work. Although the girl of a mixed pair may choose a partner similar to her twin, she should be on her guard against over-protecting him. Similarly, the DZos male may look for a strong partner on whom he can depend. However, there is no reason why they should not have happy marriages, particularly as the nature of the opposite sex will be familiar to them and they may well bring a greater understanding to the marriage than many singles or same-sex twins. If twins of any type have learned to cope with separation and to make individual friends and relationships, they will have acquired the experience and tolerance necessary to form a new partnership.

However, if twins of a pair who have decided to stay together are outward-looking they can become a very successful partnership, and by entering into joint business or other ventures they can prove that the pair is greater than the sum of its parts. Even twins who may be independent in every other way sometimes choose to work together because they complement each other so well. They may also use their joint resources in other ways, for example, in sport, or to be of service to others.

Twins as parents

Twins who become parents tend, in the author's clinical experience, to group their children into pairs, encouraging the younger child to keep up with the older one. Fairness is of paramount importance. Many twins as parents find that they have a special relationship with one of their children, and relate to them as if they were their co-twin. Sometimes they may feel that another of their children appears to be similar to themselves, so that the two members of the twinship, with all that that entails, are apparently acted out in the next generation. Many parents find that their easiest children are the ones who are not of the same sex as their twin.

In the author's clinical experience, mothers from DZos pairs may be able to be consistent with their girls and encourage independence, but can sometimes over-protect their sons and find difficulty in being firm. Mothers with triplet brothers may also have the same problem. On the other hand, twins may try harder to give their children the time and attention they can feel was lacking in their own childhood and make particularly good parents.

References

Adam, P., Matheny, A.J., Wilson, R.S., Dolan, A.B. and Krantz, J.Z. (1981) 'Behavioural contrasts in twinships, stability and patterns of differences in childhood', *Child Development* 52, 579–588.

Athanassiou, C. (1986) 'A study of the vicissitudes of identification in twins', *International Journal of Psycho-Analysis* 67, 329–335.

Bernabei, P. and Levi, G. (1976) 'Psychopathological problems in twins during childhood', *Acta Geneticae Medicae Gemellologiae* 25, 381–383.

Bouchard, C., Savard, R., Despres, J.P., Tremblay, A. and Leblanc, C. (1985) 'Body composition in adopted and biological siblings', *Human Biology* 57, 61–75.

Bowlby, J. (1988) *A Secure Base. Clinical Applications of Attachment Theory*, London: Routledge.

Burlingham, D. (1952) *Twins – A Study of Three Pairs of Identical Twins*, New York: International Press.

Byng-Hall, J. (1995) *Rewriting Family Scripts*, New York and London: The Guilford Press.

Cohen, D.J., Dibble, E. and Grawe, J.M. (1977) 'Parental style, mothers' and fathers' perceptions of their relations with twin children', *Archives of Genetic Psychiatry* 34, 445–451.

Crisp, A.H., Hall, A. and Holland, A.J. (1985) 'Nature and nurture in anorexia nervosa: a study of 34 pairs of twins, one pair of triplets and an adoptive family', *International Journal of Eating Disorders* 4 (1), 5–27.

Fisher, S. (1986) 'The metaphor of twinship in personality development', *British Journal of Psychotherapy* 4, 271–280.

Klaning, V., Mortensen, P.B. and Kyvik, K.O. (1996) 'Increased occurrence of schizophrenia and other psychiatric illnesses among twins', *British Journal of Psychiatry* 168, 688–692.

Lewin, V. (1994) 'Working with a twin. Implications for the transference', *British Journal of Psychotherapy* 10 (4), 499–510.

Luria, A.R. and Yodovitch, F.I. (1959) *Speech and the Development of Mental Processes in the Child*, London: Staples Press.

Lytton, H. (1980) *Parent–Child Interaction: The Socialisation Observed in Twin and Singleton Families*, New York: Plenum Press.

Matheny, A.J., Wilson, R.S., Dolan, A.B. and Krantz, J.Z. (1981) 'Behavioural contrasts in twinships – stability and patterns of differences in childhood', *Child Development* 52, 579–588.

Pinker, S. (1997) *How The Mind Works*, London: Allen Lane, The Penguin Press.

Preedy, P. and Lowe, M. (1998) *Multiple Voices*, Tamworth, Staffs: The Wine Press.

Robin, M., Josse, D. and Towette, C. (1988) 'Mother–twin interaction during early childhood', *Acta Geneticae Medicae et Gemellologiae* 37, 151–159.

Rosambeau, M. (1987) *How Twins Grow Up*, London: The Bodley Head.

Sandbank, A.C. (1988) 'The effect of twins on family relationships', *Acta Geneticae Medicae et Gemellologiae* 37, 161–171.

Sandbank, A.C. (1991) *Twins and The Family*, South Wirral, UK: Tamba.

Sandbank, A.C. and Brown, G.A. (1990) 'An examination of the psychological and behavioural factors in the development of language retardation in twins', *Acta Geneticae Medicae et Gemellologiae* 39, 497–500.

Segal, N.L. (1982) *Co-operation, Competition and Altruism Within Twin Sets – A Reappraisal*, Chicago, IL: University of Chicago Press.

Wallace, M. (1986) *Silent Twins*, London: Chatto & Windus.

Woodward, J. (1998) *The Lone Twin*, London and New York: Free Association Books.

Zazzo, R. (1960) *Les Jumeaux – Le Couple et la Personne*, Paris: Presses Universitaires de France.

Zazzo, R. (1976) 'The twin condition and the couple effect on personality development', *Acta Geneticae Medicae et Gemellologiae* 25, 343–352.

11 The death of a twin

Elizabeth M. Bryan

Introduction

Not surprisingly, the death of a twin will have much the same sort of effect on members of the family as the death of any other child: they will go through the same stages of grief, of shock followed by denial, anger, of later depression and, in most cases, final acceptance.

Yet following a twin's death there are some aspects of the bereavement which are different. The surviving twin will never have known life without a (mostly constant) partner of the same age and may find the loss deeply disturbing. The parents' loss is also different and is too often underestimated.

Parents who lose both of their twins suffer an obvious tragedy. Yet they will also receive the unqualified sympathy of relatives, friends and the medical profession. The attitudes of the same people tend to be very different and ambivalent if 'only' one baby has died. Parents who grieve for one twin can even be seen as being somehow ungrateful for the living one. This is particularly so where one twin dies before birth or within the first few days.

Friends, family and carers tend to have their own internal needs to downplay the tragedy and may seem to leap upon such phrases as 'How lucky that you still have a healthy baby!' or 'Two babies would have been such a handful'. The parents themselves may well have ambivalent feelings and find it very difficult to grieve for one baby while delighting in the survival of the other.

A mother who loses one child from a multiple pregnancy – or later in life – suffers a double bereavement. Not only does she lose a precious child but also what she may see as her special achievement in having twins. Many more parents of twins have to cope with the tragedy of bereavement than those whose children are singletons:

from the time of conception the mortality rate of twins is much higher, and for triplets higher still.

Intra-uterine death

The 'vanishing twin' syndrome

Boklage (1990) suggests that for every pair of twins born, at least a further nine pairs are conceived where only one of the babies develops beyond the early part of the pregnancy. Many of these lost fetuses will be unknown and unrecorded. The effect on the mother of early unrecognised losses is unknown but the awareness of early twin pregnancy will certainly increase as parents more often see both babies on ultrasound scans. Mothers especially will begin to develop a relationship with each twin at a stage when they would previously not even have known they were carrying twins.

Should parents be told when a multiple pregnancy is diagnosed early and hence risk later disappointment? Many parents prefer to know from the outset but generalisation is impossible and, because of the risk of one fetus 'vanishing', obstetricians remain divided on when to tell the parents of a multiple pregnancy. However, when parents are told in the first trimester they should also be warned of the substantial risk of losing one fetus. Recent studies of the intra-uterine behaviour of twins suggest that many fetuses respond to each other during pregnancy (see Chapter 2). Some twins appear to experience a profound sense of loss without the conscious knowledge that they had a twin. There is therefore a case for the surviving child being made aware of the early twinship so that they can be offered appropriate help with any sense of loss.

Death later in pregnancy

A fetus papyraceous (a fetus that dies in the second three months of pregnancy and becomes compressed and parchment-like) no longer comes as a surprise to the obstetrician in this era of routine ultrasound monitoring of pregnancies. Parents can therefore be told in advance what the fetus will look like. However, some professionals still discourage parents from seeing the baby (Bryan 1989). This can not only cause resentment but delay the grief work. A mother who had not been allowed to see her dead fetus following a selective fetocide for a congenital anomaly said, 'I wanted to know. I kept asking. They wouldn't show it. They just took it away.' (Another mother was angry when a post-mortem was performed without her permission: 'How dare he do it without me knowing? – As if the baby had nothing to do with me! – This was the baby I had been relating to.') The fantasy may be much worse than the reality with both congenital anomalies and a fetus papyraceous.

Because of earlier detection and intensive monitoring, many fetal deaths occur after some weeks of anxiety and treatment as, for example, in the twin transfusion syndrome (a condition in which there is an unequal blood flow between two monozygotic twins sharing a placenta). In such situations nurses and others concerned with the mother's care are the only people who 'knew' their babies, so the mothers may well wish to keep in touch and to talk over their loss with them.

Selective fetocide and fetal reduction

If one twin fetus is found to have an abnormality such as Down's syndrome or spina bifida the superficially easy solution is selective fetocide (the intra-uterine killing of the abnormal fetus). But this course of action will seem bizarre and horrifying to many doctors as well as to many parents.

Careful exploration and counselling are necessary in such cases: the final decision must of course be that of the parents. There are clearly many uncomfortable ethical issues in such situations and can seem to be uneasy associations with eugenics. Thus it is all the more important to identify and clarify these issues and the powerful emotions that are stirred up. For example, the thought of a live baby lying for many weeks by the side of his dead twin can be very disturbing. On the other hand, grieving may be delayed because the dead baby has not been aborted and its death is therefore more easily denied. Buried unconscious guilt and anxiety may add to the difficulties and further impair grieving. For many parents the full impact of the bereavement is not felt until the delivery, many weeks later, of a solitary live baby. By this time the carers may have 'forgotten' the twin and this failure to acknowledge and respect the dead baby is bound to add to the mother's distress. A photograph of the ultrasound scan showing both babies may later be precious and unique proof that the parents had indeed had twins.

The parents also have a painfully increased awareness of the baby that might have been in the vivid presence of the surviving twin. The bereaved mother, in particular, will have the difficult emotional task of grieving for a lost baby during a continuing pregnancy and after a live birth.

New techniques in the treatment of infertility have resulted in a worrying increase in the number of higher order pregnancies. The offspring of such pregnancies are much more vulnerable than single-tons and even twins. They have a higher risk of perinatal death and of long-term disability in addition to the inevitable financial, physical and emotional stress that so many babies impose on parents. Couples who are expecting three or more babies may wish to consider redu-cing the number of viable fetuses to two (or even one) or be advised to do so. The procedure is usually performed between the tenth and twelfth weeks of the pregnancy by injecting one or more of the fetuses.

The balance of risk and advantage will be different for each couple but for all there will be a sense of responsibility and much anxiety. Not surprisingly, partners sometimes disagree. There can be no sim-ple 'right' decision applying to all cases. For most people, the main concern will be the healthy survival of their babies. Parents' concern about the physical, emotional and financial demands will vary greatly between couples and will not necessarily correlate with their socio-economic status.

Parents may be distressed by the seemingly (and often actual) arbitrary choice as to which fetus should live and which should die. Some will not even have heard of the procedure and be horrified by the very idea. As yet no studies have been reported on the long-term psychological effects on parents and the surviving children but in the short term, at least, the surviving children appear to be developing normally and the parents rarely regret their decision. However, in contrast to studies on perinatal bereavement, a substantial number of parents decline to participate, being reluctant to talk or write about their feelings (personal experience and Garel *et al.* 1997).

Stillbirth and infant death

The risk of a stillbirth in twins is over twice that for singletons; and of a neonatal death five times higher. The incidence of the Sudden Infant Death Syndrome (SIDS) among twins is also higher. This is partly, but probably not entirely, due to the adverse factors known to be associated with both twinning and SIDS such as prematurity and low birthweight (Beal 1983).

After months of expecting a life-to-be there is no greater anticlimax than the birth of a dead baby. Society shuns it. Even the medical profession often does so. People try their best to forget that the baby ever was (Bourne 1968), and they manage to do this distressingly quickly (at least in the parents' eyes) even with the death of a single-ton. When one twin dies this reality avoidance can be accomplished even more easily. Giving attention to the surviving twin provides a ready escape route. By concentrating on the live baby it is quite possible, once out of the delivery room, never to mention the lost baby. Some mothers have found that midwives whom they have known well throughout their pregnancy do not – perhaps cannot – even refer to it.

But the mother, and often the father too, usually want to talk about the stillborn baby. They need to ask questions about how and why it happened; to vent anger; to attribute blame. They have an under-standable need to share their feelings, rational or not. Mothers invariably feel shame and to some extent guilt that somehow they must be responsible for the baby's death. They may even feel that they have 'killed' their baby. The mother's guilt can only be increased by misguided remarks such as 'How lucky you still have another child'. No one would say such a thing to parents who have lost one of two singletons.

The mother especially will be confused by the contradiction in her feelings as she rejoices in the new life and grieves for the death of the other simultaneously. It is only by allowing, indeed encouraging a mother to think and talk about her dead baby that the normal mourning process can take place (Lewis 1979) and her full love can be released to the survivor.

If a mother is forced to concentrate on the healthy baby to the exclusion of the dead twin she may start to idealise the dead one and to positively alienate herself from the survivor. Its normal crying, feeding behaviour or restlessness may irritate her quite unreasonably. She may feel she is being punished by him. Some parents have been led to commit child abuse in such circumstances (Bluglass 1980).

To facilitate her mourning, the mother needs to mentally distin-guish between the two babies with all the clarity she can. Having seen and handled him will greatly help her to recognise the lost child as a person in his own right. But the process will be helped by assembling or creating substantive memories of the dead baby. Photographs should always be taken, preferably of the two babies together. This should be done even if the parents show little interest at the time. If the opportunity is missed, a photographic department can usually join two separate photographs later.

Some artists are prepared to make attractive sketches using the original photographs. This will be the more appropriate choice where one baby is disfigured or has died some time before delivery. Many people like to have a memorable funeral for their baby and an individual grave or memorial. It is especially wise for even a stillborn baby to be given a name, if only to enable the survivor to more easily refer to his twin in later life. But a name should help everyone involved to constellate the various memories and memorabilia into a single helpful image.

When both babies are born alive but one is likely to subsequently die from, say, gross malformations or severe birth anoxia (lack of oxygen to the baby's brain during delivery), parents should be encouraged to give much of their time to the ill baby rather than the healthy one. Most parents will in any case want to do all they can for their sick baby, while they can. This will also reduce any guilt they may feel about the twin's death and provide extra treasurable memories over the years. As long as there are no medical contra-indications, the babies should spend some time together so that the survivor can later be told of this closeness he had with his twin. Where appropriate, photographs can be taken and even a video film made.

Death in childhood

In childhood, twins have only a slightly higher chance of dying than singletons. But when a twin dies in childhood – be it from an accident, chronic illness or acute infection – the effects on the survivor can be devastating (Bernabei and Levi 1976). The effects are of course greater where the twins have had little experience of being separated or where the one who died was the 'leader'. In some African tribes the spirit of the dead twin must be preserved by the survivor to ensure his or her wholeness (Elniski 1994). For such survivors this belief may appear to be frighteningly apt. Single surviving Yoruba twins from Nigeria carry a wooden image representing their dead twin around their neck or waist – often into adulthood – which is said to provide a refuge for the spirit of the dead twin and hence also company for the survivor.

People who are not themselves twins rarely recognise how intimate and constant is the twin–twin relationship. One psychotherapist, Joan Woodward (1998), explores this relationship with reference to Bowlby's theory of attachment (Bowlby 1971). The fact is that twins see much more of each other than they do of either parent or anyone else. Their relationships, even with the mother, are essentially triadic.

Many twins even create their own language (see Chapter 4). The loss of this partner can therefore be at least as profound as the loss of any partner.

The healthy twin should therefore be as closely involved with his brother or sister's illness and death as his level of understanding allows. Only thus can he be adequately prepared for life without his previously constant partner. At the same time the survivor will need reassurance that she or he will not catch the same illness or, indeed, die. Euphemistic substitutes for the word 'death' such as 'long sleep' can lead to the survivor fearing sleep and 'lost' may precipitate anger about the parents' carelessness. It also gives false hope of the twin's 'awakening' or return.

The unknown and unseen are often more incomprehensible and frightening than reality. For a twin with an active imagination this can be especially relevant. There are therefore advantages both to the chronically ill child and the healthy twin in being together through the final weeks and any other siblings being involved too. Janet Goodall and the parents of a terminally ill 5-year-old (a singleton in this case) helpfully described how they coped at home rather than in hospital. Both older and younger sisters were enabled to come to terms with the death of their brother much more easily than if they had been excluded from the whole experience (Cotton *et al.* 1981).

When the brother died, the parents employed the image of moving house. His body, the house, was no longer needed now that he had moved to a new one. This image may help families who are uncomfortable with 'heaven' as the new home. Books like *Waterbugs and Dragonflies* (Stickney 1982) can help children to understand the concept of moving to a new but unseen life: waterbugs are unable either to see or imagine the dragonflies which they are soon to become.

When the ill child has to be admitted to hospital, the twin should often accompany him not only for mutual comfort but for the mother's practical convenience. One mother told how she had to stop breastfeeding when one of her babies went into hospital with pyloric stenosis, an obstruction caused by the thickening of the muscle around the outlet (pyloric) valve to the stomach, because she was not allowed to bring the twin in with her. It can plainly be extremely painful for both twins when the stress of illness in hospital causes their first experience of separation. It can amplify the sense of crisis, and even children who are used to separation will often get great comfort from each other's presence at such a time. Some hospital authorities are still hard to convince that twins should be admitted together. However, it is necessary always to respect each child's individual needs. Plainly there will be times when each child will want parents to herself or himself.

A surviving twin may well feel guilty, after the death, that she or he was the one chosen to live. This guilt, of course, is compounded if she comes to think that she was directly or indirectly responsible for the twin's death and even more so if the parents seemed to have preferred the other child to live. It is all too easy for parents to idealise the dead child and forget that he too would sometimes have been lazy, untidy or otherwise irritating.

Single survivors will also feel more inadequate if parents – as many do – place undue store on being 'parents of twins' and too obviously betray this aspect of their grief.

The dying child may have outstanding business to settle before he dies, such as deciding to whom his special possessions should go. The survivor should then be involved in the process of sorting out his twin's belongings after death. One mother described how, after the accidental death of her 14-year-old identical twin son, his brother tidily preserved the twin's part of their bedroom for many months. Gradually, however, there were stages of replacement and finally he decided which of the possessions should become his own and which should be given away. He then took over the whole room for himself, keeping just one shelf of his brother's treasures – perhaps a helpful image of successful grief work. It is worth noting that some time after the accident in which he too was injured, the same boy was distressed to find that all signs of his twin had been removed from their school and that he had not even been involved in the reallocation of his brother's coat hook. This boy also assumed some of his brother's qualities, having previously been the less responsible and tidy one. Several adult twins, notably Norris McWhirter whose twin brother was murdered, have described how twinship had enhanced the performance of both (the pacer and runner effect) but that after the bereavement the choice seemed to be either to exist painfully as half a person or to take on the strength of both.

Young children have great difficulty in understanding death's finality (Goodall 1994), and that their twin will never return. One 3-year-old, whose brother had died in hospital six months earlier, insisted on taking some of his toys to the doctor at Christmas-time so that they could be given to his twin.

After the death the questions arise of whether the twin should see his dead sibling and also whether he should attend the funeral. This must be the parents' decision, but even a young child may have his own clear wishes. For many children it can be reassuring to see how peaceful their brother or sister looks after they have died. (They might otherwise create horrifying images.) Some children may like to help prepare the coffin. One 9-year-old, whose brother had died of leukaemia, spent some time carefully arranging football boots, cap and football in the coffin.

Many parents, while still grieving themselves, find the survivor's disturbed behaviour extremely stressful. One two-and-a-half-year-old who had suddenly lost his MZ twin brother from bacterial meningitis became silent, despite having had normal speech development as well as a shared 'twin language'. Six weeks later his mother showed him his face in the mirror to point out some blackcurrant juice marks. His expression lit up for a few seconds only to turn to anguish as he realised the reflection was his own, not that of his missing twin. He refused to go near a mirror again and became increasingly withdrawn and destructive. There may be profound psychic injuries that do not show any immediate overt symptoms, so close attention to the surviving twin and careful reassurance may be crucial.

Some children's difficult behaviour can disrupt family life and parents may well disagree profoundly – in complete good faith – on the best response. Marital discord over this is common. All families should therefore be offered support and bereavement counselling from the outset to prevent or reduce both the child's difficulties and the family's tensions.

A child whose twin has died in the perinatal period may later feel distress, anxiety or even just curiosity about it. They should feel free to talk about their feelings and not suppress them because they fear upsetting their parents. If their parents cannot talk about the dead sibling it is vital to find someone else with whom they may comfortably do so.

I have met many adult twins who were quite unable to talk to their parents about the loss of their twin. Others have experienced profound relief when finally able to do so. One surviving twin talked to her mother for the first time about her stillborn brother twenty-two years later. It came as a relief to them both and led to their holding a memorial service at the unmarked grave.

I believe all single surviving twins should hear about their twinship, preferably from the start, and be encouraged to ask questions and express their feelings, whether or not they are considered rational. Many feel angry: angry with the twin for deserting them; angry for causing such unhappiness in the family; angry for making them, as the survivors, feel guilty. They may also feel anger towards their parents for 'allowing' the twin to die. As I said earlier, we have yet to learn how survivors of selective fetocide and fetal reduction will feel towards their parents. Hopefully most will accept that what happened was intended for the benefit of them, the survivor, as well as, in the case of selective fetocide, for the affected child's sake. Some may feel critical and even angry.

Reactions to the news of a previously unknown twinship are unpredictable. One mother waited seven years before, with great trepidation, she told her son of his stillborn twin. The child's reaction astonished her: he was elated. He rushed into school the next day to tell his teacher and friends, 'I was a twin'. Some find that the twinship explains a long-held inner feeling of loneliness, even of loss. Many twins will treasure mementoes of their twin and some will enjoy making their own scrapbook or collection of mementoes. They may add their own drawings. One of the frequent difficulties for both the parents and the twin is at what age to picture the dead child.

Other surviving twins will have more complex feelings. Some have secret fantasies, and these can be frightening. One 5-year-old feared the ghost of his twin. He was reluctant to go upstairs on his own and was unable to put his hand out from his blankets to get a drink. It was only through talking about, and drawing, these fears that he was gradually enabled to accept that the ghost would do him no harm. Indeed he came to think of him as a friend.

Attitudes to the surviving twin

The mother's attitude

Most mothers have ambivalent feelings towards the surviving twin. Some over-protect the survivor, others reject him, many do both. They are thankful to have this baby (or child) to love, yet also feel him to be in some way responsible for the other twin's death. Did the survivor take an unfair share of the intra-uterine nutrition? With an older child, the mother may feel that the accident which killed one was somehow the fault of the other. Sometimes, tragically, this is true.

Many parents are haunted by the vision of their dead child in the living twin, especially where they were monozygotic twins. One mother dreaded washing her 2-year-old's hair: with wet hair he looked most like his dead brother. Another mother described how her 18-month-old daughter acquired a number of mannerisms that had once been peculiar to her dead MZ twin. Such ever-present reminders of the lost child can be so painful that the mother may for a while reject the twin and give an unfair amount of attention to other siblings.

This problem may even arise with the stillborn. A mother who had never seen her stillborn baby found that whenever she looked at his live twin she could not help wondering what the dead one was like.

The father's attitude

Fathers of twins may be especially affected by the death of a twin baby or child. Right from the start they are likely to have been more involved with twins than with a singleton. Many are also less used to discussing their feelings. Sometimes, of course, the father may cope with his loss much less easily than the mother but he will in any case need a lot of support in coping with her grief and the reactions of the surviving twin and of any other siblings.

Most fathers are extremely proud of having twins but unfortunately, in the early years, some of them persist in thinking of them as a single unit, 'the twins'. The destruction of this unit may therefore seem to him to leave an incomplete child, one whom the father may reject. After the loss of his 2-year-old twin son, one father insisted on removing all photographs of the pair. But the twins had never been photographed separately, so this meant removing all photographs of the live twin too. Indeed he wanted nothing to do with the MZ twin, who was too painful a reminder of the lost son and the lost twinship. He gave all his love and attention to the 5-year-old sister.

The surviving twin

The number of single surviving twin children in the UK is difficult to determine, but estimates range between 5 and 15 per cent of all twin pairs (Bryan 1992).

The cost of being a single survivor may be very high. Some of the surviving twin's characteristic problems both in his relationship with his parents and within himself have been discussed, but many are still ill-understood.

Grieving

Even those twins who appear psychologically and socially unscathed may suffer profoundly yet silently from their bereavement. Too often their dead twin is never mentioned. It is rare, for instance, for a teacher at school, or even in a playgroup, to know of a twin who died at birth, or soon after, even though the child's first drawings may be about his twinship. There may be a recurring second figure. One 3-year-old, whose twin was stillborn, was time and again attracted to depleted objects (Lewis 1983) – the toy car without a wheel, the doll missing an arm and so on.

For a monozygotic twin especially, he himself is a constant reminder of his twin and this may be deeply painful. One young man I knew, whose twin died when they were 20, grew a beard because the daily shave too agonisingly recalled the face of his twin. The survivor may have not only survivor guilt but also a terrible feeling of vulnerability and of the seemingly arbitrary nature of survival.

The work of Joan Woodward, a psychotherapist in Birmingham, teaches much about the profound and unique sense of loss felt by many adult single surviving twins. Her own twin sister died in early childhood. She interviewed over 200 bereaved twins, including many who had lost their twin at birth or in infancy, and this special kind of loss is therefore now better understood (Woodward 1988).

It was mentioned earlier how some twins whose partner was stillborn believe that their parents blame them for their twin's death. Surviving twins have reported comments such as 'Because I was the bigger baby I was told I had taken my brother's food' and 'I was untwinned at birth when my dear sister died having been starved (the doctor said) and finally kicked out by me'. A number of survivors sense that their mother would have preferred their twin to have survived instead, particularly where it was of the opposite sex.

Twins who suffer survivor guilt may strive to make up to their parents for the loss, trying to live for two. Inevitably they suffer intense feelings of failure when their unrealistic goals are not achieved. The survivor's guilt is of course the greater if he feels directly or even indirectly responsible for his twin's death. If the death resulted from, say, some prank they were involved in together, the survivor may need a lot of help in coping with his remorse, however irrational.

Following the death of a twin in later childhood or early adulthood, the surviving twin will be that much more conscious of the parents' intense grief and may strive to conceal his own emotions so as not to add to their burden. But this suppression of grief may deceive not only the parents but the survivor himself, leaving deep scars which may only surface many years later.

Mythology provides many examples of the sense of desolation felt by the survivor at the loss of his twin. Castor and Pollux were the twin sons of Leda by Tyndareus and Zeus, who had powers over the wind and waves and became known as the seafarers' guardians. When Castor was killed in battle, Pollux was so desolate that he begged his father to allow him to join his brother and so they became the heavenly constellation Gemini.

Narcissus, from whom the derogatory term 'narcissism' or self-worship is derived, is thought by some to have been a twin, albeit a much maligned one. It is suggested that Narcissus had a twin sister to whom he was devoted. After she died he spent long hours looking at his own reflection in a pool but, in this interpretation, this was not vanity but a profound longing for his lost twin.

The death of an older twin leaves a survivor who must often endure an agonising period of readjustment. No other bereavement threatens someone's identity to the same degree. Great as is the tragedy of losing a spouse or a child, at least the bereaved person has been possessed of a clear identity since before he or she became a spouse or a parent. A twin is and remains a twin from the time of conception and the loss of this most intimate and defining of all relationships can undermine the survivor's basic sense of identity. Many twins have never even imagined, let alone risked, life without their twin. They assume they will share their old age together.

Whether MZ twins in general feel the loss more than DZ is not known. The indications are that this is so. Early adulthood seems to be a particularly difficult time to lose a twin. Many such twins will not yet have embarked on independent lives. Some will be sharing careers. Some will just be embarking on the process of finding their separate selves. The loss of their twin is not only the loss of their lifelong companion and best friend but also of part of their living support system.

One of the beliefs held firmly by some twins is that, after his or her death, the twin not only survives in spirit, but is in some sense available and indeed is actively guiding them through life. For some twins this may be a way of dealing with the intense loneliness which so many of them feel.

As a result of Joan Woodward's work, a group of thirty bereaved twins met in London in 1989. The great majority of them had never knowingly met another bereaved twin before. Following this meeting and the widespread interest it created, a Lone Twin Network was established in the UK which allows bereaved adult twins to be in touch with others who have lost a twin. There are twins on this register who have lost their twins at all ages from before birth to 84 years. Many have never before had the chance to share their experiences. The relief in doing so can be profound.

Support from self-help groups

Most parents continue to think of their single surviving child as a twin even if the co-twin was stillborn, and they like other people to do so too. Some parents who have lost a twin continue to join in active membership of their local twins club and this is generally well understood by the other parents. Not surprisingly, other bereaved parents find such contact too painful. They may however welcome an opportunity to share their feelings with other bereaved parents, particularly those who had twins. The Twins and Multiple Births Association Bereavement Support Group (Tamba) in the UK provides such contacts individually or via its newsletter. It also holds three-monthly lunchtime meetings at the Multiple Births Foundation (MBF) (at Queen Charlotte's and Chelsea Hospital, London). The MBF also offers professional support and a specialised Bereavement Clinic to parents, bereaved children and bereaved adults. Adult twins can get in touch with other such bereaved adults through the Lone Twin Network in the UK. This also provides a regular newsletter and regional and national meetings. In the USA there is a support group called 'Twinless Twins'.

References

Beal, S. (1983) 'Some epidemiological factors about sudden infant death syndrome (SIDS) in South Australia', in J.T. Tildon, L.M. Roeder and A. Steinschneider (eds) *Sudden Infant Death Syndrome*, New York: Academic Press.

Bernabei, P., Levi, G. (1976) 'Psychopathologic problems in twins during childhood', *Acta Geneticae Medicae et Gemellologiae* 25: 381–383.

Bluglass, K. (1980) 'Psychiatric morbidity after cot death', *Practitioner* 224: 533–539.

Boklage, C.E. (1990) 'Survival probability of human conceptions from fertilisation to term', *International Journal of Fertility* 33: 75.

Botting, B., Macdonald-Davis, I., Macfarlane, A. (1987) 'Recent trends in the incidence of multiple births and their mortality', *Archives of Disease in Childhood* 62: 941–950.

Bourne, S. (1968) 'The psychological effects of stillbirths in women and their doctors', *Journal of the Royal College of General Practitioners* 16: 103–112.

Bowlby, J. (1971) *Attachment*, Harmondsworth: Penguin.

Bryan, E.M. (1989) 'The response of mothers to selective fetocide', *Ethical Problems in Reproductive Medicine* 1: 28–30.

Bryan, E.M. (1992) 'Death of a twin', in *Twins and Higher Multiple Births. A Guide to their Nature and Nurture*, Sevenoaks: Edward Arnold.

Bryan, E.M. (1994) 'Problems surrounding selective fetocide', in L. Abramsky and J. Chapel (eds) *The Human Side of Prenatal Diagnosis*, Oxford: Chapman and Hall.

Bryan, E., Higgins, R. (1995) 'Embryo reduction of a multiple pregnancy: an insoluble dilemma?', in *Infertility. New Choices. New Dilemmas*, London: Penguin.

Cotton, M., Cotton, G., Goodall, J. (1981) 'A brother dies at home', *Maternal and Child Health*, 6: 288–292.

Elniski, J. (1994) 'Finding one's twin', *Parabola* 19: 47–51.

Garel, M., Stark, C., Blondel, B., Lefevre, E., Vautier-Brohzers, D., Zorn, J.R. (1997) 'Psychological reactions after multiple pregnancy reduction: a 2-year follow-up study', *Human Reproduction* 12: 12–22.

Goodall, J. (1994) 'Thinking like a child about death and dying', in L. Hill (ed.) *Caring for Dying Children and their Families*, London: Chapman and Hall.

Lewis, E. (1979) 'Mourning by the family after a stillbirth or neonatal death', *Archives of Disease in Childhood* 54: 303–305.

Lewis, E. (1983) 'Stillbirths: psychological consequences and strategies of management', in A. Mulinsky, E.A. Friedman and I. Gluck (eds) *Advances in Perinatal Medicine* 3, New York: Plenum.

Lewis, E., Bryan, E. (1988) 'Management of perinatal loss of a twin', *British Medical Journal* 297: 1321–1323.

Stickney, D. (1982) *Waterbugs and Dragonflies*, Oxford: Mowbray.

Woodward, J. (1988) 'The bereaved twin', *Acta Geneticae Medicae et Gemellologiae* 37: 173–180.

Woodward, J. (1998) *The Lone Twin. Understanding Twin Bereavement and Loss*, London: Free Association Books Ltd.

Further reading

Bryan, E.M., Hallett, F. (1997) 'The impact of multiple births. Guidelines for professionals', in *Bereavement*, Section 3, London: MBF.

Higher Multiple Pregnancies (1996) Fetal reduction, London: MBF.

Multiple Pregnancy (1996) Selective fetocide, London: MBF.

Read, B., Bryan, E., Hallett, F. (1997) *When a Twin or Triplet Dies. A booklet for bereaved parents and twins*, London: MBF.

Useful addresses

International Society for Twin Studies (ISTS)
Dr Jaako Kaprio, Secretary General
Department of Public Health
PO Box 52
FIN – 00014 University of Helsinki
FINLAND

Multiple Births Foundation (MBF)
Queen Charlotte's and Chelsea Hospital
Goldhawk Road
London
W6 0XG

Tel: 0181 383 3519

Tamba
Harnott House
309 Chester Road
Little Sutton
South Wirral
L66 1QQ

Tel: 0870 121 4000/0151 348 0020
Fax: 0870 121 4001/0151 348 0765

Index